Communications
in Computer and Information Science   **1631**

More information about this series at https://link.springer.com/bookseries/7899

Indhumathi Raman · Poonthalir Ganesan ·
Venkatasamy Sureshkumar ·
Latha Ranganathan (Eds.)

Computational Intelligence, Cyber Security and Computational Models

Recent Trends in Computational Models, Intelligent and Secure Systems

5th International Conference, ICC3 2021
Coimbatore, India, December 16–18, 2021
Revised Selected Papers

 Springer

Editors
Indhumathi Raman 🄳
Coimbatore, India

Poonthalir Ganesan 🄳
Coimbatore, India

Venkatasamy Sureshkumar 🄳
Coimbatore, India

Latha Ranganathan 🄳
Coimbatore, India

ISSN 1865-0929   ISSN 1865-0937 (electronic)
Communications in Computer and Information Science
ISBN 978-3-031-15555-0   ISBN 978-3-031-15556-7 (eBook)
https://doi.org/10.1007/978-3-031-15556-7

This Springer imprint is published by the registered company Springer Nature Switzerland AG
The registered company address is: Gewerbestrasse 11, 6330 Cham, Switzerland

Preface

With the advent of massive information growth in all facets of human life, there have been continuous demands in exploiting new knowledge and striving for more technical advancements. Recent trends in big data analytics, natural language processing, artificial intelligence, and secure digital communication have created the need to explore new arenas to foster societal activities. To enhance novel ideas in the theory and progress of cyber security, as well as computational advancement for modeling and intelligence, the Department of Applied Mathematics and Computational Sciences of PSG College of Technology, India, organized the 5th International Conference on Computational Intelligence, Cyber Security and Computational Models (ICC3 2021), which was held online during December 16–18, 2021. The aim of this conference series is to serve as a platform to explore new research directions and to promote practical innovations and the state of the art.

The conference was organized under the theme "Recent Trends in Computational Models, Intelligence and Security Systems" in order to highlight the importance of developing secure and intelligent models of computation, which forms the basis for the theory of computational methods. As a curtain-raiser to ICC3 2021, a pre-conference workshop on "Cyber-physical Systems" was initiated, which took place in virtual mode during December 13–14, 2021, encompassing IoT, smart grids, robotics, and autonomous systems. The conference was financially sponsored by DRDO and Robert Bosch.

Computational intelligence is a set of nature inspired computational methodologies and techniques to address complex real-world problems encompassing neural networks, fuzzy logic, and evolutionary computation as its main key elements. The aim of computational intelligence is to develop a new arena for analyzing and creating effective processing elements with adequate knowledge on sensing, interpreting, learning, thinking, and remembering to aid intuitive information processing systems.

Cyber security is becoming an increasingly central facet of national security strategies. Both the private and public sectors are now relying on cyber security. Secure network and information systems are essential to keep the online economy in shape and to ensure progress. Being aware of potential cyber security threats, building a threat-resistant and agile infrastructure, and adopting best practices to mitigate operational hiccups and security risks are the most pertinent needs of every application sector.

Computational modeling formulates and models real-world problems and then uses computing to develop solutions. Computational models help various stakeholders to visualize, predict, optimize, regulate, and control complex systems using high-end computing technology. Computational models evolve over time, as abstractions are introduced to eliminate unnecessary details and clarify the important design principles.

ICC3 2021 featured keynote talks by 23 eminent academicians from across the globe: 12 from Asia (of which five were from India), eight from Europe, six from the USA, and one each from Africa and Australia. There were 84 paper submissions, out of which 14 papers (16.67%) were accepted for presentation. Each submitted paper underwent a rigorous (double-blind) review process. This edition of ICC3 saw an increase in the number of international members in every committee of the conference.

We, the organizers, express our sincere gratitude to all the keynote speakers and all the peer reviewers for their valuable comments that ensured the quality of the proceedings. We also express our sincere thanks to the Advisory Committee, the Technical Program Committee, and the authors for their invaluable contributions to the success of this conference. We extend our warmest gratitude to Springer for their support in publishing the ICC3 proceedings. The conference saw the culmination of novel ideas of various speakers across the globe from academia and industry and has encouraged the audience to pursue research in the domains of the conference. We hope to take forward this tradition in all our future editions.

June 2022

Indhumathi Raman
G. Poonthalir
V. Sureshkumar
R. Latha

Organization

Chief Patron

L. Gopalakrishnan   PSG & Sons Charities Trust, India

Patron

K. Prakasan   PSG College of Technology, India

Organizing Chair

R. Nadarajan   PSG College of Technology, India

Program Chair

Indhumathi Raman   PSG College of Technology, India

Computational Intelligence Track Chair

G. Poonthalir   PSG College of Technology, India

Cyber Security Track Chair

V. Sureshkumar   PSG College of Technology, India

Computational Models Track Chair

R. Latha   PSG College of Technology, India

Advisory Committee

S. Lakshmivarahan   University of Oklahoma, USA
Mika Sato-Ilic   University of Tsukuba, Japan
Sateesh K. Peddoju   IIT Roorkee, India
S. K. Hafizul Islam   IIIT Kalyan, India
R. Anitha   PSG College of Technology, India
G. Sai Sundara Krishnan   PSG College of Technology, India
R. S. Lekshmi   PSG College of Technology, India
M. Senthilkumar   PSG College of Technology, India

Technical Program Committee

Andrew H. Sung	University of Southern Mississippi, USA
Manuel Grana	University of the Basque Country, Spain
Manu Malek	International Journal of Computers and Electrical Engineering, USA
Adrian Fiech	Memorial University, Canada
Mika Sato-Ilic	University of Tsukuba, Japan
Abdel-Badeeh M. Salem	Ain Shams University, Egypt
Rufus O. Oladele	University of Ilorin, Nigeria
Anton Satria Prabuwono	King Abdulaziz University, Saudi Arabia
Kevin Curran	Ulster University, UK
Rein Nobel	Vrije Universiteit Amsterdam, The Netherlands
Gyoo-Soo Chae	Baekseok University, South Korea
Alexander Gelbukh	Instituto Politécnico Nacional, Mexico
Dariusz Jacek Jakóbczak	Koszalin University of Technology, Poland
Sucheng Haw	Multimedia University, Malaysia
Ng Kok Why	Multimedia University, Malaysia
Xiao Zhi Gao	University of Eastern Finland, Finland
Xiaochun Cheng	Middlesex University London, UK
V. B. Surya Prasath	University of Cincinnati, USA
Natarajan Meghanathan	Jackson State University, USA
Sridhar Venkatesan	Peraton Labs, USA
Srinivas Chakravarthy	Kettering University, USA
Kurunathan Ratnavelu	University of Malaya, Malaysia
Anand Nayyar	Duy Tan University, Vietnam
R. Ramanujam	IMSc, India
U. Dinesh Kumar	IIM Bangalore, India
C. Pandurangan	IIT Madras, India
Phalguni Gupta	IIT Kanpur, India
Ashok kumar M.	IIT Palakad, India
S. Lavanya	IIT (BHU) Varanasi, India
Ram Bilas Pachori	IIT Indore, India
Shivashankar B. Nair	IIT Guwahati, India
R. B. V. Subramanyam	NIT Warangal, India
M. Sashi	NIT Warangal, India
A. Kandasamy	NIT Suratkal, India
Debashish Jena	NIT Suratkal, India
K. Murugesan	NIT Trichy, India
N.P. Gopalan	NIT Trichy, India
C. Mala	NIT Trichy, India
M. P. Singh	NIT Patna, India
Sadagopan Narasimhan	IIITDM Kancheepuram, India

V. Masilamani	IIITDM Kancheepuram, India
Ashok Kumar Das	IIIT Hyderabad, India
Ruhul Amin	IIIT Naya Raipur, India
S. K. Hafizul Islam	IIIT Kalyani, India
Elizabeth Sherly	IIITM-K, India
Rishi Ranjan Singh	IIIT Allahabad, India
G. Sethuraman	Anna University, India
J. BaskarBabujee	Anna University, India
G. Sai Sundarakrishnan	PSG College of Technology, India
E. Chandra	Bharathiyar University, India
P. V. S. S. R. Chandramouli	Central University of Tamil Nadu, India
H. S. Ramane	Karnatak University, India
B. H. Shekar	Mangalore University, India
M. Senthilkumar	PSG College of Technology, India
K. S. Sridharan	Sri Sathya Sai Institute, India
P. Balasubramaniam	Gandhigram Rural Institute, India
B. K. Tripathy	VIT, Vellore, India
Aswani Kumar Cherukuri	VIT, Vellore, India
Uma Maheswari	PSG College of Technology, India
M. Sethumadhavan	Amritha Vishwa Vidyapeetham, India
Latha Parameswaran	Amritha Vishwa Vidyapeetham, India
Sudha Sadasivam	PSG College of Technology, India
K. Somasundaram	Amritha Vishwa Vidyapeetham, India
Manish Shukla	TCS Innovation Lab, India

Sponsors

Defence Research and Development Organisation (DRDO)

Robert Bosch

Contents

Computational Models

Computational Intelligence

Iris Recognition Using Symmetric Graph Structure Based Pattern Matching

Aniruddh Kr. Shukla[1], Himanshu Aditya[1], Kundan Kr. Singh[1], Rinku Datta Rakshit[2],
Deep Suman Dev[1(✉)], and Dakshina Ranjan Kisku[3]

[1] Department of Computer Science and Engineering, Neotia Institute of Technology,
Management and Science, Sarisa, South 24 PGS, Kolkata, West Bengal, India
deepsumandev@yahoo.co.in

[2] Department of Information Technology, Asansol Engineering College, Asansol, West Bengal,
India

[3] Department of Computer Science and Engineering, National Institute of Technology,
Durgapur, West Bengal, India
drkisku@cse.nitdgp.ac.in

Abstract. Automatic human identification using biometric information like Iris, leads on to the significant progress in the field of computer vision as it returns better authenticity and accuracy compared to other biometric recognition. This is because of its non-contact acquisition and user-friendly interface. But for unconstrained environment, it suffers when facial expression changes and light intensity differs. In this work, a novel approach for iris recognition called Multi Variant Symmetric Ternary Local Pattern (MVSTLP) is presented using the fundamental idea of pattern matching with the aim to find similarity between scene iris image and query iris pattern image by extracting distinctive features from them, where scene iris image is logically divided into number of query pattern size candidate windows. MVSTLP focuses on neighbour pixels selection in symmetric way within small image area and has unique ability to prioritize distinct feature extraction by establishing strong association between pixels. In effect of these, it can track very minute variations in image property and able to localize iris pattern within the scene iris image very accurately.

Keywords: Iris recognition · Local-feature descriptor · Symmetric patterns

1 Introduction

Historically, authentication conventions were based on things one possessed (a passport, a key, or identity credential), or things which are known (the answer of security question, a password, or a PIN). This information is mainly required to discourse privileges or confirm identity. However, these conventions could be conciliated as – possession of the requisite knowledge by the unauthenticated individual could lead to security breaches.

Biometrics is a mechanism that estimates distinctive physiological and behavioural characteristics of human being for authentication. These characteristics are proven to be more reliable than the traditional mechanisms for their uniqueness and accuracy. Iris,

I. Raman et al. (Eds.): ICC3 2021, CCIS 1631, pp. 3–17, 2022.
https://doi.org/10.1007/978-3-031-15556-7_1

palm print, footprint, face, fingerprint are the physiological characteristics and keystroke, signature and voice are the behavioural characteristics of human being. Out of these characteristics, Iris recognition [1, 2] gained an exceptional acceptance in recent times for its distinctive features with intricate pattern, non-contact acquisition and user-friendly interactive interface. Recognition means whether in the iris image, iris features are present or not. Detection or localization means in which part of the iris image have feature similarity with the features of query pattern iris image. Moreover, Iris has discriminative phase information with span about 249 degrees of freedom [1]. These features make it reliable and help to do accurate biometric authentication.

Iris features become more distinctive by forming different complex and random structures for instance rings, ridges, furrows, freckles, crypts, corona. These features minimize the chances of having similarity between iris patterns of different individuals. Moreover, Iris features are very substantial and is imperceptive to environment and age. Iris recognition has been enforced widely in many large-scale identity authentication systems, such as UID project of India, border control system in docks, airports, hilly regions, access control in factories etc. and in some small-scale applications like, getting access in laboratories, mobile phones, workstations, Automatic Teller Machines (ATM), evidence rooms of police etc. due to its reliability and higher recognition rates.

Key features of Iris are:

- Reliability and Accuracy – Discriminative phase information with span about 249 degrees of freedom, makes Iris recognition very reliable and accurate compared to other biometric identification.
- Uniqueness – Iris of any human being is unique because of the iris pattern structures (instance rings, ridges, furrows, freckles, crypts, corona). No two human beings have same iris pattern structure and it does not also depend on heredity.

The three main operational stages of iris recognition are: image pre-processing, feature extraction and pattern matching. To obtain informative iris region, image pre-processing is done in three steps: iris localization, iris normalization and image enhancement. Inner and outer borderlines are revealed by iris localization, preferably modelled in circular shape. Iris region covered by eyelashes and eyelids are identified and removed for better accuracy. Iris image is converted to Polar coordinates from Cartesian coordinates using iris normalization. The converted image seems to be a rectangular image with angular resolution. Factors like non-uniform illumination and low contrast due to position of light source are handled by image enhancement. Before the feature extraction and pattern matching, pre-processed iris scene image is logically divided into couple of candidate windows of iris query pattern image size following the need of pattern matching process. This entire methodology is based on the principle of pattern matching where candidate window formation is an integral phase. Because, feature matching cannot be initiated between two images with varying size. Followed by feature extraction from candidate windows of scene iris image and query iris image. To assess the similarity, features extracted from query iris image is compared with features extracted from each candidate windows of scene iris image. Iris image portion with the best similarity score will be localized. Generic iris recognition flow diagram is shown in Fig. 1.

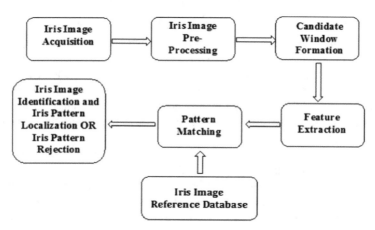

Fig. 1. Generic flow diagram of iris recognition

In Iris recognition, the most challenging factors are iris region partitioning and localization. Wrong partitioning and localization may raise the possibility to have poor outcomes and will degrade the efficacy of the iris recognition process. Image property variation such as, brightness, noise, contrast, blur, varying pigmentation levels, occlusion due to eyelashes, false rejection, false acceptance and environmental obstacles are putting the iris recognition process in challenge to achieve high degree of iris recognition accuracy.

Efficient feature extraction and accurate matching process help to achieve high degree of recognition accuracy. Intensity value of pixel in image, reflects image property. Image property will be changed if there is change in pixel intensity value. Feature extraction algorithm must be efficient to keep track of this change. To keep track of image property variations due to brightness, noise, contrast, blur, occlusion, false rejection, false acceptance and environmental obstacles, close correspondence between pixels in small image regions must be implemented. To implement this, graph structure based local descriptor is a very good candidate. Graph structure is nothing but the pixel orientation within an image area and the close coordination between pixels are implemented by forming pixel sequence path which looks like a graph structure. In image-based graph structure, graph is undirected. Pixel intensity value of an image represents "node" of the graph. Neighbour pixel of any pixel are connected through the line called "edge". Local descriptor identifies any node within a small image area as source or center pixel and refers the nearest neighbour pixels around that source or center pixel to extract distinct informative features. On the other hand, iris matching process can be done using the process of pattern matching. Pattern matching [3, 4] is one of the most advanced and improvised fields of research in terms of biometric and pattern recognition [5]. It has fascinating applications which include object tracking, image localization, image classification [6], shape matching, face tracking [7], face detection [8, 9], etc. Pattern matching process has the basic need of candidate window formation. Because, matching cannot be possible between two different size images. Large scene image is logically fragmented into small size image portions which are of query pattern image size and then comparison is done between candidate windows and query image. This process makes pattern matching very accurate while recognizing and localizing any pattern in large image.

Effective iris matching algorithm using pattern matching methodology with a high degree of matching accuracy and less dependency on computational resources under strict requirements of the matching process and various image complexities together is not achieved yet. Moreover, accurate localization of pattern, make the entire process more challenging.

While localizing an iris query pattern image, similarity measurement based on liner value proven to be inaccurate way to solve the problems because of not considering the measures of statistic like Sum of Squared Difference (SSD), Sum of Absolute Difference (SAD), Euclidian Distance, Mean Squared error (MSE) and Standard Deviation. Two matched patterns can have same MSE but may be different slightly in reality. So, all the factors of pattern must be considered for accurate localization.

2   Literature Survey

Iris features proven to be more unique and consistent compared to other biometric features of human being. It is also a proved fact that, no two persons can have the similar iris features as instance rings, ridges, furrows, freckles, crypts, corona properties vary from person to person.

Authors of [10] suggested that, various iris recognition methodologies can be fused and that can be utilized on non-perfect visible wavelength iris images taken in unimpeded environment. However, it suffers in terms of accuracy. In [11], an iris recognition strategy was proposed which uses different iris attributes present in iris images. But it is tested only on visible light iris images. It seems to be less efficient. By using Top hat filtering and Randon Transform, a flexible Iris recognition process is proposed in [12] and for feature extraction, DWT and DCT were used. It increases time complexity for real time applications. To escalate the recognition rate in noisy condition, a neural network structure was proposed in [13]. Computation time also became a factor here. Authors of [14] suggested a model for heterogeneous iris recognition, where weight map calculation is formulated depending on binary codes present in iris template. In [15], an iris encoding along with matching process was elaborated for noisy iris images. However, the multimodal procedure is not considered in this approach. Reflection and eyelash detection-based Iris segmentation is proposed in [16]. In [17], eyelid, eyelash and shadow localization are implemented as an integral part of iris recognition. Model presented in [18], based on Parabolic Hough model and Otsu's thresholding method, is used for eyelid and eyelash detection in normalized iris image. Gabor wavelet based genetic algorithm is used for iris feature extraction in [19]. A noise removal approach is introduced in [20] for non-cooperative iris recognition.

In [21] demonstrated a nonlinear mechanism which represents the local region consistency of iris bits. Also, this mechanism uses weight map to encode iris bits. This weighted calculation attains more informative elements of local iris features. An enhanced Daugman iris recognition algorithm is proposed in [22] by incorporating improvement needed for iris confinement and iris encoding. It has improved the speed of overall process to some extent. A center key point-based feature extraction process was delineated in [23] by doing productive fusion of SIFT features. It shows substantial improvement in recognition rate. So, it has been seen that feature, extracted on implementation of close correspondence between pixels in local region, gives a certain edge to the recognition algorithm and side-by-side helps to return higher matching accuracy.

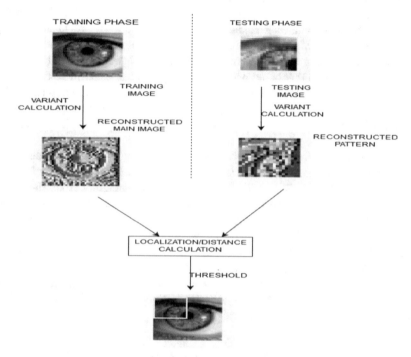

Fig. 2. Iris matching using MVSTLP based pattern matching process

Local Binary Pattern (LBP) [24], extracts local image information by comparing intensity value of the center pixel with intensity values of all its neighbours present in 3×3 small image area. Local graph structure (LGS) [25, 26] extract features from image using the concept of graph structure. It overrules the limitation present in LBP, by considering maximum feature in working grid area. LGS 3×4 structure refers neighbour pixels asymmetrically from left and right side of a source pixel. Illumination invariantness is one of the key properties of LGS. However, it struggles sometimes for its asymmetric graph structure and redundant relationship implementation between pixels. Improvement over LGS was done and reported as Symmetrical Local Graph Structure (SLGS) in [27]. It refers neighbour pixels of target pixel in a balanced symmetric way within a 3×5 small image area. SLGS reduces the number of redundant relationship implementations between pixels to maximum extent. A logical extension over LBP was proposed in [28] as Local Ternary Pattern (LTP) which also works in 3×3 small image area to extract features. These graph structure based local descriptors showed their proficiency in biometric application like face recognition with different image property variations. So, local graph structure-based descriptor can be a good candidate for iris recognition.

In this paper a novel approach, MVSTLP, has been proposed with a focus to maximize recognition rate compared to others by overcoming the limitations of existing methods. Variant formation for MVSTLP is done by comparing center pixel and its neighbour pixels within the small image area, followed by categorization of variants in different pixel groups. Similarity estimation is evaluated with Euclidean distance by comparing iris pattern with each candidate windows formed from individual iris image of the database. Candidate window with best similarity score will be considered as the best possible image area where presence of iris pattern image portion can be seen. Iris recognition using MVSTLP based pattern matching process is shown in Fig. 2. Here feature extraction and image reconstruction are the steps with great importance before the model being tested. Using local descriptor, local image features are extracted in terms of optimal weighted value of interest pixels. From these values image is reconstructed to have better image property clarity.

Iris recognition is done in this paper using graph structure based local descriptor. Local descriptor still has not been used for this purpose. Local descriptor basically works in small image area and extracts local image information by establishing close correspondence between pixels present within that area. To extract informative image information, pixel references surrounding an interest pixel should be symmetric (equal in count) in all direction. While fetching image information, different pixel orientation returns different image information. From that informative unique one will be selected. For these reason, multivariant symmetric approach is important.

Rest of the paper is delineated as follows. Novel MVSTLP based iris matching approach is presented in Sect. 3. Experimental evaluation is elaborated in Sect. 4. Concluding remarks is mentioned in the last section.

3 Proposed Iris Recognition Methodology Using Multi Variant Symmetric Ternary Local Pattern (MVSTLP)

3.1 Problem Formulation

The process of iris recognition with principle of pattern matching contains couple of sequential stages and they are iris image acquisition, iris image pre-processing, candidate window formation, feature extraction, matching and identification of iris pattern and iris pattern localization. In the iris image acquisition stage, iris images are acquired and stored in the database. Iris images are normalized and enhanced in the iris image pre-processing stage. Candidate windows of iris pattern image size are formed by logically dividing the input iris image for more accurate identification of iris pattern. Candidate windows of pattern image size are formed because matching cannot be formulated between different size if images. Suppose, input iris image size is $M_1 \times M_2$ pixels and query iris pattern image size is $Q_1 \times Q_2$ pixels where $Q_1 < M_1$ and $Q_2 < M_2$. MVSTLP works with 3×5 image area to extract the close association between the pixels present within that area. It calculates updated weighted decimal value for each interest pixel by forming variants with different orientation of neighbour pixels for that interest pixel. This helps to figure out distinctive feature points from both the iris image samples and iris pattern image. Then histogram is generated for both candidate windows and query iris pattern image and the histograms are compared to check for similarity. In the iris pattern localization stage, the matched portion in the iris image is localized with respect to query iris pattern image.

3.2 Proposed Methodology – Multi Variant Symmetric Ternary Local Pattern (MVSTLP)

The proposed MVSTLP algorithm which works on a fixed matrix size of 3×5 and updates the intensity value of the interest pixel based on the intensity values of the neighbour pixels. It covers the wide range of pixels within 3×5 image area. This algorithm gives a unique insight where it constructs a new image using feature extraction methodology. The variant calculation is the new add on to this algorithm. For example, pixel intensity values of the pixels present in an assumed 3×5 image area is shown in Table 1.

Table 1. Pixel intensity values in an assumed 3×5 image area

126	131	108	141	150
208	217	190	177	100
215	233	215	114	175

The pixel association with center pixel (CP) or interest pixel is shown in Fig. 3 following MVSTLP. The numbers marked from 0–5 denote the index of the pixels. MVSTLP generates local ternary patterns by referring neighbour pixels symmetrically in three-pixel groups using Eq. 1.

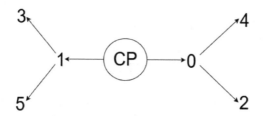

Fig. 3. Position wise neighbour pixels for center pixel (CP)

$$\sum_{i=0}^{N/3} [S(n_{2i} - n_{2i+1})3^i] \tag{1}$$

where N is the number of reference neighbour pixels and for MVSTLP, $N = 6$. Following Eq. 1, the loop will move from $i = 0$ to $i = 2$. Three groups will be formed and, in each group, there will be 2 pixels. For first group (PG 1), where i = 0, neighbourhood reference pixels at positions 0 and 1 are selected with respect to center pixel (CP). For second group (PG 2), where i = 1, neighbourhood reference pixels at positions 2 and 3 are selected with respect to center pixel (CP). For third group (PG 3), where i = 2, neighbourhood reference pixels at positions 4 and 5 are selected with respect to center pixel (CP). With respect to the reference neighbourhood pixel selection different pixel association can be formed with different orientation, which are known as 'variants'. Pixel group and variant formation are shown in Table 2.

Table 2. Pixel group and different variants of MVSTLP with respect to center pixel (CP)

Pixel group	Candidate pixels (index)	Variants		Updated decimal values
PG 1	0th and 1st	V1	(CP-0)(CP-1)(CP-2)(CP-3)(CP-4)(CP-5)(2-3)(4-5)	186
		V2	(CP-0)(CP-1)(CP-2)(CP-3)(5-4)(3-2)(5-CP)(4-CP)	186
		V3	(CP-4)(CP-5)(2-3)(5-4)(CP-0)(CP-1)(CP-2)(CP-3)	187
		V4	(5-4)(3-2)(5-CP)(4-CP)(CP-0)(CP-1)(CP-2)(CP-3)	171
PG 2	2nd and 3rd	V5	(CP-0)(CP-1)(CP-2)(CP-3)(CP-4)(CP-5)(0-1)(4-5)	184
		V6	(CP-0)(CP-1)(CP-2)(CP-3)(5-4)(1-0)(5-CP)(4-CP)	190
		V7	(CP-4)(CP-5)(0-1)(4-5)(CP-0)(CP-1)(CP-2)(CP-3)	139
		V8	(5-4)(1-0)(5-CP)(4-CP)(CP-0)(CP-1)(CP-2)(CP-3)	235
PG 3	4th and 5th	V9	(CP-0)(CP-1)(CP-2)(CP-3)(CP-4)(CP-5)(0-1)(2-3)	185
		V10	(CP-0)(CP-1)(CP-2)(CP-3)(3-2)(1-0)(5-CP)(4-CP)	182
		V11	(CP-4)(CP-5)(0-1)(2-3)(CP-0)(CP-1)(CP-2)(CP-3)	155
		V12	(3-2)(1-0)(5-CP)(4-CP)(CP-0)(CP-1)(CP-2)(CP-3)	107

Optimal updated intensity value of center pixel is calculated using Eq. 2.

$$\left(avg \sum_{PG=1}^{3} \left(avg \sum_{V=1}^{4} set\ V \right) \right) \quad (2)$$

where PG = Pixel Group and V = variant number. Average of 4 variants is taken for each pixel group, so total 3 average values from 3 pixel groups are obtained. After that, again average value from those 3 average values is calculated, which is the optimal updated intensity value of the corresponding center pixel.

3.3 Steps of MVSTLP Based Iris Recognition Process

Step 1: Read query iris image and stored iris images.
Step 2: Divide each stored iris images into candidate windows (shown in Fig. 4) of query iris pattern image size.

Step 3: Apply local feature descriptor "Multi Variant Symmetric Ternary Local Pattern (MVSTLP)," on query iris pattern image and on all candidate windows formed from stored iris images to extract features.

Step 4: MVSTLP works on 3 × 5 reference image area (keeping interest pixel at center of 3 × 5 image area). For each 3 × 5 image area of query iris image and of each candidate window, extract features by calculating binary value and corresponding decimal value using MVSTLP.

Step 5: Generate histogram for each 3 × 5 block with the updated weighted value (applicable for query iris pattern image and each candidate window).

Step 6: Marge all histograms to get one histogram (applicable for query iris pattern image and each candidate window).

Step 7: Distance is calculated between each candidate window histogram with the query iris pattern image histogram using Euclidian Distance metrics.

Step 8: Comparison (distance calculation) gives recognition accuracy.

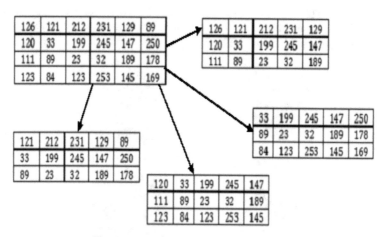

Fig. 4. Sliding candidate window formation

Dividing the stored image at every time means forming the candidate windows of iris pattern image size, is a basic structural need of any recognition using pattern matching concept.

4   Experimental Evaluation

Initially, iris database images are logically divided into number of candidate windows of iris pattern image size. Followed by calculation of optimal weighted value for the center pixel within each 3 × 5 area using MVSTLP. Similarity proximity is calculated with Euclidean distance by comparing iris pattern histogram with each candidate histograms formed from individual iris image of the database. Candidate window with best similarity score will be treated as the most possible image area where iris pattern image portion is present.

The proposed iris recognition process is evaluated on 400 iris images chosen from CASIA-Iris V.3-Interval database. The format of iris images is 8-bit gray level JPEG and the images are captured under near infra-red (NIR) illumination about 700–900 nm. A sample iris image is shown in Fig. 5.

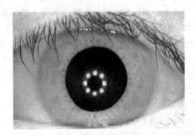

Fig. 5. A sample image from CASIA-Iris V.3-Interval database

Sample iris image, iris pattern image, reconstructed iris and iris pattern image using MVSTLP are shown in Fig. 6. Iris pattern localization using MVSTLP based iris recognition process is shown in Fig. 7.

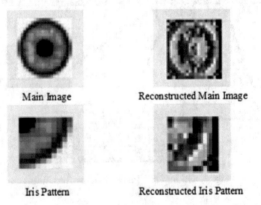

Main Image   Reconstructed Main Image

Iris Pattern   Reconstructed Iris Pattern

Fig. 6. Sample main and Iris pattern image with initial and reconstructed view using MVSTLP

Fig. 7. Iris pattern localization using MVSTLP

To show the efficiency of the proposed MVSTLP based iris recognition process, it was tested along with existing iris recognition processes [16–20] and few local descriptors-based processes by determining essential parameters such as False Rejection Rate (FRR)

with assuming False Acceptance Rate (FAR) = 0.001%, Equal Error Rate (ERR) and Correct Recognition Rate (CRR). In candidate windows, it has been seen that pattern appearance may match in more than one candidate windows. However, it is not possible to take all. The more likely candidate window will be selected. So, how much methods are able to discriminate these negligible candidate windows, that is the matter of concern. For that, FAR is assumed to be fixed with 0.001% and FRR is calculated. Comparative study is conducted on normal image and noisy converted image types of the above mentioned database.

4.1 Results on Iris Images (Normal Type)

For any recognition, feature study is the main step. Extracted feature will include not only image property, but also image property deviation due to noise, blur etc. For this reason, along with other recent state-of-the-art methods, methods delineated in [16–19] and [20] are tested because of their motivation towards iris recognition.

The comparative study between the other processes and proposed MVSTLP based iris recognition process on normal type images is shown in Table 3 and Fig. 8. By keeping FAR = 0.001%, it has been seen that FRR of the process in [20] is less than of the method in [18], but they have shown their competitiveness with similar CRR. Proposed MVSTLP has appeared better than other methods with less FRR and good CRR. Though LGS, SLGS and LTP are tested on face recognition previously, but they have also shown their effectiveness in iris recognition.

Table 3. Recognition accuracies on Iris images (normal type)

Author name/Approach name	FRR (%) @ FAR = 0.001%	ERR (%)	CRR (%)
Kong and Zhang [16]	2.57	0.59	99.14
He et al. [17]	1.90	0.46	99.28
Min and Park [18]	2.37	0.53	99.34
Hamed Ghodrati et al. [19]	3.16	0.93	98.42
Hamed Ghodrati et al. [20]	1.51	0.40	99.34
LGS [26] based approach	3.05	0.86	98.56
SLGS [27] based approach	2.81	0.64	98.87
LTP [28] based approach	2.72	0.61	99.02
MVSTLP based approach	1.46	0.38	99.43

4.2 Results on Iris Images (Noisy Type)

Performance of the algorithms are also tested on noisy converted images of the CASIA-Iris V.3-Interval database. Iid zero-mean Gaussian noise with noise level 100 is applied on the images to make them noisy.

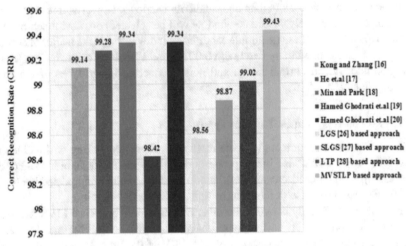

Fig. 8. Comparative accuracy measurement on Iris images (normal type)

The performance of the different recognition processes on noisy type images is shown in Table 4 and Fig. 9. Methods of [17, 18, 20] are good in performance and also competitive to SLGS and LTP based recognition process. Though MVSTLP based recognition process come with little bit higher FRR than method of [20] but surpasses all other methods with very high CRR.

Table 4. Recognition accuracies on Iris images (noisy type)

Author name/Approach name	FRR (%) @ FAR = 0.001%	ERR (%)	CRR (%)
Kong and Zhang [16]	3.17	0.71	98.59
He et al. [17]	2.35	0.58	99.02
Min and Park [18]	2.84	0.62	99.16
Hamed Ghodrati et al. [19]	3.44	0.96	98.77
Hamed Ghodrati et al. [20]	1.78	0.51	99.21
LGS [26] based approach	3.61	0.97	98.02
SLGS [27] based approach	2.68	0.67	99.07
LTP [28] based approach	2.34	0.59	99.18
MVSTLP based approach	1.79	0.38	99.29

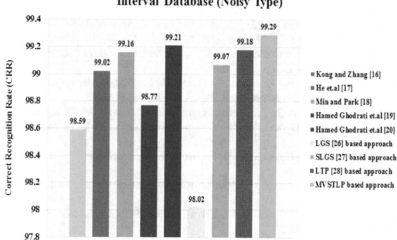

Fig. 9. Comparative accuracy measurement on Iris images (noisy type)

5 Conclusion

This paper has presented an effective local descriptor (MVSTLP) based iris recognition methodology. It has minimized the limitations of other local descriptors such as LGS, SLGS and LTP. For its dominant feature extraction structure and pattern matching procedure in the process of iris identification and localization, it tries to overcome the challenges of other iris recognition processes and increases the matching accuracy also. Another point for any biometric authentication method is that, the captured images not always be without any image property variations, there may be some variations due to image property change. MVSTLP extracts the features in more symmetric way from 3 × 5 small image area by referring unique neighbour pixels. Different variants are formed to extract informative and distinct features. As, MVSTLP works in small image area to extract distinct features, it can identify each image property variations accurately. In addition to this, the distinct feature extraction process of MVSTLP helps to prove its efficacy not only on normal images but also on noisy images. As it is very effective on normal and noisy images, it can also be very effective on blurred, contrast enhanced and noisy (with Gaussian, Brownian, Periodic, Impulse Valued, Quantization noises) images. MVSTLP based matching process can also be used in other biometric identifications like, face, palm print, fingerprint, footprint etc.

References

1. Daugman, J.: How iris recognition works. IEEE Trans. CSVT **14**(1), 21–30 (2004)
2. https://www.irisid.com/productssolutions/technology-2/irisrecognitiontechnology

3. Lewis, J.P.: Fast template matching. In: Vision Interface 95, Canadian Image Processing and Pattern Recognition Society Conference, Quebec City, Canada, pp. 120–123 (1995)
4. Mahalakshmi, T., Muthaiah, R., Swaminathan, P.: An overview of template matching technique in image processing. Res. J. Appl. Sci. Eng. Technol. 4(24), 5469–5473 (2012)
5. Chen, J., Shan, S., Zhao, G., Chen, X., Gao, W., Pietikainen, M.: A robust descriptor based on weber's law. In: IEEE Conference on Computer Vision and Pattern Recognition (CVPR 2008), Anchorage, Alaska, pp. 1–7 (2008)
6. Lyons, M.J., Budynek, J., Akamatsu, S.: Automatic classification of single facial images. IEEE Trans. Pattern Anal. Mach. Intell. 21(12), 1357–1362 (1999)
7. Samaria, F.S., Harter, A.C.: Parameterization of a stochastic model for human face identification. In: 2nd IEEE Workshop on Applications of Computer Vision, Sarasota, Florida, pp. 138–142 (1994)
8. Zong, W., Huang, G.B.: Face recognition based on extreme learning machine. J. Neurocomput. 74, 2541–2551 (2011)
9. Li, S., Gong, D., Yuan, Y.: Face recognition using Weber local descriptors. J. Neurocomput. 122, 272–283 (2013)
10. Santos, G., Hoyle, E.: A fusion approach to unconstrained iris recognition. Pattern Recogn. Lett. 33(8), 984–990 (2012)
11. Tan, T., Zhang, X., Sun, Z., Zhang, H.: Noisy iris image matching by using multiple cues. Pattern Recogn. Lett. 33(8), 970–977 (2012)
12. Dhage, S.S., Hegde, S.S., Manikantan, K., Ramachandran, S.: DWT-based feature extraction and radon transform based contrast enhancement for improved iris recognition. Procedia Comput. Sci. 45, 256–265 (2015)
13. Hajari, K., Gawande, U., Golhar, Y.: Neural network approach to iris recognition in noisy environment. Procedia Comput. Sci. 78, 675–682 (2016)
14. Liu, N., Liu, J., Sun, Z., Tan, T.: A Code-level approach to heterogeneous iris recognition. IEEE Trans. Inf. Forensics Secur. 12(10), 2373–2386 (2017)
15. Tan, C.W., Kumar, A.: Efficient and accurate at-a-distance iris recognition using geometric key-based iris encoding. IEEE Trans. Inf. Forensics Secur. 9(9), 1518–1526 (2014)
16. Kong, W.K., Zhang, D.: Accurate iris segmentation based on novel reflection and eyelash detection model. In: International Symposium on Intelligent Multimedia, Video & Speech Processing, Hong Kong, China, pp. 263–266 (2001)
17. He, Z., Tan, T., Sun, Z., Qiu, X.: Robust eyelid, eyelash and shadow localization for iris recognition. In: Proceedings of the International Conference on Image Processing, San Diego, California, USA, pp. 265–268 (2008)
18. Min, T.H., Park, R.H.: Eyelid and eyelash detection method in the normalized iris image using the parabolic Hough model and Otsu'sthresholding method. Pattern Recogn. Lett. 30, 1138–1143 (2009)
19. Ghodrati, H., Dehghani, M.J., Danyali, H.: Iris feature extraction using optimized Gabor wavelet based on multi objective genetic algorithm. In: International Symposium on Innovations in Intelligent Systems and Applications (INISTA), Dogus University, Istanbul, Turkey, pp. 159–163 (2011)
20. Ghodrati, H., Dehghani, M.J., Danyali, H.: A new accurate noise-removing approach for non-cooperative iris recognition. J. Signal Image Video Process. 8(1), 1–10 (2014). https://doi.org/10.1007/s11760-012-0396-z
21. Tan, C.W., Kumar, A.: Accurate iris recognition at a distance using stabilized iris encoding and zernike moments phase features. IEEE Trans. Image Process. 23(9), 3962–3974 (2014)
22. Peng, Z., Wang, H., Wu, J., Li, J.: An improved Daugman method for iris recognition. Wuhan Univ. J. Nat. Sci. 20(3), 229–234 (2015). https://doi.org/10.1007/s11859-015-1086-9

23. Alvarez-Betancourt, Y., Garcia-Silvente, M.: A keypoints-based feature extraction method for iris recognition under variable image quality conditions. Knowl.-Based Syst. **92**, 169–182 (2016)
24. Rahim, M.A., Hossain, M.N., Wahid, T., Azam, M.S.: Face recognition using Local Binary Patterns (LBP). Glob. J. Comput. Sci. Technol. Graphics Vision. **13**(4), 1–7 (2013)
25. Chen, L., Yang, Y., Chen, C., Cheng, M.: Illumination invariant feature extraction based on natural images statistics—Taking face images as an example. In: IEEE Conference on Computer Vision and Pattern Recognition, Providence, RI, USA, pp. 681–688 (2011)
26. Ayoob, M.R., Mathusoothana, R., Kumar, S.: Face recognition using symmetric local graph structure. Indian J. Sci. Technol. **8**(24), 1–5 (2015)
27. Mankar, V.H., Bhele, S.G.: A review paper on face recognition techniques. Int. J. Adv. Res. Comput. Eng. Technol. **1**, 339–346 (2012)
28. Tan, X., Triggs, B.: Enhanced local texture feature sets for face recognition under difficult lighting conditions. IEEE Trans. Image Process. **19**(6), 1635–1650 (2010)

Program Architecture for Structural Health Monitoring of Pamban Bridge

Shivani Chiranjeevi[1], R. Manimegalai[2]([mail]) [iD], and U. Saravanan[3]

[1] Iowa State University, Iowa, USA
[2] PSG Institute of Technology and Applied Research, Coimbatore, India
drrm@psgitech.ac.in
[3] Indian Institute of Technology Madras, Chennai, India

Abstract. Structural Health Monitoring (SHM) is a damage detection and characterization strategy for mechanical systems and infrastructures. SHM has been used recently for evaluating and monitoring structural health of bridges under operational condition. A SHM system is implemented for a truss bridge in a marine corrosive environment in India, the Pamban Bridge at Rameshwaram in Tamil Nadu. A wired sensor network is deployed that monitors the strain, temperature, and acceleration. All sensors have been linked to form a network and the readings, in binary format are sent over to cloud storage. The readings are converted to ASCII format and analyzed for any abnormality. A notification system is designed and implemented. The proposed SHMON-PB, an IoT based Structural Health Monitoring for Pamban Bridge, alerts all stakeholders if an anomaly is detected. It is hoped that the SHM would eliminate the need for manual inspection which saves a significant amount of cost, effort and resources.

Keywords: Structural Health Monitoring · Wired sensor networks · Cloud storage · Truss bridge · Notification · Authentication and Authorization

1 Introduction

The Pamban bridge serves as a vital link to connect Rameshwaram with mainland is in the world's second most corrosive environment. The bascule section of the Pamban bridge connecting the mainland India to Rameshwaram, is monitored with wired sensors. The truss bridge made of steel is corroding. The corrosion causes a reduction in the cross-sectional area and hence the stiffness of the bridge decreases. Decrease in stiffness causes excessive deflection and hence failure to meet the serviceability condition of the bridge. Since, deflections are not amenable to continuous measurement, acceleration at node points and axial strain in members are measured along with temperature. The abstract architecture of the implemented SHM is shown in Fig. 1. The sensors, namely, the accelerometers, strain gauges and the temperature sensors are distributed over the truss measure and transmit the data over cloud. The measured unstructured data need to be formatted and analyzed to check whether all the parameters under consideration are within limits. The proposed SHM system monitors the bridge for potential inappropriate

I. Raman et al. (Eds.): ICC3 2021, CCIS 1631, pp. 18–30, 2022.
https://doi.org/10.1007/978-3-031-15556-7_2

loss in cross sectional area due to corrosion. Custom analysis software is used to simulate the behavior of the structure for a moving train. As a first diagnostic if the sensed values exceed a predetermined threshold, indicative of a possible damage, an alert notification is sent to the concerned. This would initiate more closer look into the data for damage identification and localization.

2 History of Structural Health Monitoring (SHM)

SHM has evolved greatly from the earliest methods of recurrent hammer strikes at the specimen known as the hammer test and continuous visual inspection for cracks, faults or any other visible deformations. This is primarily because of the widespread civilization resulting in rapid development of concrete structural projects and that these methods were very becoming inefficient as reliable methods of inspection. For the same reasons, the above methods don't formally count as SHM. Inefficiency of the visual inspection methods due to drastic increase in the structures has necessitated development of more reliable methods of health monitoring [1]. Roover et al. [2] have proposed a Digital Image Correlation (DIC) that uses multiple digital cameras. The pictures are captured from time to time and stored to determine strain. These patterns are compared with the currently captured pictures to identify the patterns for damage. Chain Dragging has been implemented by Scott et al. [3]. This involves dragging the chain around the structure and listening to the acoustic reflex from the structure to detect subsurface abnormalities. The accuracy and the reliability of the method depend on the inspector who listens to the sound and analyses it for any damages. Fibre optics are widely used in many projects and it can be used to measure various parameters such as strain, temperature and is used for both local and global monitoring. One such system has been designed by Casas et al. [4]. Using ultrasonic waves has been a popular method of non-destructive evaluation in many fields and has been used extensively in bridge health monitoring. When these waves hit the surface, the reflections of the wave are read by a transducer and the impact of the waves implies details about the areas of damage as suggested by Iyer et al. [5].

Another well-known technique is to make strain measurements by using the electrical resistance strain gauges that has been proposed by Dally et al. [6]. A commonly used sensor for continuous monitoring of the structure is accelerometer which measures acceleration. The vibrations caused by a moving object over the bridge are captured by the sensor. This strategy has been put into use by Park et al. [7]. Acoustic Emission (AE) generally uses piezoelectric sensors to detect the minimal amount of energy released from points of damage from where the energy is emitted as stress waves [8]. The release of energy is usually due to any crack, faults and corroded regions. The faults in any part of the structure can be detected with this sensor but a major disadvantage is the intervention of the background noise with the sound signal which affects the results. Many sensors ranging from the acoustic emission sensors, fibre optic sensors to the commonly used accelerometers are either used individually or in combination according to the needs.

3 Literature Survey

Matthew et al. [9] have proposed a continuous vibration and periodic strain-based monitoring to track the health of a highway bridge. The authors have proposed a system

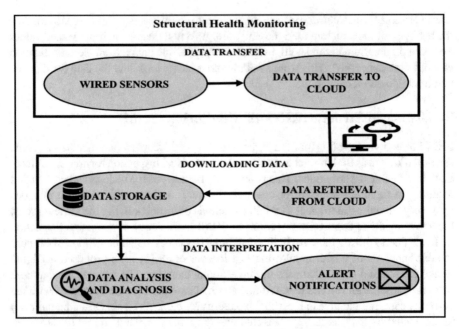

Fig. 1. Block diagram of a typical Structural Health Monitoring system

that uses three sensors namely, the strain transducers to derive the structural characteristics, the temperature sensors to monitor the temperature and the accelerometers to measure the vibration values. It emphasizes on the transmission of data at a high rate with minimal to no loss of packets with dedicated hardware. Though data success rate over a 11-sample duration was 99.999%, the high data transmission rate causes the external buffer to overrun when any interrupts irrelevant to the current task arises. Gregory et al. [10] have proposed a simple system of wireless sensor network (WSN) primarily for its low expenses in terms of easy installation and maintenance for SHM of a truss structure. The sensors are organized to form a centralized network architecture. The sensors are required to transmit the entire raw sensor readings. Consequently, this causes increased network overhead. Decentralized algorithms such as Damage Location Assurance Criterion (DLAC) were used previously for damage localization but it has many disadvantages. The nodes only transmit the intermediate results that are relevant to the flexibility calculations which in turn reduce both the energy and bandwidth usage. The sensor nodes are organized into a hierarchical decentralized architecture which uses clusters. A clustering algorithm is often complex to be implemented and often involves extra computations to re-elect the cluster head if the existing fails.

A WSN consisting of accelerometers which measures the vibration values of different regions of a highway bridge giving information about the structural health of the bridge has been proposed by Li et al. [11]. The sensor measures the vibration values at different times under different loads. Finite Element Analysis (FEA) is carried out and the vibration values are simulated for given load conditions. The simulation results are compared with the actual values to analyse the condition of the bridge. An enhancement is proposed where a database is to be created which will observe the frequency reductions throughout the lifetime of the bridge. An enhanced SHM System using Stream processing and Artificial Neural Network technique (SPANNeT) has been proposed by Khemapech et al. [12]. It provides real time monitoring of the bridges and a warning system which alerts the concerned. The WSN collects the sensor data and on-the-go processing of the data happens and an artificial neural network is built to handle the strain values of different regions of the bridge which is subject to loads only in the vertical direction. The success of the message transfers is 90% which makes the SPANNeT a reliable implementation.

The SPANNeT Weighted Acyclic Graph (WAG) unlike the normal WAG is capable of concurrent verifications. The usage of decentralized systems for SHM poses a variety of problems. The significant being, it requires the real time data to be persisted and also in order to perform any computations on it. Since a huge volume of data is being generated every day, storing such volume causes serious storage issues. Harms et al. [13] have focused on a more power efficient alternative to the above proposal using the Smart Brick technology that uses both on-board and external sensors for measuring both external and structural phenomena and a quad-band modem for long range communication. One major drawback is the cost of the modem and the major advantage being the increased power and data transmission efficiency. SHM has been proposed for industrial and residential buildings by Giammarini et al. [14]. The system uses WSN which is also energy and cost efficient. A real time data acquisition of data must be done to prevent or monitor in case of any unpredictable events such as earthquakes. The cost of the microcontroller, communication modules and sensor nodes used for data acquisition and transfer are very feasible cost wise. The system is centralized meaning all the sensor nodes are connected to it and exchange data with it. This could possibly cause a communication overhead and storage burden due to the large volumes of data generated. The analysis of the entire data collected is the sole responsibility of the data centre which might cause computation overhead and total failure of the system if the central server fails.

Lei et al. [15] have implemented a SHM system for a curved girder skew bridge. The types of monitoring done are environment, static and dynamic monitoring using the respective sensors. The built-in packages in LabView are integrated with the communication modules to collect data, pre-process it and apply algorithms for data analysis and it makes the entire process more reliable and precise. Swit et al. [16] have proposed an Acoustic Emission (AE) based SHM for a cable-stayed bridge in Vietnam. When any micro fracture occurs, energy is released in the form of an AE wave. The sensor captures this wave and converts it to an electrical wave for further analysis. The AE method identifies earlier stages of damage and enables retrofitting to the existing structures by identifying the matured damage prone regions. There is also a high possibility of external noises interfering with the sensing system resulting in false alarms. Patil et al. [17] have used a combination of ultrasonic sensors and accelerometers. The accelerometers measure the tilting angle of the bridge pillar whereas the ultrasonic sensors measure the level of water. Though the use of a centralized server has many disadvantages, the data transmission packet loss rate is significantly improved in this implementation.

4   The Proposed Structural Health Monitoring System

The purpose of the proposed SHM system in the bridge is to determine the overall axial stiffness of each of the members of the truss that make the bridge. The ideal method to find the axial stiffness of the members of the truss is by measuring the displacement at all the nodes of the truss. However, continuous measurement of the displacement is not possible leading one to seek alternative methods. If the truss is statically indeterminate internally, the overall member axial stiffness could be estimated from the axial strain in the members, but this is not possible in case of internally statically determinate truss. Further, only the locomotive would have a constant axle load. The wagon axle load depends on the passenger/goods carried. Hence, the forces coming on the truss is also an unknown. In other words, based on the measured response of the truss to an unknown forcing function, its characteristics must be determined. Towards this, 84 of the 92 members of the truss is instrumented with electrical strain gauge to measure the axial strain. These measured axial strains would facilitate in the estimation of the axle loads of the train moving over it. It also would provide localized estimate of the stiffness of the member. Apart from this the truss is instrumented with 40 accelerometers. 20 of them measuring the vertical acceleration of the bridge at 20 nodes of the truss and the remaining measure the axial acceleration of the bridge at the same 20 locations. Apart from these there are 10 temperature sensors. While the sampling rate of the strain gauges is 100 Hz that of the temperature gauges is only 1 Hz. However, since it is desired that the accelerometer readings need to be integrated to get displacements after suitable filtering to remove the noise and the initial conditions, each accelerometer is sampled at 600 Hz.

The system is configured such that if the reading in the trigger accelerometers exceed a threshold due to the passage of a train, the data acquisition system wakes up and start recording the data for around 500 s. The recordings of the accelerometer, strain and temperature sensors are stored and transmitted in separate files. Thus, a train pass generates around 100 MB of data. The data is stored locally as well as transmitted to the cloud. The data generated over a day is to be analyzed at a prefixed time. For this the data is to be downloaded from the cloud, the file format must be converted from binary to ASCII and the data analyzed. The analysis of data consists of three checks: (*i*) ensure that the sensed values are within acceptable limits (*ii*) the sensed values of various sensors are correlated and hence it is checked if these correlations hold (*iii*) estimate the axle loads and axial stiffness of the members and to ensure they are within limits. Custom algorithms implemented in MATLAB performs the analysis and generates a report and a warning message, if required.

5   Data Retrieval from Sensors

The sensors set up at multiple locations along the bridge collect the measurements when the train passes over the bridge. The collected files are transmitted over to a cloud server in binary format as the size of the file is minimal and transmission rates are fast.

5.1   Data Storage in the Proposed SHM Using Cloud

The proposed health monitoring system uses Microsoft's OneDrive cloud platform for storing the data. It first was launched by Microsoft in August 2007. Users store their files and the data can be synced across multiple devices. OneDrive for Business is used for commercial purposes where the organization must pay for the usage. A Python script is used to download the files from OneDrive. Authorization and authentication are required to access the data from OneDrive. Authentication is the process of proving the identity of the user. Authorization is the act of granting an authenticated party permission to perform a particular action. It specifies what data the entity can be accessed and what operations can be performed on the data. Microsoft identity platform which is explained in the following section implements the OpenID Connect protocol for handling authentication and OAuth 2.0 protocol for handling authorization.

5.2   Microsoft Identity Platform and Graph API

Microsoft Identity Platform (MIP) is a platform that allows applications developed to sign into Microsoft accounts. It provides authorized access to APIs such as Microsoft Graph which is the gateway to data in Microsoft 365 such as One Drive by providing a unified programmability model. MIP authenticates users and provides security tokens that provide a client application access to the protected resources on a resource server. Before MIP, Azure Active Directory (Azure AD) Developer Platform v1.0 was deployed for this purpose. MIP evolved from Azure AD. Azure AD uses Azure AD Authentication Library (ADAL) and MIP uses Microsoft Authentication Library (MSAL). OAuth 2.0 and OpenID Connect (OIDC) are the security standards used to achieve the authorization and authentication by MIP respectively. Microsoft Graph API is a RESTful web API that allows users to access the Microsoft cloud resources. It exposes REST APIs and client libraries to access the data on One Drive.An application can interact with data pertaining to all the services in Microsoft 365 using a single endpoint called graph.microsoft.com as shown in Fig. 2. Microsoft Graph API is secured by MIP and an application must get access token from MIP and attach it to each Graph API request.

5.3   Scopes and Permissions

The app requires permissions for performing operations such as reading a file, writing to a file. The users or administrators can either approve or deny the requests that the Client app requests. It is a safe practice for the app developers to request only for the permissions they need for the app to function. The permissions are referred to as scopes and they are represented by a string. The requests for the scopes can be made in the authorization request using the scope parameter. The Microsoft Identity Platform provides provisioning for the following types of permissions [18]:

Delegated Permissions: The app requires certain permissions to be provided if it must perform the files uploaded to the cloud. These permissions require a user signed into the Microsoft OneDrive account to consent to the permissions asked for. Some high privileged permissions require the administrator of the account to consent to the permissions. The app which requests the consent may not have more privileges than the user who consents to these permissions. **Application Permissions:** These permissions do not require a signed in user to consent to the permissions. They are consented by the administrator account.

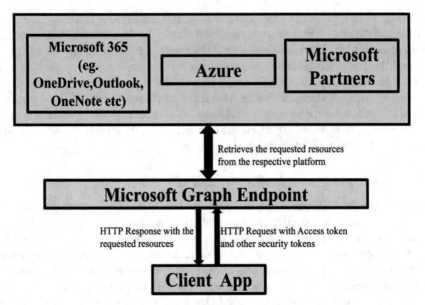

Fig. 2. Data access using Microsoft Graph API

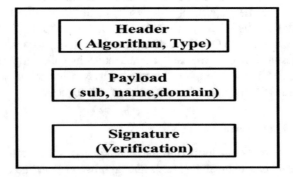

Fig. 3. Access token structure

5.4 Security Tokens Used in OAuth 2.0 and OIDC

Access Tokens: Access Tokens are security tokens which are issued by MIP endpoint. These security tokens are JSON Web Tokens (JWTs), Base 64 encoded JSON objects signed by Azure. Client receives the access token from the Azure v2.0 endpoint. Access tokens are given in response to the GET request to the endpoint where the Client includes the permissions it requires along with other details. The response contains information such as the expiry period of the token, the scopes/permissions granted and other metadata about the token. The contents of the tokens are called claims. The token is split into three parts namely the header, payload and the signature, each separated by a period and Base64 encoded as depicted in Fig. 3. The Client treats the token as an opaque string.

ID Tokens: ID tokens are security tokens used to verify the identity of the user by the Client as a part of the OIDC protocol to enable a single sign-on that can be used across multiple applications. This is returned to the Client along with access token. ID tokens are JWTs similar to the access tokens. The claims for ID tokens are the same as that of the access tokens. Here the payload contains the information that the Client wants to know about the user.

5.5 OAuth 2.0 Authorization Protocol

OAuth 2.0 [18] is a security protocol used solely for the purpose of authorization as depicted in Fig. 4. It gives an application i.e. the Python script, the permission to access the resources stored in OneDrive on behalf of the user without the user having to give his or her credentials. The app must post a HTTP request to the authorization endpoint of MIP to receive the authorization code. This code is exchanged with the token endpoint of MIP to receive access token. Access token provides access to the Microsoft Graph API protected Azure AD. The Resource owner in this protocol is the user who owns the data One Drive. Client is the app created with Azure AD which requires APIs to access the data. Authorization server is the MIP which is capable of providing and revoking access to resources and issuing tokens. Resource server is the platform where the data resources are hosted. The interactions between the entities of OAuth 2.0 protocol and how tokens are exchanged from endpoints are illustrated in Fig. 4 and Fig. 5. OAuth 2.0 only provides authorization not authentication. Open ID Connect (OIDC) is used for this purpose. It is an authentication protocol heavily based on and is an extension of OAuth 2.0 protocol. It ensures that a user signs into a web application securely. It differs from OAuth 2.0 mainly in the use of an ID token. This ID token helps the Client app to verify the identity of the user by reading the profile details of the user. This in turn enables the user to experience a Single sign-on (SSO) at the Client. The ID Token is typically a JWT. The Client app can acquire an access token as it is an extension of OAuth 2.0 protocol. The OIDC varies from the OAuth in the scopes mentioned in the initial GET request. The offline_access scope of OIDC is used here. In the HTTP response, an access token and an ID token is returned.

OAuth 2.0 only provides authorization not authentication. Open ID Connect (OIDC) is used for this purpose. It is an authentication protocol heavily based on and is an extension of OAuth 2.0 protocol. It ensures that a user signs into a web application securely. It differs from OAuth 2.0 mainly in the use of an ID token. This ID token helps the Client app to verify the identity of the user by reading the profile details of the user. This in turn enables the user to experience a Single sign-on (SSO) at the Client. The ID Token is typically a JWT. The Client app can acquire an access token as it is an extension of OAuth 2.0 protocol. The OIDC varies from the OAuth in the scopes mentioned in the initial GET request. The offline_access scope of OIDC is used here. In the HTTP response, an access token and an ID token is returned. Before the authorization code flow starts, the Client app must be registered with the Azure AD and the necessary configurations for the app. The app name is given, supported account types are selected and the point from where tokens are to be received and requests are to be submitted i.e. redirect URI is selected. Client ID, an object ID and a directory ID are created which

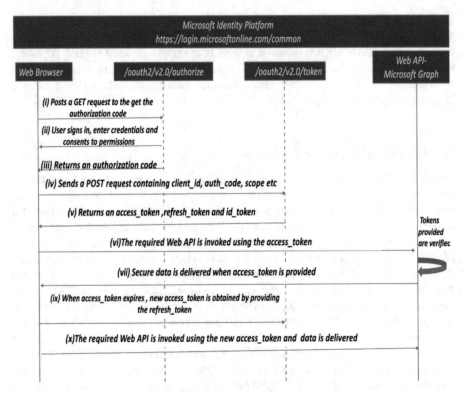

Fig. 4. OAuth authorization protocol

is noted down for obtaining the tokens at a later point. The details of the app created are displayed on the Azure Dashboard. The devices on which the app would be used are selected and any default redirect URI provided is selected for use. Redirect URI is typically where the app can send and receive authentication requests and responses. The redirect_uri is assigned by default according to the platform the app is used on. The API permissions are chosen according to the operation that would be performed over the files. If the permissions require admin consent, it has to be approved by the admin. To obtain the authorization code or the auth_code, a GET request is made with the redirect URI with parameters such as the client_id, scopes. In the response, the auth_code is returned which is saved to obtain the access token in the next step. The process of submitting the request and obtaining the token from the endpoint is illustrated in Fig. 6.

The user is requested to sign in at this step to verify his/her credentials to proceed to get the auth_code. A successful response returns two parameters, the code and state. The former contains the authorization code and the latter is a verification parameter for the app to check if the values in it are identical during both the request and response. If the response is unsuccessful, an error code and the error description is returned. Now a POST request of type FORM URL Encoded is made where the body contains the following parameters (*i*) grant_type, (*ii*) client_id and (*iii*) code. The body of the

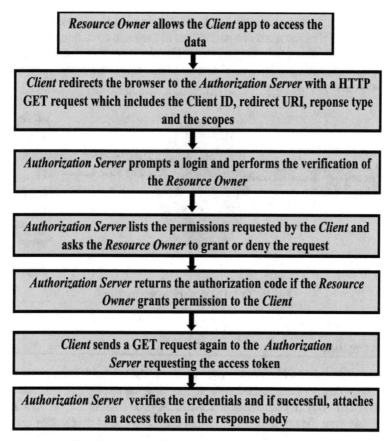

Fig. 5. Workflow of OAuth 2.0 authorization protocol

response contains an access token and a refresh token which expires in the time specified in the expiry_period in the response body. Access tokens come with an expiry period which is typically 3600 s. They must be refreshed occasionally to have continued access to the resources. A POST request must be made again to the token endpoint but the refresh_token parameter must be passed in the body of the request instead of the code where we had passed the auth_code previously. This token is applicable to all the permissions the app had received consent to. A successful JSON response contains the requested access_token, token_type, expires_in, scope,refresh_token and id_token parameters.

The error response contains the error code, the error description, list of error codes that helps in diagnosis of the error, timestamp specifying the time when the error occurred, a trace ID and a correlation ID. The files are generated whenever the train passes over the bridge. The files need to be downloaded and analysed once in a day. The file to be downloaded is achieved by posting a GET request containing the path of the file and the accesstoken. A folder is generated each day which contains the date it was generated. The system's date is computed and only the folder containing the files of that specific date are downloaded into the local computer into folders organized by date and type. Initially, a GET request to search the files in the drive containing today's files is made. The files are stored in a list and these files alone are downloaded everyday by making a GET request again instead of downloading all the files in the drive folder for efficient storage.

Fig. 6. Twilio SMS sending mechanism

6 Automation

The sensors record data whenever the train runs over the bridge. It is unreliable to have a person download the files, run the code and retrieve the results. So, the code must be run at the end of every day automatically. Also, the code must be run on boot up of the system eliminating the need for any user intervention. The system's date is retrieved using the date time package and any folder with the date is matched and the files inside those folders are used for processing. This process is done at 23:00 h every day. The module from the Python library that is used is *schedule*. The code is required to run on windows start up. This enables the program to be run every time the system starts up. In the Users folder, Hidden Apps on top of the menu bar of the file explorer is clicked. The App Data is selected and further navigated to the Startup folder. The Windows Registry is a collection of databases of configuration settings for Microsoft Windows operating systems. The Windows Registry stores much of the information and settings for software programs, hardware devices, user preferences, and operating system configurations. The Python script that must be automated is added to the Windows Registry and this is also done using a Python script where the Windows registry key must be edited. Registry has a list of programs that must be executed when the user logs onto the system. The Python script that must be automated along with its path must be added to the registry. The Python code which adds the script to the windows registry should be run as the administrator when it is done for the first time.

7 Conclusions and Future Work

The developed system for SHM was successfully able to retrieve the binary sensor measurement readings from Microsoft's OneDrive. Authorization and authentication protocols are implemented that ensure that only protected access to the resources is permitted. The data conversion takes place at the local computer where the header information is also extracted and processed separately. The converted data values are analysed further to check if they lie in the optimal range. If not, an alert system was developed to intimate the concerned persons for further measures to be taken. This greatly avoids the need for manual inspection at sites where such tasks are difficult to be carried out. An efficient mechanism that downloads the files automatically as soon as it becomes available to process and analyse the conditions on the go could be integrated with the existing modules. This effectively would make the analysis and notification modules more dynamic and relevant to the needs.

References

1. Gastineau, A., Johnson, T., Schultz, A.E.: Bridge health monitoring and inspection–a survey of methods. University of Minnesota, Technical Report (2009). www.lrrb.org/pdf
2. De Roover, C., Vantomme, J., Wastiels, J., Taerwe, L.: DIC for deformation assessment: a case study. Eur. J. Mech. Environ. Eng. **48**(1), 13–19 (2003)
3. Scott, M., et al.: A comparison of nondestructive evaluation methods for bridge deck assessment. NDT&E Int.. **36**, 245–255 (2003)
4. Casas, J., Cruz, P.: Fiber optic sensors for bridge monitoring. J. Bridg. Eng. **8**(6), 362–373 (2003)
5. Iyer, S., Schokker, A., Sinha, S.: Ultrasonic c-scan imaging: preliminary evaluation for corrosion and void detection in post tensioned tendons. Transp. Res. Rec. **1827**, 44–52 (2003)
6. Dally, J., Riley, W.: Experimental Stress Analysis. 4th ed. College House Enterprises, LLC (2005)
7. Park, H.S., Lee, H.M., Adeli, H., Lee, I.: A New Approach for Health Monitoring of Structures: Terrestrial Laser Scanning. Computer-Aided Civil and Infrastructure Engineering. **22**(1), 19–30 (2007)
8. Baifeng, J.I., Weilian, Q.U.: The research of acoustic emission techniques for non destructive testing and health monitoring on civil engineering structures. In: International Conference on Condition Monitoring and Diagnosis, p. 57 (2008)
9. Whelan, M.J., Gangone, M.V., Janoyan, K.D.: Highway bridge assessment using an adaptive real-time wireless sensor network. IEEE Sens. J. **9**(11), 1405–1413 (2009)
10. Hackmann, G., Guo, W., Yan, G., Sun, Z., Lu, C., Dyke, S.: CyberPhysical codesign of distributed structural health monitoring with wireless sensor networks. IEEE Trans. Parallel Distrib. Syst. **25**(1), 63–72 (2014)
11. Li, F.X., Islam, A.A., Jaroo, A.S., Hamid, H., Jalali, J., Sammartino, M.: Urban highway bridge structure health assessments using wireless sensor network. IEEE Topical Conf. Wirel. Sens. Sens. Netw. (WiSNet) **2015**, 75–77 (2015)
12. Khemapech, I., Sansrimahachai, W., Toahchoodee, M.:A real-time health monitoring and warning system for bridge structures. In: 2016 IEEE Region 10 Conference (TENCON), pp. 3010–3013 (2016)
13. Harms, T., Sedigh, S., Bastianini, F.: Structural health monitoring of bridges using wireless sensor networks. IEEE Instrum. Meas. Mag. **13**(6), 14–18 (2010). https://doi.org/10.1109/MIM.2010.5669608
14. Giammarini, M., Isidori, D., Concettoni, E., Cristalli, C., Fioravanti, M., & Pieralisi, M.:Design of wireless sensor network for real-time structural health monitoring. In: 2015 IEEE 18th International Symposium on Design and Diagnostics of Electronic Circuits & Systems, pp. 107–110 (2015)

15. Lei, S.S., Gao, Y.T., Pan, D.G.: Comprehensive real time bridge health monitoring system of tongtai bridge. In: MATEC Web of Conferences, vol. 31, p. 11003. https://doi.org/10.1051/matecconf/2015311100358 (2015)
16. Swit, G., Krampikowska, A., Luong, M.C.: A prototype system for acoustic emission-based structural health monitoring of Mỹ Thuận Bridge (2016). https://doi.org/10.1109/PHM.2016.7819877
17. Patil, P.K., Patil, S.R.: Structural health monitoring system using WSN for bridges. In: 2017 International Conference on Intelligent Computing and Control Systems (ICICCS), pp. 371–375 (2017). https://doi.org/10.1109/ICCONS.2017.8250746
18. Wike, R.: Permissions and consent in the Microsoft identity platform endpoint. Microsoft identity platform- Azure, 01–2020. Technical report (2020). https://docs.microsoft.com/en-us/azure/active-directory/develop/v2-permissions-and-consent

Masking Based De Trop Noise Exclusion and Image Inpainting Instance Restoration

S. Gopikha$^{(\boxtimes)}$ and M. Balamurugan

School of Computer Science and Engineering, Bharathidasan University, Tiruchirappalli, India
gopikha.in@gmail.com, mbala@bdu.ac.in

Abstract. Skin cancer has shown a rapidly growing event rate, highlighting skin cancer as a significant issue for general well-being. Impediment due to artifacts in dermoscopic images impacts the analytic activity and decreases the precision level. In this work, the De Trop Noise Exclusion - Inpainting (DNE-INPAINT) approach is proposed for the errand of artifacts evacuation and posterior mending on dermoscopic images. The methodology eliminates forefront white matter artifacts and reconstruction of missed pixels by a sequence of vintage boosting, Gray contrast stretching, filtering, mask creation for the noise existence areas and inpaint the masked areas relative with a source image. The experiments use the ISIC 2019 and ISIC 2018 dataset to prove the exhibition of the proposed technique that is demonstrated to be superior to other methods. To survey the quality of the outcomes acquired by the proposed methodology, concerning the original images, various metrics such as Mean Squared Error (MSE), Peak Signal-to-Noise Ratio (PSNR), Structural Similarity Index (SSIM) and some other parameters, which are deliberated in result section.

Keywords: Artifacts · Inpainting · Gray contrast stretching · Vintage boosting

1 Introduction

At present days, skin cancer is the world's fastest growth tumors, and melanoma is a form of skin cancer that is most life-threatening [1, 2]. Since the diagnosis of skin cancer might confront various human problems and entails some cost and morbidity, researchers aim to automate this assessment to verify whether it is harmless or dangerous. High efficiency computer helped the doctors avoid misdiagnosis using diagnostics systems. However, computer-aided diagnosis of skin illness is one of the most troublesome challenges in the processing of medical images [2–4]. This helps dermatologists to choose whether a tumor in the skin is benign or malignant. Unfortunately, at some point in the acquisition and communication stage the skin picture gets damaged by noise. Noise corruption in factual life is unavoidable in the process of sensing images and could suggestively affect the quality of the image. Thus the picture content cannot be readily observed and the bright image can affect tasks of high vision. Therefore, removing noise at various image processing and vision tasks from the observed image is an integral step [5, 6]. Denoising has therefore considered a classical but demanding study of medical images.

© The Author(s), under exclusive license to Springer Nature Switzerland AG 2022
I. Raman et al. (Eds.): ICC3 2021, CCIS 1631, pp. 31–48, 2022.
https://doi.org/10.1007/978-3-031-15556-7_3

A great number of denoising approaches to recover the pure image from the noisy remark were proposed during the last decades. And the following characteristics should be a beautiful image denotation algorithm: (1) The clean images with unidentified noise are to improve sufficiently [7]. In other words, a single model may retrieve different noisy images. (2) The recovery of noisy images should be effective and not take too long. (3) The original image information must be preserved while it is denounced, particularly the high-dimensional image texture data that is readily misconstrued for noise. Many approaches have been proposed for denouncing images, including previous methods based on picture [8, 9] and discriptive methods of image denouncement based learning [10–14] in recent decades. One of the classic denoisers is Block matching and 3D (BM3D) [7], an image denoisers benchmark. For BM3D, the related blocks in the picture are usually searched and grouped first.

After that, co-operative filtering denotes comparable blocks. Finally, the blocks are fused with varied weights into the original image. BM3D is quicker than other image-based algorithms, but when the noise is complicated, it will deteriorate. Although BM3D performs well in terms of denoising, it is insufficient for denoising pictures polluted by high amounts of noise. In other words, as the noise level upsurges, so does the performance of BM3D. Although previous techniques are capable of achieving promising denotational performance, they confront the challenges of manually defined parameters and sophisticated optimum algorithms. In order to tackle these challenges, many descriptive strategies for learning the previous picture models were presented. In order to train a denoising ideal based on a picture of the field of experts with degree of decline inference, Chen et al. created a trainable, nonlinear reaction diffusion scheme [10]. Chen et al. Although these methods work well for denotation of images, the applicability are limited by the precursors utilized. In order to acquire the optimum settings [12], a number of hand-tuned parameters are also needed. Moreover, for a particular noise level, the previous methods are useless for blind denoising.

To tackle the issues, DNE-INPAINT approach is proposed to solve the evacuation and posterior patching on input dermoscopic images. The artifacts of forefront white matter is eliminated and damaged pixels restoration is done with the process.

1)   Vintage boosting helps to improve the radiant of the image.
2)   Gray contrast stretching stretches the image intensities of the image this tends to enhance contrast more precisely.
3)   Filtering technique to observed hair in order to detect the hair outline
4)   Mask created in the presence of artifacts areas and
5)   Reconstruct the missed pixels is done by comparing with the source image area from the donor pixel near the area boundary to paint over the masked area.

The experimental study uses the two publicly available datasets to authenticate the effective of proposed DNE-INPAINT technique with existing techniques. The remaining paper is ordered as follows: Sect. 2 presents the study of existing techniques with its limitation. Section 3 describes the proposed practise along with algorithm. The validation of the proposed methodology with existing techniques in terms of various parameters are given in Sect. 4. Lastly, the research study conclusion is deliberated in Sect. 5.

2 Literature Review

Skin cancer has drawn the attention of the medical and scientific community in the past years due to its high occurrence and severe treatment. Although noise in medical images is a trouble for the reason that it can obscure and blur important characteristics in images, many of the noise reduction techniques have own problems.

Khan et al. [15] present an efficient technique for enhancing dermoscopic images by eliminating a hair and extra artifacts by black-hat morphological dispensation and total variant inpainting. Furthermore, to demonstrate the impact of augmentation of dermoscopic images, a scheme is projected to achieve skin lesion classification results comparable to deep neural networks at the same cheap cost as Conv 2-D by acting two dimensional convolution on images. To cater information thoroughly, this system goes through 3 convolution streams. The suggested model is tested on a public Skin Lesion database of 2000 images. When hair and artifacts are removed using the suggested method, the classification accuracy of three classes, and Seborrheic Keratosis (SK), improves. The segmentation process is not carried out by this technique.

Lyakhova and Lyakhov [16] suggested a technique for recognizing and cleaning hair, as well as assessing the technique's performance using a pre-trained neural network. Hair in image can conceal key diagnostic information when studying pigmented lesions, lowering the usefulness and excellence of examination results. The MatLab R2019b software package is used to model clinical dermatoscopic pictures from the open record ISIC Melanoma Project. The classification for dermatoscopic images of pigmented skin formations with an initial phase of hair removal will allow doctors to boost the efficacy and speed of diagnosis and begin disease treatment earlier. The reconstruction of missed pixel areas are not concentrated by this method.

Javaid [17] used machine learning to develop a system for classifying and segmenting skin lesions as benign or malignant. A novel approach of contrast stretching of dermoscopic images, which is based on the approaches of mean values and pixels standard deviation. The OTSU thresholding algorithm is then used to segment the image. Following segmentation, characteristics such as the GLCM for texture documentation, the Histogram of Oriented Gradients (HOG) object, and color identification features are recovered from the segmented pictures. For dimensionality reduction, HOG features are reduced using Principal Component Analysis (PCA). To address the class imbalance issue, Synthetic Minority Oversampling Method (SMOTE) sampling is used. For classification, classifiers such as Quadratic Discriminant, SVM, and Random Forest are utilized. The suggested method is validated using the publicly available ISIC-ISBI 2016 dataset. The Random Forest (RF) classifier achieves the highest level of accuracy. On ISIC-ISBI 2016, the system with the RF classifier had a classification accuracy of 93.89%. However, Random Forest takes very long time for training, when compared with SVM and other machine learning technique.

Ramella, [18] suggested a simple approach for detecting and removing hair from dermoscopic images. Initially, the regions to examine as candidate hair regions, as well as the border/corner components placed on the image frame, are discovered automatically. The hair areas are then determined using saliency, shape, and image color information. Finally, the discovered hair areas are recreated using a straightforward inpainting technique. The approach is tested using a publicly available dataset of 340 image in total. We also suggest a way for evaluating a hair removal procedure on a qualitative and quantitative basis. The evaluation results are promising since the detection of hair regions is accurate, and the performance results are acceptable in comparison to other existing hair removal technologies. However, the inpainting techniques requires modification for better classification accuracy.

Attia [19] suggested a deep learning strategy for hair segmentation using feebly labeled data that is built on a hybrid network of recurrent and convolutional layers. The method relied on deep encoded features to recognize and delineate hair in skin images. After that, the encoded structures are input into recurrent neural network layers, which encode the spatial relationships between fragmented patches. The studies are carried out on a publicly accessible dataset titled "Towards Melanoma Detection: Challenge". The technique outperformed the state-of-the-art method in terms of segmentation accuracy, with a Jaccard Index of 77.8% versus 66.5% reported by the method. In addition, the method achieved a tumor disrupt pattern as low as 14%, associated to 23% for the existing technology. Using inadequately labeled ground truth for training, the hybrid construction for segmentation was able to precisely distinguish and separate the hair from the background, with lesions and the skin. The results will be poor while the hybrid technique is implemented with larger datasets.

Dhabal, [20] anticipated the differential evolution based slap swarm algorithm (DESSA) as improved denoising method. The improved performance of SSA is used to optimally obtain the different combinations of filters and cascaded arrangement of filters are carried out in this process. The DESSA method is used to effectively remove the three different noises such as speckle noise, gaussian noise, salt and pepper noise. The method used the CEC2014 datasets in terms of PSNR and SSIM. However, the method didn't focus on the segmentation process that increases the PSNR value.

Recovering an unpolluted image was suggested by Tian, [21], the Dual Denoising Network (DudeNet). By extracting both global and local data and fusing them to attain salient features, DudeNet's sparse technique effectively trades denoising performance for processing speed. Additionally, the author advocated for the use of compression blocks to eliminate redundant data and reduce computational and memory usage. DudeNet's great visual quality and computing efficiency have been demonstrated in a large number of studies. Multiple low-level vision responsibilities, such as image super-resolution and deblurring, are inaccessible to the DudeNet.

For the purpose of achieving high perceptual quality results while maintaining a small MSE, Kawar, [22] developed a novel stochastic denoising approach. With Langevin dynamics, we sample from the posterior distribution to reconstruct the image, which is then applied repeatedly to any given MMSE denoiser. Our approach for solving the inpainting problem has been extended to recover missing pixels and remove noise from partially provided data while recovering missing pixels. For the denoising solution, this method must develop uncertainty measures in order to reveal and quantify the range of probable outcomes.

Ohayon, [23] have took a different approach, aiming to produce sharp and aesthetically pleasing denoised images that remain true to their clean sources. According to the rules, the objective is to obtain excellent perceptual quality while minimizing unwanted distortion. Using a stochastic denoiser trained as a generator within conditional generative adversarial networks, this is accomplished by taking samples from the posterior distribution (CGAN). The penalty term introduced to the CGAN goal in this study is theoretically grounded and does not impose a distortion requirement on individual samples, as is the case with distortion-based regularization terms.

Chen, [24] developed a play-and plug medical image denoising framework, namely Lesion-Inspired Denoising Network (LIDnet), to collaboratively improve both denoising performance and detection accuracy of denoised medical images. Specifically, to insert the feedback of downstream detection task into existing denoising framework by jointly learning a multi-loss objective. Instead of using perceptual loss calculated on the entire feature map, a novel region-of-interest (ROI) perceptual loss induced by the lesion detection task is to further connect these two tasks. To achieve better optimization for overall framework, a customized collaborative training strategy is developed for LIDnet. On consideration of clinical usability and imaging characteristics, three low-dose CT images datasets are used to evaluate the effectiveness of the LIDnet.

Talavera-Martinez [25] to use convolutional neural networks (CNN) in conjunction with an encoder-decoder architecture to detect and restore the hair's pixels from dermoscopic images prior to performing hair removal. It's also worth noting that, during the network's training phase, an entirely new combined loss function is implemented that incorporates the L1 distance as well as the total variation loss as well as the structural similarity index metric. When evaluating the efficacy of this technique using simulation, researchers turn to tools like PH2, dermquest, EDRA2002, dermis and the ISIC Data Archive. These algorithms don't seem to be able to tell the difference between lighter and darker hairs.

In dermoscopic pictures, Talavera-Martnez, [26] created a model based on CNN for hair removal. The model's restoration ability is improved using a joint loss function during the network's training. We pretend the existence of skin hair in hairless image used from publicly known datasets such as the PH2, EDRA2002, dermquest, dermis and the ISIC Data Archive in order to train the CNN and objectively assess its performance. Using a more comprehensive system for skin lesion analysis and using the resulting information to extract additional characteristics will not work with this technique.

A novel blind picture denoising method, devised by Wang, [27] have utilizes the asymmetric GAN. The novel method utilizes adversarial learning to optimize high-dimensional image information denoising in order to attain a good balance between noise removal and detail preservation. An image down-sampling layer is inserted among the generating model and the discriminating model to overawed the unstability of the GAN training and increase the discriminative performance of the discriminating model. The complete image's feature is extracted, and the noise effect on training images is reduced, using a multi-scale feature down-sampling layer. The ID-AGAN algorithm's performance is thoroughly tested using a variety of diverse experimental setups. However, the more texture information in the image will be lost if this algorithm is used.

Image denoising scheme (BM3D) and Wiener filter (which is at the core of the BM3D algorithm) were thoroughly examined by Hasan, [28]. After that, an enhanced Wiener filter tailored to SSIM, greatly improving BM3D's performance. Using BM3D's upgraded Wiener filter, researchers were able to demonstrate that high-quality image denoising may be achieved.

For picture denoising, Wang, [29] created a new low-rank matrix recovery technique. Using an existing reweighted low-rank matrix approach, we integrate a total variation (TV) norm and a pixel range restriction to achieve structural smoothness and considerably increase the recovered image's quality. Low-rank matrix recovery is mathematically formulated by using the nuclear norm, TV normal and l1 norm together, which allows the low-rank things of natural images to be utilized, the structural smoothness to be enhanced and massive sparse noise to be detected and removed. The suggested difficult non-convex optimization issue is solved using iterative alternating direction and fast gradient projection approaches. All of the hyperspectral images or video in the studies were processed with the same set of settings. The parameters, on the other hand, should be altered based on the problem at hand.

Denoising convolutional neural networks (DnCNNs) were developed by Zhang, [12] to take use of recent advances in deep architecture, learning algorithms, and regularization procedures for picture denoising. Using batch normalization and residual learning, training can be sped up while denoising performance is improved. Instead of using a model trained for additive white noise at a particular level of noise, DnCNN trains a model for Gaussian denoising with an uncertain noise level. DnCNN implicitly eliminates the latent clean image from the hidden layers when utilizing the residual learning technique. This method, on the other hand, is ineffective for restoring images with genuine complex noise or for other types of general picture restoration.

3   Proposed Methodology

In this section, hair removal process is carried out by various processes, which is labelled in the Fig. 1. Initially, the input image is taken from ISIC challenging datasets of 2019 and 2018. To remove the hair from the input images, five process are presented in the proposed research that includes vintage boosting, gray contrast stretching, filtering, mask creation and DeTrop Noise Exclusion using inpainting. These five processes are briefly described in the following below section.

3.1   Dataset Description

Here, the two challenging dataset are described as follows:

- ISIC 2019

    The dataset is acquired from ISIC (International skin imaging collaboration) 2019 challenge dataset archive which contains benign and malignant skin lesions dermoscopy images. There are 2637 images of training images and 660 testing image.
- ISIC 2018

    The dataset is acquired from ISIC 2018 challenge dataset archive which contains benign and malignant skin lesions dermoscopy images. There are 2650 images of training images and 712 testing image.

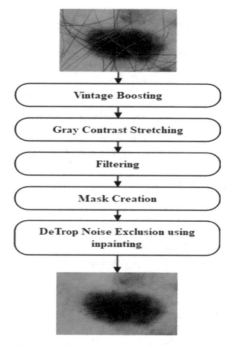

Fig. 1. Workflow of proposed methodology.

3.2 Vintage Boosting

In this research work, new idea (vintage boosting) is developed to increase the pixel brightness in input images. Vintage Boosting is a term characterized as the intensity of a pixel comparative with another pixel. The following equation is used to compute the vintage boosting:

$$Compute = (maxintensity/p) * (sourceimage/(maxintensity/q)) * 0.9 \quad (1)$$

where, $p = 1$ *and* $q = 1$. Here, the vintage factor is 0.9, which is used to increase the intensity of the images. Algorithm 1 describes the process of vintage boosting that is as follows:

Algorithm 1: Vintage Boosting

Input: $N \times I = 1,2, ... n$ set of Noise image
Output: $VB(NX_{I=1....n})$Denoise image
Read $N_{x1}, N_{x2} .... n$
Evaluate N_{xI}(A range(max_I))
Fix $\sigma = 1, \Omega = 1$
Read pixel $N_{xI}(R_{y1}, G_{y1}, B_{y1}) ... R_{yn}, G_{yn}, B_{yn}))$
For each NX_I
Compute$(^{max_I}/_\sigma) \times (^{NX_I}/_{(Max_I}/_\Omega)}) \times$ VF
Return $VB(NX_I = 1....n)$
Where,
NX_I is the noise input image.
max_I is maximum intensity of the image
VF is the vintage factor (set as 0.9)
$VB(NX_I = 1....n)$ is vintage boosting input noise image

3.3   Gray Contrast Stretching

This paper processed 2-dimension still image which is represented in $M \times N$ matrix form, where M and N are the width and height of the image. The matrix can be treated as 2- dimension array, representing x and y coordinates. Contrast stretching can be done by employing Gray Scale Transform function as shown in Eq. 2:

$$K_0 = G(K_i - P) + P \tag{2}$$

where, the pixel value of output image is given as K_0, the pixel value of input image is described as K_i, the contrast strength coefficient is represented as G and P is the grayscale value that is used as center of contrast. Figure 2 shows the output sof gray contrast stretching.

The following Algorithm 2 presents the description of gray contrast stretching.

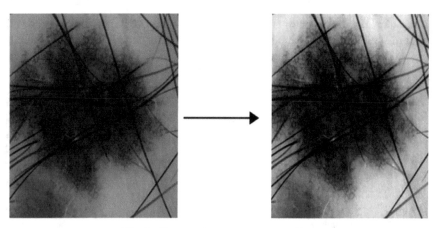

Fig. 2. Output of gray contrast stretching

Algorithm 2: Gray contrast stretching

Input: $VB(N_{XI=1,\dots n})$
Output:$GR_s(N_{XI=1,\dots n})$

For each $VB(N_{XI} = 1, \dots . n)$
     $VBNX_I \rightarrow \quad GR(NX_I)$
     Evaluating /Evaluate $GR(NX_I)(max), GR(NX_I)(min)$
     Compute $(255/(GR(NX_I)(max) - GR(NX_I)(min)) \times (GR(NX_I) -$
 $GR(NX_I)(min) + SF)$
     Return $GR_s(NX_{I=1,\dots n})$
     Where,
 $VB(NX_{I=1,\dots n})$ is the vintage boosting input noise image.
 $GR(NX_I)$ is the grayscale input image with noise
 $GR(NX_I)(max)$ is maximum element of the grayscale input image
 $GR(NX_I)(min)$ is minimum element of the grayscale input image
 SF is the stretching factor (set as 0.7)
 $GR(NX_I)$ is gray contrast stretched noise image.

3.4 Filtering

We use a morphological operator to filter the observed hair in order to detect the hair contour. The image is subjected to a blackhat (bottom-hat) transform with a size of 20×20 pixels. The difference between the closing and input images is known as the blackhat transform. This morphological filter highlights dark pixels with a high contrast to their surrounding environment, as shown in the dermoscopic image. The final step is to threshold the generated image. This threshold is equal to twice the mean of the entire image. The mean over the entire image helps to account for global lighting, whereas a mean calculated locally would be more sensitive to slight fluctuations in brightness in the image. It is worth noting that the blackhat filter highlights the dermoscopic pictures' border and pictogram. However, by employing this filter, a big portion of the image is removed, and the frequency of false alarms is minimized. Algorithm 3 explains the process of filtering.

Algorithm 3: Filtering

Input: $GR_s(NX_{=1,...nl})$
Output: $BFLT(NX_{I=1,...n})$
Fix $ST(shape, (y, t))$
For each $GR_s(NX_I = 1, ... n)$
Compute $\qquad\qquad BFLT(NX_I = 1, ... n) = MORPH_{Close}GR_s(NX_I) - GR_s(NX_I), ST(shape, (y, t))$
Return $BFLT(NX_{I=1,...n})$
Where,
St is structuring element
(y, t) is the size of CF kernel (set as 20×20)
$BFLT(NX_I)$ is black hat filter image
$MORPH_{Close}$ is the morphological closing operation.
Closing with a 20×20 kernel, perform back hat filter on grayscale image to find hairs

3.5 Mask Creation

Binary Thresholding is used to create the mask, where thresholding is one of the simplest mask creation methods. Basic method exchanges each pixel $P_{i,j}$ in the image for black or white pixel according to intensity I of the pixel. Thresholding input value is fixed constant called threshold. If $P'_{i,j}$ is thresholded version of $P_{i,j}$ according to intensity $I(P_{i,j})$ and T is threshold then:

$$P'_{i,j} = \begin{cases} 1 & \text{if } I(P_{i,j}) >= T \\ 0 & \text{otherwise} \end{cases} \tag{3}$$

The following Algorithm 4 describes the proposed mask creation.

Algorithm 4: Mask creation

Input: $BFLT(NX_{I=1,...n})$
Output: $Mask(BFLT)(NX_{I=1,...n})$
Read $BFLT(NX_I = 1, ... n)$
Compute $\qquad$ Mask $\qquad (BTH)(NX_{I=1,...n}) \rightarrow BFLT(NX_{I=1,...n}),$ $Min_I(u, v), Max_I(u, v)$
Return Mask $(BTH)(NX_{I=1,...n})$
Where,
Mask (BTH) is binary threshold mask
$Min_I(u, v)$, is the maximum threshold value
$Max_I(u, v)$ is the minimum threshold value

3.6 DeTrop Noise Exclusion Using Inpanting

Digital inpainting allows for the rebuilding of minor damaged areas of an image. Digital inpainting can be used to remove text and logos from still images or films, recreate scans of damaged images by eliminating scratches or stains, or create aesthetic effects. The missing area should be inserted to estimate the gray value and gradient from that area when it is inserted. Navier-Stokes [30] is used to perform inpainting in the proposed method.

Inpainting is an incompressible fluid according to Navier-Stokes. The picture intensity function serves as the stream function, with isophote lines defining the flow's streamlines. The method given here does not need the user to specify the source of the fresh knowledge. This is done robotically (and fast), allowing numerous regions with completely distinct structures and surrounding backgrounds to be filled in at the same time. Furthermore, no constraints are placed on the topology of the region to be painted. The program just requires one human interaction: marking the areas to be inpainted. Algorithm 5 will describe the DeTrop Noise exclusion procedure.

Algorithm 5: DeTrop Noise Exclusion using In-painting

Input: $Mask(BTH)(NX_{I=1,...n})$
Output: $De(NX_{I=1,...n})$
Compute
$De(NX_I = 1,...n)$
$\quad\quad\quad\quad\quad \rightarrow ((NX_{I=1,...n}), Mask(BTH)(NX_{I=1,...n}), inpainting$
$\quad\quad\quad\quad\quad - rad, Inpaint - NS)$
Return $De(NX_{I=1,...n})$
Where,
NS Navier strokes

Figure 3 shows the sample output of 2019 challenging dataset using each step for hair removal process.

4 Results and Discussion

In this section, the proposed DeTrop Noise Exclusion using Inpainting with existing techniques is described. The section consists of performance metrics, quantitative and qualitative analysis. The proposed system is implemented using Python with 4 GB RAM, 1 TB hard drive and a 3.0 GHz Intel i5 processor.

4.1 Performances Metrics

The various performance metrics with its equations are given in this section.

Mean Square Error (MSE) and Peak Signal Noise Ratio (PSNR)
Initially, the PSNR and MSE formulas are presented as:

$$PSNR = 20log_{10}(\frac{MAX_f}{\sqrt{MSE}}) \tag{4}$$

Input image	Vintage Boosting	Gray contrast stretching	Filtering	Mask creation	De Trop Noise Exclusion using Inpainting

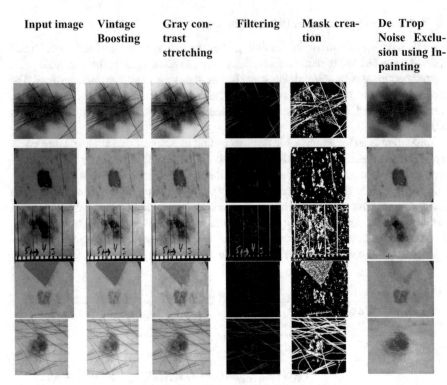

Fig. 3. Sample output for hair removal

$$MSE = \frac{1}{mn} \sum_0^{m-1} \sum_0^{n-1} \|f(i,j) - g(i,j)\|^2 \qquad (5)$$

where, f as the original image matrix data,

 g represent as a degraded image matrix data,

 j represent as index of that column,

 n represent as sum of columns of pixels

 m represent as sum of pixels rows

 i represent as index of that row,

 $MAXf$ represent as maximum signal value that occurs in our original.

The modified version of PSNR is

$$PSNR - H = 10log\left(\frac{255^2}{MSE_H}\right) \qquad (6)$$

In this expression, MSE_H is calculated taking into account Human Visual System according to approach described in [31]:

$$MSE_H = K \sum_{i=1}^{I-7} \sum_{j=1}^{J-7} \sum_{m=1}^{8} \sum_{n=1}^{8} ((X[m,n]_{ij} - X[m,n]_{ij}^e)T_c[m,n])^2 \qquad (7)$$

where I, J signify as the image size, $K = 1/[(I-7)(J-7)64]$, Xij are DCT coefficients of 8×8 image block for which the organizes of its left upper corner are equivalent to i and j, X_{ij}^e are the DCT constants of the consistent block in the unique image, and Tc represent as the matrix of correcting factors.

Structural Similarity (SSIM) Index
The common form of the SSIM index among signal x and y is distinct as:

$$SSIM(x, y) = [l(x, y)^\alpha . [c(x, y)]^\beta . [s(x, y)]^\gamma]$$ (8)

where α, β and γ are relative position of the three components. Exactly, we set $\alpha = \beta = \gamma = 1$ and resulting SSIM index is given by

$$SSIM(x, y) = \frac{(2\mu_x\mu_y + C_1)(2\sigma_{xy} + C_2)}{(\mu_x^2 + \mu_y^2 + C_1)(\sigma_x^2 + \sigma_y^2 + C_2)}$$ (9)

This satisfies the subsequent circumstances:

1. Symmetry: $SSIM(x, y) = SSIM(y, x)$
2. Boundedness: $SSIM(x, y) \leq 1$;
3. Unique maximum $SSIM(x, y) = 1$ if and only if $x = y$

$$SSIM(x, y) = [I_M(x, y)]^{\alpha M} \prod_{j=1}^{M} [c_j(x, y)]^{\beta_j} [s_j(x, y)]^{\gamma_j}$$ (10)

where, M is a scale obtained after $M - 1$ iterations. At the j-th scale.

Universal Image Quality Index
To comprehend this, we rewrite the Q description of as a product of three components

$$Q = \frac{\sigma xy}{\sigma_x \sigma_y} . \frac{2\overline{xy}}{(\overline{x})^2 + (\overline{y})^2} . \frac{2\sigma_x \sigma_y}{\sigma_x^2 + \sigma_y^2}$$ (11)

The correlation coefficient among x and y measures the degree of linear correlation among x and y and has a dynamic range of $[-1, 1]$. When $y_i = ax_i + b$ for all $i = 1, 2, \ldots N$, where a and b are constants and $a > 0$, the optimal value is 1. Even if x and y are linearly connected, relative distortions between them may exist. The second element, with a value range of $[0, 1]$, measures the proximity of the mean brightness between x and y. It equals 1 if and only if $\overline{x} = \overline{y}$, σ_x and σ_y can be considered as estimates of x and y's contrast, hence the third component measures how comparable the images' contrasts are. Its value range is also $[0, 1]$, with the best value 1 obtained if and only if $\sigma_x = \sigma_y$.

Visual Information Fidelity (VIF)

$$VIF = \frac{\sum_{j \in subbands} I(\overrightarrow{C}^{N,j}; \overrightarrow{F}^{N,j}|s^{N,j})}{\sum_{j \in subbands} I(\overrightarrow{C}^{N,j}; \overrightarrow{E}^{N,j}|s^{N,j})}$$ (12)

where, we sum over the sub bands of interest, and $\overrightarrow{C}^{N,j}$ represent N elements of the random field C_j that defines the coefficients from sub-band j, and so on.

4.2   Performance Analysis of DeTrop Noise Exclusion Using Inpainting

Initially, first 10 images are taken from the ISIC-2019 dataset for validation and analysed with various metrics, which is shown in Table 1.

Table 1. Comparative analysis of proposed method for ISIC-2019 dataset.

S.No	MSE	PSNR	SSIM	RMSE	VIF	UQI	MSSSIM	PSNR (HVS)
1	27.847	35.137	0.926	7.798	0.525	0.997	0.978	36.802
2	258.347	26.080	0.867	14.126	0.526	0.991	0.870	25.078
3	103.903	29.785	0.885	9.207	0.499	0.996	0.934	29.404
4	404.366	27.001	0.851	15.485	0.402	0.990	0.917	26.248
5	175.303	29.158	0.890	11.032	0.531	0.995	0.945	28.455
6	221.346	26.570	0.864	13.287	0.509	0.992	0.875	25.519
7	55.311	33.096	0.921	6.318	0.592	0.997	0.955	33.005
8	330.123	28.135	0.834	14.234	0.524	0.994	0.934	25.541
9	278.267	26.452	0.871	13.897	0.478	0.993	0.852	35.550
10	189.356	30.119	0.882	12.672	0.421	0.992	0.934	28.398

While experiments are carried out in terms of PSNR, the first and seventh images provide better results than other images. For instance, the PSNR of 1st image is 35.137, but more than two images provide low performance. This proves that the quality of the image is depends upon PSNR values. The error rate of MSE and RMSE is also considered for experiments, which shows that 4th and 8th images have high error rates than other images. Higher the SSIM gives the best output results for hair removal. Therefore, SSIM of 1st and 7th images have nearly 92%, where other images have nearly 85% to 88% of SSIM. The quality index is high for all the input images, where 1st and 7th images have the higher UQI. The following Table 2 displays the comparative analysis of proposed scheme for first 10 images from ISIC 2018 dataset in terms of various parameter metrics.

For the experiments in terms of PSNR, the best values (33%) are provided by first and last images, where the fourth image provides low PSNR value (23.48%). The other remaining images provide nearly 28% to 30% of PSNR. The RMSE is low (9.21%) only for first image, where the 6th image has high RMSE (15.56%). While comparing with ten input images, the first image shows better performance in terms of UQI, PSNR (HVS) and MSSSIM. The 5th image has highest VIF (0.598), where the 10th image has low VIF (0.419). From these experimental results, it is proved that the first image has better PSNR, UQI, MSSSIM and PSNR.

Table 2. Comparative analysis of proposed method for ISIC-2018 dataset.

S.No	MSE	PSNR	SSIM	RMSE	VIF	UQI	MSSSIM	PSNR (HVS)
1	325.613	33.165	0.827	9.211	0.545	0.984	0.976	35.261
2	302.234	30.221	0.898	10.876	0.5135	0.952	0.953	24.243
3	120.458	26.764	0.854	12.954	0.4491	0.974	0.924	28.762
4	220.674	23.482	0.863	11.546	0.462	0.998	0.912	25.341
5	256.887	28.987	0.876	14.741	0.598	0.948	0.935	28.633
6	130.546	30.186	0.835	15.568	0.573	0.946	0.968	25.319
7	187.234	29.186	0.812	14.381	0.491	0.912	0.989	27.553
8	175.654	29.158	0.856	13.925	0.535	0.935	0.987	31.054
9	240.124	26.570	0.898	11.248	0.487	0.928	0.964	29.604
10	198.981	33.096	0.934	12.369	0.419	0.915	0.934	33.458

4.3 Quantitative Analysis

The next Table 3 shows the average comparative analysis of proposed method for overall data of both datasets and also compared with some existing techniques.

Table 3. Quantitative analysis of proposed method with existing methods.

Methods	Dataset	MSE	PSNR	SSIM	RMSE	VIF	UQI	MSSSIM	PSNR (HVS)
Ref. [32]	**100 dermoscopic images**	258.347	26.080	0.867	14.226	0.526	0.991	0.870	24.628
Ref. [33]	**20 clinical image**	404.366	27.001	0.851	15.485	0.402	0.990	0.917	25.738
Ref. [34]	**50 dermoscopy image**	221.346	26.570	0.864	13.287	0.509	0.992	0.875	25.065
Ref. [35]	**50 dermoscopy image**	103.903	29.785	0.885	9.207	0.499	0.996	0.934	28.681
Proposed	ISIC-2019	204.416	29.153	0.879	11.086	0.5	0.9937	0.919	29.4
Proposed	ISIC-2018	215.84	29.081	0.865	12.681	0.507	0.949	0.954	28.922

From the above table, it is clearly stated that overall data analysis has lower performance than single image analysis. However, ISIC-2019 has higher PSNR (29.153%) value than ISIC-2018 dataset that has only 29.081%. The UQI of 2019 dataset has 0.993, where 2018 dataset has only 0.949. But the MSSSIM of 2018 dataset has high value than 2019 dataset. The error rate of RMSE and MSE is low (11.086% and 204.416%) in ISIC-2019 dataset, where the 2018 dataset has 12.681% of RMSE and 215.84% of MSE. From this experiment, it is proved that ISIC 2019 dataset has better performance in terms of MSE, PSNR, SSIM, RMSE, UQI and PSNR (HVS) than 2017 dataset.

5 Conclusion

In this paper, DeTrop Noise Exclusion using inpainting for evaluation of image visual quality is proposed. In this proposed technique, five major steps are included namely vintage boosting, gray contrast stretching, filtering, mask creation and inpainting based on Navier-Stokes. The two publicly available datasets such as ISIC-2019 and 2018 challenging dataset for validating the performance of proposed technique. The experimental results show the advantages of the proposed method in terms of PSNR, MSE, RMSE, SSIM, UQI, VIF, PSNR (HSV) and MSSSIM. It is worth noting that we tested our ideal in dermoscopic images with real hair, achieving good visual results and confirming its usefulness. In some cases, when high strands of hair dermoscopic images are denoised, the quality of the images is diminished. In the future, we hope to apply our approach to a more comprehensive skin lesion analysis scheme using machine learning techniques for leveraging the knowledge to extract other features.

References

1. Alasadi, A.H.H., Alsafy, B.M.: Diagnosis of malignant melanoma of skin cancer types. Int. J. Interact. Multim. Artif. Intell. **4**(5), 44–49 (2017)
2. Abdullah, H.N., Abduljaleel, H.K.: Deep CNN based skin lesion image denoising and segmentation using active contour method. Eng. Technol. J. **37**(11A), 464–469 (2019)
3. Sheha, M.A., Mabrouk, M.S., Sharawy, A.: Automatic detection of melanoma skin cancer using texture analysis. Int. J. Comput. Appl. **42**(20), 22–26 (2012)
4. Sharma, D., Srivastava, S.: Automatically detection of skin cancer by classification of neural network. Int. J. Eng. Tech. Res. **4**(1), 15–18 (2016)
5. Fan, L., Zhang, F., Fan, H., Zhang, C.: Brief review of image denoising techniques. Vis. Comput. Ind., Biomed., Art **2**(1), 1–12 (2019). https://doi.org/10.1186/s42492-019-0016-7
6. Goyal, B., Dogra, A., Agrawal, S., Sohi, B.S., Sharma, A.: Image denoising review: from classical to state-of-the-art approaches. Inf. fusion **55**, 220–244 (2020)
7. Dabov, K., Foi, A., Katkovnik, V., Egiazarian, K.: Image denoising by sparse 3-D transform-domain collaborative filtering. IEEE Trans. Image Process. **16**(8), 2080–2095 (2007)
8. Xu, J., Zhang, L., Zhang, D., Feng, X.: Multi-channel weighted nuclear norm minimization for real color image denoising. In: Proceedings of the IEEE International Conference on Computer Vision, pp. 1096–1104 (2017)
9. He, N., Wang, J.B., Zhang, L.L., Lu, K.: An improved fractional-order differentiation model for image denoising. Signal Process.s **112**, 180–188 (2015)
10. Chen, Y., Pock, T.: Trainable nonlinear reaction diffusion: a flexible framework for fast and effective image restoration. IEEE Trans. Pattern Anal. Mach. Intell. **39**(6), 1256–1272 (2016)
11. Mao, X., Shen, C., Yang, Y.B.: Image restoration using very deep convolutional encoder-decoder networks with symmetric skip connections. Adv. Neural. Inf. Process. Syst. **29**, 2802–2810 (2016)

12. Zhang, K., Zuo, W., Chen, Y., Meng, D., Zhang, L.: Beyond a gaussian denoiser: residual learning of deep cnn for image denoising. IEEE Trans. Image Process. **26**(7), 3142–3155 (2017)
13. Lefkimmiatis, S.: Non-local color image denoising with convolutional neural networks. In: Proceedings of the IEEE Conference on Computer Vision and Pattern Recognition, pp. 3587–3596 (2017)
14. Zhang, K., Zuo, W., Zhang, L.: FFDNet: toward a fast and flexible solution for CNN-based image denoising. IEEE Trans. Image Process. **27**(9), 4608–4622 (2018)
15. Khan, A. H., Iskandar, D.N.F., Al-Asad, J.F., El-Nakla, S.: Classification of skin lesion with hair and artifacts removal using black-hat morphology and total variation. Int. J. Comput. Digit. Syst. **10**, 597–604 (2021)
16. Lyakhova, U. A., Lyakhov, P. A.: Method of cleaning hair structures for intellectual image classification of skin neoplasms. In: 2021 Ural Symposium on Biomedical Engineering, Radioelectronics and Information Technology (USBEREIT), pp. 0020–0023. IEEE (2021)
17. Javaid, A., Sadiq, M., Akram, F.: Skin cancer classification using image processing and machine learning. In: 2021 International Bhurban Conference on Applied Sciences and Technologies (IBCAST), pp. 439–444. IEEE (2021)
18. Ramella, G.: Hair removal combining saliency, shape and color. Appl. Sci. **11**(1), 447 (2021)
19. Attia, M., Hossny, M., Zhou, H., Nahavandi, S., Asadi, H., Yazdabadi, A.: Digital hair segmentation using hybrid convolutional and recurrent neural networks architecture. Comput. Methods Program. Biomed. **177**, 17–30 (2019)
20. Dhabal, S., Chakrabarti, R., Mishra, N.S., Venkateswaran, P.: An improved image denoising technique using differential evolution-based salp swarm algorithm. Soft. Comput. **25**(3), 1941–1961 (2020). https://doi.org/10.1007/s00500-020-05267-y
21. Tian, C., Xu, Y., Zuo, W., Du, B., Lin, C.W., Zhang, D.: Designing and training of a dual CNN for image denoising. Knowl.-Based Syst. **226**, 106949 (2021)
22. Kawar, B., Vaksman, G., Elad, M.: Stochastic image denoising by sampling from the posterior distribution. arXiv preprint arXiv:2101.09552 (2021)
23. Ohayon, G., Adrai, T., Vaksman, G., Elad, M., Milanfar, P.: High perceptual quality image denoising with a posterior sampling cgan. arXiv preprint arXiv:2103.04192 (2021)
24. Chen, K., Long, K., Ren, Y., Sun, J., Pu, X.: Lesion-Inspired denoising network: connecting medical image denoising and lesion detection. arXiv preprint arXiv:2104.08845 (2021)
25. Talavera-Martinez, L., Bibiloni, P., Gonzalez-Hidalgo, M.: Hair segmentation and removal in dermoscopic images using deep learning. IEEE Access **9**, 2694–2704 (2020)
26. Talavera-Martínez, L., Bibiloni, P., González-Hidalgo, M.: An encoder-decoder CNN for hair removal in dermoscopic images. arXiv preprint arXiv:2010.05013 (2020)
27. Hou, X., et al.: Learning deep image priors for blind image denoising. In: Proceedings of the IEEE/CVF Conference on Computer Vision and Pattern Recognition Workshops (2019)
28. Hasan, M., El-Sakka, M.R.: Improved BM3D image denoising using SSIM-optimized Wiener filter. EURASIP J. Image Video Process. **2018**(1), 1–12 (2018). https://doi.org/10.1186/s13640-018-0264-z
29. Wang, H., Cen, Y., He, Z., He, Z., Zhao, R., Zhang, F.: Reweighted low-rank matrix analysis with structural smoothness for image denoising. IEEE Trans. Image Process. **27**(4), 1777–1792 (2017)
30. Ebrahimi, M.A., Lunasin, E.: The Navier–Stokes–Voight model for image inpainting. IMA J. Appl. Math. **78**(5), 869–894 (2013)
31. Egiazarian, K., Astola, J., Ponomarenko, N., Lukin, V., Battisti, F., Carli, M.: New full-reference quality metrics based on HVS. In: Proceedings of the Second International Workshop on Video Processing and Quality Metrics, vol. 4 (2006)
32. Abbas, Q., Celebi, M.E., García, I.F.: Hair removal methods: a comparative study for dermoscopy images. Biomed. Signal Process. Control **6**(4), 395–404 (2011)

33. Huang, A., Kwan, S.Y., Chang, W.Y., Liu, M.Y., Chi, M.H., Chen, G.S.: A robust hair segmentation and removal approach for clinical images of skin lesions. In: 2013 35th Annual International Conference of the IEEE Engineering in Medicine and Biology Society (EMBC), pp. 3315–3318. IEEE (2013)
34. Toossi, M.T.B., Pourreza, H.R., Zare, H., Sigari, M.H., Layegh, P., Azimi, A.: An effective hair removal algorithm for dermoscopy images. Skin Res. Technol. **19**(3), 230–235 (2013)
35. Bibiloni, P., González-Hidalgo, M., Massanet, S.: Skin hair removal in dermoscopic images using soft color morphology. In: Ten Teije, A., Popow, C., Holmes, J.H., Sacchi, L. (eds.) AIME 2017. LNCS (LNAI), vol. 10259, pp. 322–326. Springer, Cham (2017). https://doi.org/10.1007/978-3-319-59758-4_37

Extending Machine Learning Techniques Using Multi-level Approach to Detect and Classify Anomalies in a Network on UNSW-NB15 dataset

Utkarsh Rodge$^{(\boxtimes)}$ (ID) and Vinod Pathari (ID)

National Institute of Technology Calicut, Kerala 673601, India
rodgeutkarsh@gmail.com

Abstract. With the increase in the number of internet-connected devices and widespread adoption of IoT devices, there is a massive growth in network activity and along with it, the attack surface has also increased. IDS and IPS play a crucial role in detecting and thwarting the increasing attacks day by day. Traditional security measures like iptables and similar rule-based filtering mechanisms have become insufficient to meet these new challenges. With the power of machine learning, these attacks can be more efficiently and accurately identified. This paper proposes an IDS with a multi-level approach by extending machine learning techniques to detect anomalies in a network. We have shown that a multi-level machine learning model is more accurate in classifying the attacks than a single machine learning model using the UNSW-NB15 dataset. Our work achieves the aim of improving the accuracy of identifying anomalous network packets and classifying them into their respective attack category.

Keywords: Anomaly detection · Misuse detection · Network intrusion detection · Machine learning · Network security

1 Introduction

With the rapid pace of development, hackers are also evolving at a similar rate in their capabilities. Thus Intrusion Detection System (IDS), responsible for identifying intrusions that violate security policies, forms a critical component of any computing environment. Of different types of IDS, the focus of this work is on Network IDS. They can be classified into misuse-based or signature-based and anomaly-based depending on the detection mechanism.

Anomaly Detection: Anomaly Based IDS tries to create a profile for Normal or Anomalous activity. Depending upon the deviation of any activity above a certain baseline, away from Normal profile or towards Anomalous profile, the activity is flagged as an Anomaly or Normal activity, as the case may be.

Misuse Detection: Misuse-based IDS, also called Signature-based IDS, compares every activity or the flow of activity with the available attack signatures already stored with it to determine if the activity is regular or a type of intrusion.

I. Raman et al. (Eds.): ICC3 2021, CCIS 1631, pp. 49–59, 2022.
https://doi.org/10.1007/978-3-031-15556-7_4

Both these mechanisms have their drawbacks and advantages. Misuse detection can identify the type of attack, which can help trigger prevention mechanisms associated with that type of attack but cannot identify new or unknown attacks. This is possible using Anomaly detection. A hybrid-based IDS combines both anomaly-based and misuse-based IDS.

With the ready availability of tools used for hacking and increasing development in the security field, the attacks are growing in complexity. There is a need for improvement in IDS to increase the discovery of such attacks. Machine learning (ML) is an evolving field that can allow a system to evolve and adapt by using previous data. A solid static system can work with ever-increasing and changing attacks. ML techniques can be fine tuned to detect new attacks which the system has never seen, using just the historical data. Due to this, there is an increasing number of IDS based on the ML.

In this research, architecture with a hybrid-based IDS approach, which combines both Anomaly-based and Misuse-based IDS, is proposed by extending ML techniques to obtain more accurate results. Averaged one-dependence estimators (AODE), J48, and Random Forest (RF) ML algorithms are used to demonstrate the proposed architecture. AODE is a probabilistic classification algorithm developed to address the attribute independence issue of the Naive Bayes classifier. J48 algorithm is a classification algorithm used to generate a decision tree that implements classifier algorithm C4.5. Random Forest is an algorithm that generates multiple decision trees and uses their results to obtain a more accurate result.

An intrusion detection mechanism can be broadly divided into the following steps: i) Data collection, ii) Data pre-processing, iii) Learning Phase, iv) Intrusion Detection, v) Defence Response.

A large amount of network activity data is captured in the data collection phase, most commonly using tools such as Wireshark in pcap format. This data is then processed to transform it and extract essential features used for later phases. A machine learning model is created in the learning phase using the data from the previous phase, which is then used to classify a real-time activity in the next phase into anomalous or normal categories. Several approaches for the implementation of IDS are proposed using Machine Learning techniques.

The most common approach to enhance the performance of an existing ML algorithm is by feature selection. In this method, only a selection of features based on their metrics is considered to create an ML model rather than using all the features available. This methodology boosts the performance of particular algorithms along with various metrics, including accuracy and training time.

2   Dataset

Dataset selection plays an important role in determining the real-world performance of any IDS. M Ring et al. [1] did a survey on Network-based Intrusion Detection Datasets wherein they evaluated many of the available datasets based on 15 different properties. From their survey, they identified UNSW-NB15 [2] and CIC-IDS2017 datasets as the ones with recent attacks, as well as satisfying the properties set. UNSW-NB15 is chosen to evaluate the proposed system since it is widely used and can be used to compare the results with other similar research works. The distribution of attacks and normal packets present in the UNSW-NB15 dataset is given in the Table 1.

Table 1. Attack distribution in UNSW-NB15 dataset

Class	Training Set No. of Records	Testing Set No. of Records
All	175,341	82,332
Normal	56,000	37,000
Fuzzers	18,184	6062
Analysis	2000	677
Backdoors	1746	583
DoS	12,264	4089
Exploits	33,393	11,132
Generic	40,000	18,871
Reconnaissance	10,491	3496
Shellcode	1133	378
Worms	130	44

Total 47 features are extracted from the network packets, including source and destination - IP, ports and time to live values, the protocol used, sent, and received bytes. Few of the connection features are also present, generated using scripts to capture similar characteristics of the connections. The authors of this dataset have provided a subset of the same to evaluate the ML models quickly. This subset is divided into two parts used for the training and testing of any ML model. The same methodology is followed in the testing of this ML system.

3 Proposed Architecture/Methodology

3.1 Two Level System

In this paper, a System design/Architecture is proposed having two levels with specific goals defined for each of them. Both levels, when working together, result in an ML system with improved accuracy than the existing ones.

Level 1's sole responsibility is to perform anomaly detection by classifying the packets/ data instances into Normal or Anomaly. Level 2 is responsible for classifying the attacks into their basic types or classes.

The motivation for this design is based on the understanding that the ML model for multi-class classification is not as accurate as of that of an ML model for binary classification. This was observed upon experimenting with ML algorithms Averaged one-dependence estimators (AODE), K-nearest neighbors (KNN), Random Forest, J48, Naive Bayes, and Radial basis function network (RBFN). The mentioned algorithms displayed higher accuracy when classifying the instances into binary classes of Normal and Anomaly compared to multi-class classification that classifies them into their basic Normal or Attack type class.

The Level 1 binary classifying ML model acts as a filter for the Level 2 multi-class classification model, increasing the system's overall accuracy in multi-class classification. The overall accuracy of the proposed system for binary classification is the same as that of level 1. The accuracy of the proposed system for the multi-class classification is equal to the combined result of attack instances classified correctly by the level 2 ML model and normal instances classified correctly by level 1.

The architecture for the Proposed system is shown in Fig. 1.

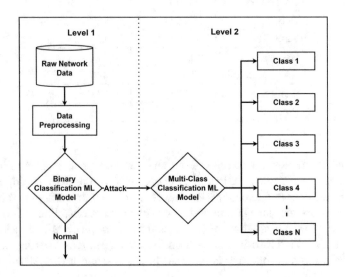

Fig. 1. Proposed multi-level architecture.

When it comes to the time taken by the system for categorizing network packet instances, it may be noted that not all of these will pass through the complete system. Most of the packets that are categorized as normal will only be processed by level 1, and the remaining packets will be forwarded to level 2. Significant growth in accuracy is observed with adding a level without the same proportional increase in processing complexity. Thus the proposed architecture provides an improvement in accuracy without much performance cost. Our approach gains efficiency with an increase in the number of instances. More of them will be filtered by the initial levels and the burden on the next level will be much less.

3.2   Level 1 - Sub-Leveling/Merging ML Models

The multi-level concept can be extended to form sub-levels into level 1. The sub-levels are composed of the ML models of different algorithms under consideration. The sub-levels together can be treated or understood as a merging process where we try to generate a new result derived from 2 ML models.

The 2 ML model results for binary classification can be merged based on the dataset's two classes: Anomaly and Normal. When considering a class, e.g., Normal class for combination, the approach is as follows.

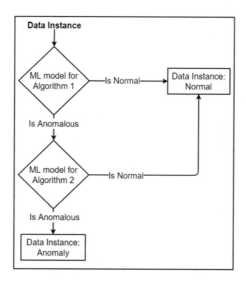

Fig. 2. Merging models based on normal class.

First, classify all the dataset instances using the classifier ML model of algorithm 1 and assign the type of packets marked normal by it as the final classification type. The instances marked as Anomaly are further evaluated using the classifier ML model of algorithm 2. Whatever the class is assigned to the instance, is the final class for it. This process can be seen visually in the following Fig. 2.

The accuracy of the system is not affected by changing the order or arrangement of the algorithms used. In terms of complexity for categorizing the instances, the placement of algorithm models in the architecture will affect it. Since the algorithm placed at the start will be responsible for significant categorization of all the network packet instances available, it will be most beneficial if a lower complexity algorithm is placed here. Thus the placement of algorithm models in decreasing order of their complexity will result in a system with comparatively lower computing complexity than other possible combinations.

The merging process involves the use of different ML models which are independent of each other for their model creation. Thus, they can be trained in parallel and distributed systems, and the models can then be consolidated to form the architecture. Using this parallel approach, the costliest algorithm will decide the overall complexity of the process.

In our experiment, we have merged the ML models based on the Normal class. When merging two ML models based upon the Normal class, the resultant model will detect more Normal instances than the two algorithms included in the process.

The merging process of extending the ML model is not limited to just 2 ML algorithms. Many algorithms can be combined similarly to improve the results obtained further. This merging process is also helpful to compensate for the shortcomings of the ML models, and the results can be further optimized. The optimization can be environment-specific too.

3.3 Constructing Model 1

The Machine learning algorithms used as a base for implementation of the proposed architecture are Averaged one-dependence estimators (AODE), J48, and Random Forest. They were found to give good results in less time compared to many other ML algorithms like that clustering-based, neural networks, and naive Bayes algorithm in terms of training time.

The binary classification accuracy of the algorithms mentioned is given in Table 2. The table also includes the accuracies for the merged ML models, which can be observed to give gradually increasing results. The normal class is used as a deciding factor for classification in the model merging process to increase the accuracy of the resultant model. As the AODE, J48, and Random Forest are much faster compared to other algorithms, merging them can lead to creating a resultant model with a little increase in training time, given how the merging process works.

Notations { A - B } denotes the merged sub-levels of the ML model of algorithms A and B.

Table 2. Accuracy of individual and combination of ML techniques.

No	ML Technique	Accuracy (%)
1	J48	87.03
2	AODE	89.83
3	RandomForest	87.45
4	RBFN	76.58
5	{AODE - J48}	90.60
6	{AODE - RandomForest}	90.47
7	{AODE - {J48 - RandomForest}}	90.87

Table 2 exhibits the success of the sub-leveling or merging process.

Table 3. Classification accuracy of ML model standalone and after Level 1 implementation

Level 1 Algorithm	ML Technique	Classification accuracy(%)
Before Level 1 Implementation		
-	AODE	73.11
-	J48	75.26
-	RandomForest	75.64
After Level 1 Implementation		
{AODE-{J48-RF}}	AODE	78.72
{AODE-{J48-RF}}	J48	80.03
{AODE-{J48-RF}}	RandomForest	79.17

Table 3 shows the accuracy of the ML models used for multi-class classification before and after implementing the proposed 2 level system. The accuracy calculation includes the correctly classified normal class instances.

The model with the highest accuracy, i.e., the one formed by merging AODE, J48, and RandomForest algorithms for level 1 and using the J48 algorithm for level 2 multi-class classification, will be hereafter referred to as Model 1 in the paper.

3.4 Optimization on Model 1 (Model 2)

Table 4 shows the attacks missed for each class by the respective ML models. It is to be noted that the ML models used in the table employ binary classification.

It can be observed from Table 4 that the fuzzers are identified in fewer numbers compared to present instances. There can be a possibility that the presence of fuzzers is decreasing the accuracy of the overall model.

Table 4. No. of attacks missed of each class by ML models.

Anomaly Class	Available	J48	RF	AODE
Analysis	677	10	2	43
Backdoor	583	2	0	1
DoS	4089	19	6	29
Exploits	11132	121	49	195
Fuzzers	6062	736	625	2043
Generic	18871	22	2	24
Reconnaissance	3496	13	2	17
Shellcode	378	1	2	24
Worms	44	1	0	0

Fuzzers try to stress a system and/or cause unexpected behavior by throwing random, invalid, or unexpected inputs. This type of attack mostly makes use of input fields to provide attack inputs. Except for the input data provided by the attacker, the activity itself might seem normal. This is the most likely reason for the decrease in accuracy of the overall ML model, where more normal instances are flagged as anomalous due to fuzzers.

Upon further experimentation, by modifying the Training part of the dataset to mark fuzzer instances as normal, the accuracy is achieved as seen in Table 5.

Table 5. Accuracy of individual and combination of ML techniques with fuzzer modification.

No	ML Technique	Accuracy (%)
1	{AODE - {J48 - RandomForest}}	90.87
2	AODE(with Fuzzer mod)	95.47
3	J48(with Fuzzer mod)	94.52
4	RandomForest(with Fuzzer mod)	95.30
5	{(1) - AODE(with Fuzzer mod)}	91.27
6	{(1) - J48(with Fuzzer mod)}	92.95
7	{(1) - RandomForest(with Fuzzer mod)}	92.98

Instead of completely giving up on detecting fuzzer instances as done by the models in the rows 2, 3 and 4 in Table 5 we have tried to merge them with the previously identified highest accuracy model to include fuzzer detection and obtained consistent higher accuracy models as observed in rows 5, 6 and 7 of Table 5.

This new model with fuzzers treated as normal can be combined with our previously obtained highest accuracy results. At the expense of fuzzers, the accuracy for detecting other attacks or normal instances increased. With this new modification, the new accuracy is increased further to 92.98% with the RandomForest algorithm.

Table 6 shows the ML models' accuracy for multi-class classification before and after implementing the proposed 2 level system with the algorithm mentioned above at level 1.

Table 6. Classification accuracy of ML model standalone and after level 1 implementation

Level 1 Algorithm	ML Technique	Classification Accuracy(%)
Before Level 1 Implementation		
-	AODE	73.11
-	J48	75.26
-	RandomForest	75.64
After Level 1 Implementation		
{{AODE-{J48-RF}} - RF(with Fuzzer mod)}	AODE	80.92
{{AODE-{J48-RF}} - RF(with Fuzzer mod)}	J48	82.22
{{AODE-{J48-RF}} - RF(with Fuzzer mod)}	RandomForest	81.31

This two level system with previously identified highest accuracy combination of AODE, J48, and RandomForest along with RandomForest with Fuzzer modification and using J48 algorithm model at level 2 will be referred to as Model 2 in the rest of the paper.

4   Evaluation Results for Proposed Models

Different metrics for the proposed Model 1 and Model 2 (Optimized on Fuzzer) are presented below.

Table 7. Evaluation metrics for Model 1 and Model 2

Metrics	Model 1	Model 2
Accuracy	90.87%	92.98%
Precision	0.919	0.878
Recall	0.874	0.979
F-measure	0.896	0.926
False Positive Ratio	0.063	0.110

Table 8. Confusion matrix for Model 1   **Table 9.** Confusion Matrix for Model 2

		Prediction	
		Normal	Anomaly
Actual	Normal	32322	4678
	Anomaly	2839	42493

		Prediction	
		Normal	Anomaly
Actual	Normal	36239	761
	Anomaly	5016	40316

5   Comparative Study

Kumar V et al. [3], in their research, proposed an integrated rule-based IDS. In all the assessments being performed on the UNSW-NB15 dataset, they claim that their model's performance is considerably higher than other decision tree models to detect the five categories of attack in the dataset.

Almomani O [4], in his research, proposed a feature selection model using five algorithms, namely particle swarm optimization, grey wolf optimizer, firefly optimization, and genetic algorithm. Using 13 Rules generated from varying combinations of the above algorithms to get a different number of features based on it, he evaluated this features selection model on J48 and SVM model using UNSW-NB15 dataset. Results were obtained in the range of 79.18%-90.48% for the J48 classifier, and for the SVM model, the accuracy range was 79.08%-90.12%.

M. Kasongo et al. [5] proposed XGBoost as a feature selection algorithm, evaluated it upon different ML models, and concluded with Decision Tree showing the highest accuracy increase from 88.13% to 90.85% on the UNSW-NB15 dataset for binary classification.

Jiang K et al. [6], in their research, used one-side selection (OSS) and Synthetic Minority Over-sampling Technique (SMOTE) to reduce noisy samples from majority class and increase minority samples to obtain/train on a balanced dataset. They then used a Convolution neural network (CNN) and Bi-directional long short-term memory (BiLSTM) to extract spatial and temporal features to form a deep hierarchical network model. Their research obtained a multi-class accuracy of 83.58% and 77.16% on the NSL-KDD and UNSW-NB15 dataset, respectively.

Y Yang et al. [7], in their study, proposed a fuzzy aggregation approach using the modified density peak clustering algorithm (MDPCA) and deep belief networks (DBNs), which resulted in a model with 90.21% accuracy on the UNSW-NB15 dataset.

Table 10. Accuracy comparison of various techniques.

ML technique	Feature Selection Method	Binary Accuracy (%)	Multi-class Accuracy (%)
DT [3]	IG	84.83	57.01
J48 [4]	PSO-FO-GO-GA	90.48	-
SVM [4]	PSO-FO-GO-GA	90.11	-
ANN [5]	XGBoost	84.39	77.51
DT [5]	XGBoost	90.85	67.57
CNN-BiLSTM [6]	OSS-SMOTE	-	77.16
MDPCA-DBN [7]	-	90.21	-
Model 1	-	90.87	80.03
Model 2	-	92.98	82.22

Table 10 shows our work in comparison to the previously mentioned similar works. The proposed model does not make use of any feature selection methods and still the results are very encouraging.

6 Conclusion

In this work, we have extended the ML model and observed a successful increase in the system's accuracy in binary and multi-class classification without any serious impact on performance.

The system can act as an adaptive and modular architecture as each model used in this architecture can be trained separately and the results integrated dynamically in the system. New ML models can also be trained, and included for possible higher accuracy. Appropriate ordering of the algorithms will ensure that the higher accuracy is achieved not at the cost of performance.

References

1. Ring, M., et al.: A survey of network-based intrusion detection data sets. In: Computer & Security 2019 (2019). https://doi.org/10.1016/j.cose.2019.06.005, arXiv: 1903.02460 [cs.CR]
2. Moustafa, N., Slay, J.: UNSW-NB15: a comprehensive data set for network intrusion detection systems (UNSW-NB15 network data set). In 2015 Military Communications and Information Systems Conference (MilCIS), pp 1–6 (2015). https://doi.org/10.1109/MilCIS.2015.7348942
3. Kumar, V., Sinha, D., Das, A.K., Pandey, S.C., Goswami, R.T.: An integrated rule based intrusion detection system: analysis on UNSW-NB15 data set and the real time online dataset. Cluster Computing **23**(2), 1397–1418 (2019). https://doi.org/10.1007/s10586-019-03008-x
4. Almomani, O.: A feature selection model for network intrusion detection system based on PSO, GWO, FFA and GA algorithms. Symmetry **12**(6), 1046 (2020). https://doi.org/10.3390/sym12061046
5. Kasongo, S.M., Sun, Y.: Performance analysis of intrusion detection systems using a feature selection method on the UNSW-NB15 dataset. J. Big Data **7**(1), 1–20 (2020). https://doi.org/10.1186/s40537-020-00379-6
6. Jiang, K., et al.: Network intrusion detection combined hybrid sampling with deep hierarchical network. IEEE Access **8**, 32464–32476 (2020). https://doi.org/10.1109/ACCESS.2020.2973730
7. Yang, Y., et al.: Building an effective intrusion detection system using the modified density peak clustering algorithm and deep belief networks. Appl. Sci. **9**(2), 238 (2019). https://doi.org/10.3390/app9020238

Evaluation and Recommendation of Fertility Hospitals Through Multi Criteria Decision Making and Rank Correlation

K. Parisa Begum[✉] and Shina Sheen

Department of Applied Mathematics and Computational Sciences,
PSG College of Technology, Coimbatore, Tamilnadu, India
{kpb.amcs,ssh.amcs}@psgtech.ac.in

Abstract. While the increase of infertility all over the world is difficult to assess given the inconsistencies in defining infertility, about 15% of couples have difficulty in conceiving a baby at some point in their lives. At the same time the growth of fertility hospitals also has multiplied in the current years. The fertility treatment involving multiple factors from basic guidance to advanced Artificial Reproduction Techniques (ART), a common man may not be able to analyze and choose the best fertility hospitals. Involving multiple criteria like facilities, cost, distance etc., the problem is suitable perfectly for Multi-Criteria Decision Making methods (MCDM) of operations research. In this work, fertility hospitals are being ranked using MCDM methods and the disagreement of ranks are studied with the help of Kendall's correlation method and the ranks of all hospitals based on multi-criteria and multiple-alternatives are provided. Sensitivity analysis of these methods are studied in view of the criteria weight assignment. The results of these experiments confirm that the proposed approach will enable to apply multiple MCDM methods to resolve the conflicting rankings and an agreement could be achieved.

Keywords: Fertility · MCDM · Ranking · Decision making · Hospital ranking · Performance analysis

1 Introduction

People generally consider that preventing pregnancy, planning conception and childbirth will be happening smoothly as they wish. People are expected to have children so that they forward their family legacies through generations. But if they are not able to produce children, it can create confusions and spoils happiness in the family. Hence it will be disturbing, humbling and emotionally destructive.

Infertility is defined as a condition of the reproductive system which prevents the formation of children. Approximately 10–15% of couples throughout the world are affected. The infertility test is recommended for couples who failed to conceive within 1 year of their attempt. For women who have crossed the age 35, this 1 year time is replaced by 6 months. This definition is meant to guarantee that people who are having difficulties that can be solved get medical help as soon as possible.

Currently the environment has become so polluted and also because of the work culture of people, many of them are being affected by infertility, which makes infertility treatment a major business.

Fertility hospitals advertise having so many facilities which may not be true always. People should consider so many factors before they choose a particular clinic. Patient's preference will play an important role and they have to decide which facilities or factors are important for them. The Human Fertilization and Embryo Authority (HFEA) [6] says that "Birth rate" is not only the factor to decide. Factors like treatments offered, how much they are comfortable with the doctors and staffs, counseling methodology, cost and location of the clinic are also to be considered. A detailed analysis about the choices should be done before making a decision. Since this problem involves multiple cost criteria and multiple benefit criteria, it is a good choice for applying multiple criteria decision making methods.

Multiple Criteria Decision Making (MCDM) is closely associated to single-objective optimality method of Operations Research which is maximizing a scalar function with respect to the given constraints. A complex problem is broken down to simple problems in MCDM, which are solved and reassembled again to be projected to the decision makers as single final picture. MCDM techniques consider disconnected choices defined by a set of criteria, where the criteria values may belong to different types like cardinal or ordinal. Many objects are being specified and compared with a number of characteristics. These characteristics are generally conflicting in nature. Aggregation in these cases is a major issue because it aims at operating and synthesis of the usually conflicting features of the objects, to achieve a goal like choosing among the objects, rank ordering them, sorting them into categories and so on [4]. Different kinds of aggregation procedures have been suggested [20].

The objectives (attributes) of a decision-making problem must be measurable, and the results can be quantified for each decision alternate. On the basis of these outcomes, comparisons of options are made, facilitating the selection of the best (satisfying) option. As a result, multi-objective optimization approaches can be used to rank or select one or more alternatives from a collection of available possibilities based on several, often competing properties. While selecting a fertility hospital, patients would seek for maximum facilities(different procedures for infertility treatment), minimal cost and minimal distance. When patients need maximum facilities, cost may increase proving the conflicting criteria. Also the hospitals which are easily reachable may also expect high cost for the stay and procedures, which could be considered as conflicting criteria. In this study, MCDM methods like Multi-MOORA, TOPSIS and WASPAS are applied in analysing the performances of fertility hospitals and ranking them.

2 Related Work

Guo et al. [7] have developed a recommender system for identifying KOL (KEY OPINION LEADERS) for any particular disease. Qualification, experience and reliability are being used for ranking the doctors in selection as KOL for a specific disease.

Vachova and Hajdikova [16] in their work have compared a group of Czech hospitals' achievement. MCDM methods have been applied based on the financial health parameter. The hospitals had been ranked and those in the top and bottom of the rank list are identified. Al-Shayea [2] in his work has measured the performance and the efficiency for nine departments at King Khalid University Hospital. Data Envelopment Analysis (DEA) is a fractional linear programming based technique that has got a wide acceptance because it is very successful in comparing competences of any company or its sector or a single department. In a year, 2 departments of 9 departments only have 100% efficiencies as per the analysis. Streisfield et al. [15] in their work have considered ten different dimensions, such as provision of information, clinic and staff competence, coordination and integration, accessibility, continuity and transition, physical comfort, staff attitude and relationship, communication, patient involvement, privacy and emotional support, and so on. In this list, provision of information was ranked first and accessibility was ranked last.

Pekkaya [14] has demonstrated that MCDM approaches may be used to order career options because more than one criterion is assessed simultaneously instead of just one. In his research, he came to the conclusion that MCDM and TOPSIS approaches are simple and typical of the other methods' performance. Janic and Reggiani [9] have implemented 3 discrete MCDM strategies to the hassle of choice of a brand new hub airport for a hypothetical EU airline. The end result implied that the weights of the standards and now no longer the MCDM strategies, have to be taken into consideration greater cautiously while coping with this and comparable MCDM problems. Leoneti et al. [11] in their study discovered that TOPSIS and SAW had internal ranking inconsistencies. As a result, while TOPSIS did a decent job of forecasting the first ranking, it had a lot of ranking dispute, which made it difficult to replace the better alternative in some cases. There was no reversibility concern with any of the methods. Li et al. [12] in their work demonstrate that the TOPSIS approach in water quality assessment is a feasible and reliable method in terms of weights sensitivity analysis. Kou et al. [10] used 10 distinct prominent MCDM methods to pick industrial robots with numerous competing criteria and a finite pool of candidate alternatives in order to decrease cost and time. It has been determined that the selection of relevant criteria and alternatives should take precedence over the selection of the appropriate MCDM method for this situation. The authors used numerous MCDM methods to solve the industrial robot selection problem, which contains multiple competing criteria and a finite collection of candidate alternatives. They came to the conclusion that when it comes to selecting an industrial robot, more emphasis should be placed on the right selection of the important parameters [3].

Marcus et al. [13] used an Internet-based survey to examine and compare different factors influencing a patient's choice of initial and subsequent in vitro fertilisation (IVF) clinics. The clinic's success rate and the quality of the treatment offered were the two most important factors influencing both initial and subsequent clinic choices. In their study, Abel et al. [1] proposed a method for aggregating the preferences of several DMs (Decision Makers) using multi-objective optimization to derive and emphasise underlying conflict between the DMs when seeking consensus. To reduce detrimental effects on decision outcomes, this strategy uses inconsistency reduction throughout the aggregation phase. This method can produce a single final solution based on global compromise information or DM weights of relevance. SAW (Simple Additive Weighting), TOPSIS (Techniques for Order Preference by Similarity to an Ideal Solution), and GRA are presented by Wang et al. [18] (Grey Relational Analysis). It uses an experimental design strategy to assign attribute weights, then integrates several MCDM assessment methods to build the hybrid decision-making model, which can help a decision maker make a sensible conclusion without having professional skills or considerable expertise. Zhang et al. [21] have proposed a hybrid optimization approach (M-BGV) that combines multi-objective artificial bee colony (MOABC), best worst (BW) method, grey relational analysis (GRA), and visekriterijumsko kompromisno rangiranje (VIKOR) to solve multi-objective optimization problems. They have suggested a multi-criteria decision-making strategy that combines GRA and VIKOR to find the best answer by analysing the Pareto set's solutions.

Problems involving multiple criteria and multiple alternative have been solved applying MCDM methods in different areas of decision making. Analysing the performance of fertility hospitals involves finding hospitals with maximum facilities, at minimum cost and minimum distance. In this paper, MCDM methods are applied for the first time for performance analysis of fertility hospitals which is appropriate in a multi-criteria and multi-alternative situation.

3 Proposed Work

The goal of the proposed research is to compare a collection of fertility centres based on facilities, cost, and distance. It entails gathering data about hospitals, transforming the data into the required format, extracting (facilities), and then selecting the suitable Multi-Criteria Decision Making procedures for the specific application. Outcome of the study would be a list of hospitals with the appropriate rankings. For the analysis of fertility hospitals, MCDM methods have not yet been applied.

3.1 System Overview

The architecture shown in Fig. 1 consists of the modules Acquirement of data, Storage and Access, Modelling and recommending.

In the Acquirement stage, the focus is on acquiring the information about the hospitals which are available as web pages on the Internet. An advanced web

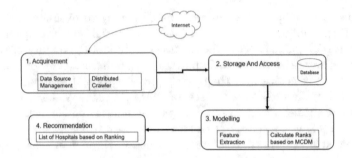

Fig. 1. Architectural overview of the system

crawler has been developed to download the open source web pages belonging to the corresponding seed URL and domain. The seed URLs are collected manually for different tier-I cities. In the Modelling stage, the data files are extracted and converted to the desired format. Multiple MCDM methods have been applied in calculating the rank for each hospital. In Recommendation module, after calculating the ranks for each hospital with different methods, a comparison is done about which method is consistent and which hospital is consistent in the ranking.

3.2   MCDM Methods

Multi-objective optimization (or programming), also known as multi-criteria is the simultaneous optimization of two or more competing attributes (objectives) based on a set of criteria. These types of challenges can be found in a variety of sectors, including product design, process design, manufacturing industry, vehicle design, and other areas where optimal decisions must be made when two or more conflicting objectives must be balanced. Multi-objective optimization problems include lowering a product's cost while maximising its profit, or optimising a component's strength while minimising its weight. The 3 important MCDM approaches that were employed in ranking fertility hospitals are TOPSIS [8], WASPAS method [19] and MultiMOORA [5].

3.3   Design and Deployment

Starting with data collection and ending with ranking, the design and deployment of the performance analysis system is covered in detail in this part.

Data Acquisition. In view of building the model, a web crawler has been built to scrape hospital web-pages, and the missing cost details were collected from other authorized websites. The location details are collected manually from the location coordinates given in their official websites and from google maps.

A web crawler is typically set in advance for each website design, making it difficult to adjust the crawler when the target site changes. The procedure for installing Web Crawler task management is outlined in the sections below.

The URLs for the home pages of the hospitals from multiple cities are collected manually and using these URLS, the URLs for the pages belonging to the same domain are collected. The architecture of the web scrapper has been explained in the following steps:

1. The client is initialized with the link address of a web page to be crawled. A task request is sent to the server along with the link address.
2. HTTP request is sent from the server to fetch the web page and returning the information required to the client.
3. Processing the information received from the server
4. The same procedure is repeated until all the URLs in the crawling list are successfully crawled

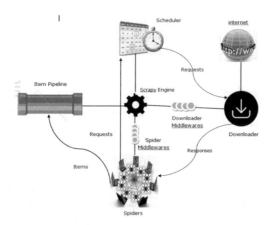

Fig. 2. Web scrapper architecture

Components of the web scrapper and the data flow are shown in Fig. 2. A crawling framework is provided for crawling different Internet contents. Each web page downloaded from the Internet through the item pipeline are stored as plain text files.

Data Processing and Analysis. The data downloaded have to be searched for the existence of the key factors. The factors to be collected for fertility hospitals can be broadly described into Basic Facilities, Facilities for International Patients, Communication, Cost information, Success Rate and Distance.

In this study, a total of 45 selection factors for the fertility hospitals are considered as criteria which are listed in Table 1. For the purpose of analysis, a list of fertility hospitals in tier-I(Metro) and tier-II cities in India were collected. In Tier-1 City-I, 11 fertility hospitals, in Tier-1 City-II, 16 fertility hospitals and 7 fertility hospitals from a Tier-2 city were used for study and the web pages for these hospitals has been downloaded. The fertility hospitals which have not been updated for a long time are removed from the study. The actual weights of

Table 1. Features table and classification

Basic Facilities
AIH, AID, IUI, IVF, Embryo transfer, Gamete Intrafallopian Tube Transfer, ICSI, MESA, PESA, Testicular Sperm Aspiration, Testicular Sperm Extraction, ED, Cryo-preservation, Freezing of semen, Embryo freezing, Oocyte cryopreservation, Ovarian tissue cryopreservation, Semen Preparation, Facilities for semen preparation and IUI, Egg sharing, Surrogacy, IMSI, Laser assisted hatching, Preimplantation genetic diagnosis, Preimplantation genetic screening, The Endometrial Receptivity Array
Hospitality and International Patients
Accommodation, Airport pick-up and drop, Translation, International Patients
Communication Facilities
MailID, Chat Facility, Phone
Cost Information
IVFCost, IUICost, Insurance, Smart Treatment Plans, Packages, Financing Options
Affiliation Information
Registration with Society for Assisted Reproduction, Indian Medical Association etc.
Research Publications
Research Publications
Success Rate Information
Success Rate details
Others
Second opinion, Psychological counseling

the criteria have a big impact on estimating the importance of the alternatives and choosing the best one. The challenges related with their estimates have been examined in both the theory and practise of MCDM approaches implementation.

The weights of the criteria can be subjective and objective in which subjective approach determines weights based on the judgement made by the decision makers. Objective method selects weights based on mathematical calculations. Hence the weights for each criteria obtained from experts from different hospitals are averaged and normalized. Normalization formula is given as

$$w_j = \frac{d_j}{\sum\limits_{j=1}^{n} d_j} \tag{1}$$

where n is the number of criteria, d_j is the subjective weight for a particular criterion.

The normalised weights calculated using Eq. 1 for each criteria are listed in Table 2. For sensitivity analysis an equal weight assignment has been done and compared with the empirical(subjective) weight assignment. Since they convey the opinions of highly competent specialists with vast experience, these subjective weights are crucial for evaluating the outcomes [17]. From this sensitivity analysis, it is easy to understand which MCDM method is having better stability with regard to the change of weights.

Table 2. Features weights - Normalized

Feature name	Normalised wt	Feature name	Normalised wt
AIH	0.0190058	PGD	0.0219298
AID	0.0190058	PGS	0.0219298
IUI	0.0233918	ERA	0.0219298
IVF	0.0277782	Second opinion	0.0204678
Embryo transfer	0.0233918	Accommodation	0.0233918
GIFT	0.0160819	Airport pick-up and drop	0.0204678
ICSI	0.0233918	Translation	0.0175439
MESA	0.0131579	International patients	0.0204678
PESA	0.0160819	Insurance	0.0233918
TESA	0.0219298	Smart treatment plans	0.0248538
TESE	0.0219298	Packages	0.0219298
OD, ED	0.0219298	Financing options	0.0204678
Cryopreservation	0.0219298	Psychological counseling	0.0219298
Freezing of semen	0.0219298	Publications	0.0175439
Freezing of embryos	0.0248538	Society for assisted reproduction	0.0263158
Oocyte cryopreservation	0.0233918	Indian medical association	0.0263158
Ovarian tissue cryopreservation	0.0219298	Success rate	0.0263158
Semen preparation	0.0248538	IVFCost	0.0263158
Facilities for semen preparation and IUI	0.0248538	IUICost	0.0263158
Egg sharing	0.0190058	MailID	0.0263158
Surrogacy	0.0204678	Chat	0.0248538
Laser assisted hatching	0.0175439	Phone	0.0263158

4   Results and Analysis

Number of the fertility hospitals chosen for study in different metros and cities
are: in Tier1 - 27 hospitals and in Tier2 - 7 hospitals. The criteria weights are
marked as a score of 10 and obtained from experts. These scores are normalized
in the range between 0 to 1. According to Table 2, criterion of IVF, Cost factors,
Communication factors, Accreditation/Affiliation, Oocyte preservation, Semen
preservation and freezing have higher weightage.

Fertility hospitals have been ordered based on the features shown in
Table 1 via the following MCDM methods: Ratio System Ranking (RSR),
Multiplicative Form Ranking (MFR), Multi-MOORA ranking (combined rank-
ing)(MMOORA), TOPSIS Linear (TOPSISL), TOPSIS Vector (TOPSISV) and
WASPAS. Each MCDM assigns rank to each hospital based on the hospital data.
The similarity between the rankings assigned by the multiple MCDM methods
is measured by applying Kendall's rank correlation method. Kendall's Tau is
a non-parametric measure for ranked data columns. Kendall's rank correlation
coefficient (Tau) is calculated between two different MCDM methods. Value of
Tau has a range of 0 to 1, with 0 denoting no relation and 1 denoting a perfect
relationship. Having a Tau value more than 0.9 for the ranking methods, means,
that the hospitals have been ordered in the same way by most of the MCDM
methods. Hence the top ranked hospitals could be recommended. The results of
the ordering evaluations via MCDM methods using Equal weights assignment
and empirical weights for the Tier-1 City1 is presented in Table 3 and Table 4.

Table 3. Tier-1 City1 hospitals - Ranking based on equal weight

Alternatives	RSR	MFR	MMOORA	TOPSISL	TOPSISV	WASPAS
Hospital1	5	4	5	4	4	4
Hospital2	1	2	1	2	1	2
Hospital3	7	8	7	8	7	8
Hospital4	2	1	2	1	3	1
Hospital5	9	9	9	9	9	9
Hospital6	8	7	8	7	8	7
Hospital7	10	10	10	10	10	10
Hospital8	3	3	3	3	5	3
Hospital9	11	11	11	11	11	11
Hospital10	4	5	4	5	2	5
Hospital11	6	6	6	6	6	6

MCDM methods WASPAS, TOPSISL and MFR are having similar behaviour in assigning the ranks in both equal weight assignment and empirical weight assignment. Hospital2 and Hospital4 are being ranked as either rank1 or rank2 by all the methods which shows the agreement between the methods. In WASPAS method's Q index calculation, equal contribution from both sum and product methods has been considered by setting the λ value as 0.5.

Table 4. Tier-1 City1 hospitals - Ranking based on empirical weight

Alternatives	RSR	MFR	MMOORA	TOPSISL	TOPSISV	WASPAS
Hospital1'	5	4	4	4	5	4
Hospital2	1	2	1	2	1	2
Hospital3	7	8	7	8	7	8
Hospital4	2	1	2	1	3	1
Hospital5	9	9	9	9	9	9
Hospital6	8	7	8	7	8	7
Hospital7	10	10	10	10	10	10
Hospital8	3	3	3	3	4	3
Hospital9	11	11	11	11	11	11
Hospital10	4	5	5	5	2	5
Hospital11	6	6	6	6	6	6

Ranks assigned by the different MCDM methods for a particular city (Tier-1 City1) is shown in Fig. 3. Sensitivity analysis to change in weights show their effect in high to middle ranks only. In lower ranks, there is no much variation.

Rankings of Multiplicative Form Ranking, TOPSIS Linear and WASPAS agree on all the hospitals. Ratio System Ranking and MMOORA methods disagree in only one rank. Out of 6 methods used in this study, only two methods MMOORA and TOPSIS Vectors have a change in their initial ranking. There are only 2 interchanges in ranks between MMOORA and TOPSIS Vector for the 4th and 5th ranks while considering the Tier-1 City1 Hospitals.

The Kendall Correlation for the MCDM methods' rank assignments for Tier-1 City1 is shown in Fig. 4. It could be understood that the degrees of disagreements on the rankings of the hospitals among MCDM methods are less. Both the hospitals in comparison have the same values for all features except Semen Preservation, Egg Sharing, Pre-implementation Genetic Screening (PGS), Pre-implementation Genetic Diagnosis and Insurance. Hence the presence of these factors (facilities) differentiates the first and second rank hospitals in Tier-1 City1 as shown in Fig. 5.

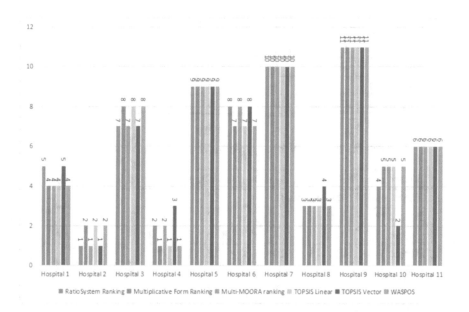

Fig. 3. Tier-1 City1 hospitals - Ranking based on empirical weight

On applying the same process for Tier-1 City2 considering 16 hospitals for the analysis, Table 5 and Table 6 show the ranking based on equal weight method and empirical weight method. MFR, TOPSIS Linear and WASPAS has given the same ranking for the hospitals, while other methods have provided different rankings.

List of top 5 hospitals remains consistent with all MCDM methods. There is no abrupt change in the rankings. The correlation matrices for the Tier-1 City2 city ranking are shown in Fig. 6 and Fig. 7. The correlation values show that the

Table 5. Tier-1 City2 hospitals ranking - Equal weights

Alternatives	RSR	MFR	MMOORA	TOPSISL	TOPSISV	WASPAS
Hospital1	12	12	11	12	11	12
Hospital2	8	6	8	6	10	6
Hospital3	5	7	5	7	1	7
Hospital4	10	13	12	13	8	13
Hospital5	6	8	6	8	4	8
Hospital6	11	9	9	9	12	9
Hospital7	14	14	14	14	14	14
Hospital8	9	10	10	10	7	10
Hospital9	7	5	7	5	9	5
Hospital10	2	1	1	1	5	1
Hospital11	4	2	2	2	6	2
Hospital12	13	11	13	11	13	11
Hospital13	16	16	16	16	15	16
Hospital14	3	4	4	4	3	4
Hospital15	1	3	3	3	2	3
Hospital16	15	15	15	15	16	15

Table 6. Tier-1 City2 hospitals ranking - Empirical weights

Alternatives	RSR	MFR	MMOORA	TOPSISL	TOPSISV	WASPAS
Hospital1	11	12	11	12	12	12
Hospital2	8	6	7	7	9	7
Hospital3	5	7	5	6	2	6
Hospital4	12	13	12	13	10	13
Hospital5	7	8	8	8	4	8
Hospital6	10	9	9	9	11	9
Hospital7	14	14	14	14	14	14
Hospital8	9	10	10	10	6	10
Hospital9	6	5	6	5	8	5
Hospital10	4	1	1	3	7	1
Hospital11	3	2	2	2	5	3
Hospital12	13	11	13	11	13	11
Hospital13	16	16	16	16	16	16
Hospital14	2	4	4	4	3	4
Hospital15	1	3	3	1	1	2
Hospital16	15	15	15	15	15	15

Table 7. Tier-2 City1 hospitals - Ranking based on equal weight

Alternatives	RSR	MFR	MMOORA	TOPSISL	TOPSISV	WASPAS
Hospital1	6	4	4	4	6	4
Hospital2	1	1	1	1	2	1
Hospital3	3	2	2	2	3	2
Hospital4	2	3	3	3	1	3
Hospital5	5	6	6	5	5	6
Hospital6	7	7	7	7	7	7
Hospital7	4	5	5	6	4	5

Table 8. Tier-2 City1 hospitals - Ranking based on empirical weight

Alternatives	RSR	MFR	MMOORA	TOPSISL	TOPSISV	WASPAS
Hospital1	6	4	4	5	6	4
Hospital2	1	1	1	1	1	1
Hospital3	3	2	2	2	4	2
Hospital4	2	3	3	3	2	3
Hospital5	5	6	6	4	5	6
Hospital6	7	7	7	7	7	7
Hospital7	4	5	5	6	3	5

rankings change in 1 or 2 grades only and overall they are similar. The top 3 ranks are shuffling among Hospital10, Hospital11, and Hospital15. Factors like GIFT, MESA, Psychological Counselling, Cost of the treatment and distance contribute for the high ranks allotted. Hence the patient could be helped in selecting a best fertility hospital based on the facilities.

The result of applying MDCM methods for the fertility hospitals in Tier-2 City1 city is shown in Tables 7 and 8. For this city in equal weight assignment the methods MFR, MMOORA, WASPAS give the same ranking for all hospitals. TOP 3 rankings are shared by Hospital2, Hospital3 and Hospital4 respectively in view of all methods.

When empirical weight method is applied, even though 3 rankings changed overall in TOPSIS Linear method, the list of top 3 rankings hospitals has not changed. The correlation of these methods is shown in Fig. 8 and Fig. 9. From the correlation chart it can be seen that all the methods behave similarly both in equal weight method and empirical method. The factors contributing for the high ranks are Cryo-preservation, Publication, GIFT, MESA, Insurance, distance and AID.

To summarize, data are collected from authorised websites of multiple hospitals (alternatives) through web scrapping and decision matrix generated. Attributes (Criteria) needed to evaluate the fertility hospitals are extracted. Two

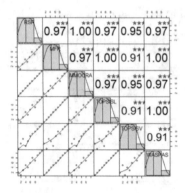

Fig. 4. Correlation among MCDM methods in equal weight assignment - Tier-1 City1

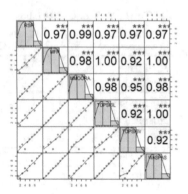

Fig. 5. Correlation among MCDM methods in empirical weight assignment - Tier-1 City1

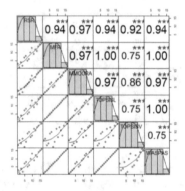

Fig. 6. Rank correlation in equal weight - Tier-1 City2

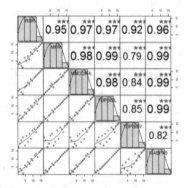

Fig. 7. Rank correlation in empirical weight - Tier-1 City2

different weight methods have been followed in this study: Subjective method (Empirical) based on the estimates assigned by experts and Objective method of assigning equal weight. MCDM methods RSR, MFR, MMOORA, TOPSIS-Linear, TOPSISVector and WASPAS have been applied and the hospitals have been ranked.

The following observations have been made:

1. Fertility hospital selection problem is a decision making problem having multiple conflicting criterion and multiple alternatives from which choosing one alternative is very tough. So in this study, MCDM methods which are good at handling these types of optimization problems are used to help people to know the top rated fertility hospitals among a set of fertility hospitals.
2. Instead of applying a single method and getting a rank, multiple methods are applied and a list of top hospitals could be found from these ranks.

3. Hospitals which have basic facilities along with the latest facilities/services get a high score. Hospitals having maximum facilities along with minimum distance are getting good score.
4. Facilities like Cryopreservation, Egg sharing, PGD, PGS, Psychological counseling, Research Publications, less cost for the treatment and less distance are factors deciding the high score
5. MCDM methods like RSR, MFR, TOPSISLinear and WASPAS produce a similar ranking. MMOORA and TOPSISVector change in rank assignment with a change in weight.
6. Rank Correlation analysis of the ranks given by these methods has been done using Kendall's Correlation method and the minimum correlation value is 0.71

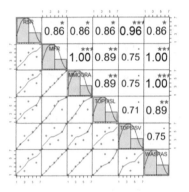

Fig. 8. Rank correlation in equal weight - Tier-2 City1

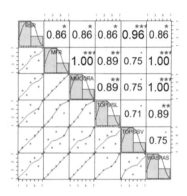

Fig. 9. Rank correlation in empirical weight - Tier-2 City1

5   Conclusion

This study shows that fertility hospitals can be ordered via MCDM methods since many criterion are considered simultaneously instead of only one criterion and includes both benefit criterion and cost criterion. Best ranking hospitals have the facilities like Cryopreservation, Egg sharing, Preimplantation genetic diagnosis(PGD), Preimplantation genetic screening(PGS), Psychological Counselling, Insurance cover, Publication, Cost of the treatments and distance etc. Hospitals which have many of these apart from the basic needs are placed in the top rankings.

Most of the methods have produced similar rankings for the selection of fertility hospitals. Methods MMOORA and TOPSIS Vector are similar in their behaviour. The other methods RSR, MFR, TOPSIS Linear and WASPAS produce a similar ranking. Hence instead of taking the result from a single method, a group of methods could be combined in taking the decisions. When applying Kendall's Rank correlation, the result of correlation shows that minimum correlation value among all 3 cities is 0.71.

For a decision maker, assigning a precise performance grade to an alternative for the criteria under consideration is quite difficult. Hence usage of fuzzy approach could be an advantage to assign weight instead of precise numbers. In this study, the ranking method is a static approach and user preference is not included. In future work, according to the user preference, the weightage could be modified. Also the user's current location could be identified dynamically from his position through a mobile application and hospitals near to him could be recommended.

References

1. Abel, E., Mikhailov, L., Keane, J.: Group aggregation of pairwise comparisons using multi-objective optimization. Inf. Sci. **322**, 257–275 (2015)
2. Al-Shayea, A.M.: Measuring hospital's units efficiency: a data envelopment analysis approach. Int. J. Eng. Technol. **11**(6), 7–19 (2011)
3. Athawale, V.M., Chakraborty, S.: A comparative study on the ranking performance of some multi-criteria decision-making methods for industrial robot selection. Int. J. Ind. Eng. Comput. **2**(4), 831–850 (2011)
4. Bouyssou, D., Marchant, T., Pirlot, M., Tsoukias, A., Vincke, P.: Evaluation and Decision Models with Multiple Criteria: Stepping Stones for the Analyst, vol. 86. Springer, Heidelberg (2006). https://doi.org/10.1007/0-387-31099-1
5. Brauers, W.K.M., Zavadskas, E.K.: Project management by multimoora as an instrument for transition economies. Technol. Econ. Dev. Econ. **16**(1), 5–24 (2010)
6. Fertilisation, T.H., Authority, E.: Getting started your guide to fertility treatment (2017). https://www.hfea.gov.uk/about-us/publications/publications-for-people-seeking-treatment/
7. Guo, L., Jin, B., Yao, C., Yang, H., Huang, D., Wang, F.: Which doctor to trust: a recommender system for identifying the right doctors. J. Med. Internet Res. **18**(7) (2016)
8. Hwang, C., Yoon, K.: Multiple Attribute Decision Making: Methods and Applications: A State-of-the-Art Survey. Lecture Notes in Economics and Mathematical Systems. Springer, Cham (1981). https://books.google.co.in/books?id=X-wYAQAAIAAJ
9. Janic, M., Reggiani, A.: An application of the multiple criteria decision making (MCDM) analysis to the selection of a new hub airport. Eur. J. Transp. Infrastruct. Res. EJTIR **2**(2) (2002)
10. Kou, G., Lu, Y., Peng, Y., Shi, Y.: Evaluation of classification algorithms using MCDM and rank correlation. Int. J. Inf. Technol. Decis. Making **11**(01), 197–225 (2012)
11. Leoneti, A.B.: Considerations regarding the choice of ranking multiple criteria decision making methods. Pesquisa Operacional **36**(2), 259–277 (2016)
12. Li, P., Qian, H., Wu, J., Chen, J.: Sensitivity analysis of TOPSIS method in water quality assessment: I. Sensitivity to the parameter weights. Environ. Monit. Assess. **185**(3), 2453–2461 (2013)
13. Marcus, H.J., Marcus, D.M., Marcus, S.F.: How do infertile couples choose their IVF centers? An internet-based survey. Fertil. Steril. **83**(3), 779–781 (2005)

14. Pekkaya, M.: Career preference of university students: an application of MCDM methods. Procedia Econ. Finance **23**, 249–255 (2015)
15. Streisfield, A., Chowdhury, N., Cherniak, R., Shapiro, H.: Patient centered infertility care: the health care provider's perspective. Patient Experience J. **2**(1), 93–97 (2015)
16. Váchová, L., Hajdíková, T.: Evaluation of Czech hospitals performance using MCDM methods. In: Proceedings of the World Congress on Engineering and Computer Science, vol. 2 (2017)
17. Vinogradova, I., Podvezko, V., Zavadskas, E.: The recalculation of the weights of criteria in MCDM methods using the Bayes approach. Symmetry **10**(6), 205 (2018)
18. Wang, P., Zhu, Z., Wang, Y.: A novel hybrid MCDM model combining the SAW, TOPSIS and GRA methods based on experimental design. Inf. Sci. **345**, 27–45 (2016)
19. Zavadskas, E.K., Turskis, Z., Antucheviciene, J., Zakarevicius, A.: Optimization of weighted aggregated sum product assessment. Elektronika ir elektrotechnika **122**(6), 3–6 (2012)
20. Zavadskas, E., Skibniewski, M., Antucheviciene, J.: Performance analysis of civil engineering journals based on the web of science® database. Arch. Civil Mech. Eng. **14**(4), 519–527 (2014)
21. Zhang, H., Peng, Y., Hou, L., Tian, G., Li, Z.: A hybrid multi-objective optimization approach for energy-absorbing structures in train collisions. Inf. Sci. **481**, 491–506 (2019)

Up-Link/Down-Link Availability Calculation in Cloud Using Ford Fulkerson Algorithm

R. Devi$^{(\boxtimes)}$ and V. Gopalakrishnan

Government College of Technology, Coimbatore 641013, Tamil Nadu, India
{r.devi,gopalakrishnan.v}@gct.ac.in

Abstract. In recent days Cloud plays a vital role in Information technology. Many customers and organization are moving towards the cloud computing environment for effective utilization of the resources. Availability of Internet is the main need for accessing the cloud. Once the customer registered for a cloud service, they can access the service from anywhere and at any time using the Internet. Normally, shortest distance between the user interface and the information server in the Internet is identified using RIP (Routing Information Protocol) or OSPF (Open Shortest Path First Protocol). Ford Fulkerson algorithm is applied to shortest path graph to identify the uplink/downlink bandwidth. Hence this algorithm helps to identify the current availability percentage of cloud services. This algorithm is efficient when compared to the existing measurement methodologies like Trouble Ticketing, Device reach-ability and SNMP (Simple Network Maintenance Protocol).

Keywords: Availability · Routing Information Protocol · Open Shortest Path First · Ford Fulkerson · Cloud providers · Cloud customers

1 Introduction

INTERNET is intended to serve as a backbone for Cloud services. Definitions of the key terms that are used frequently are described here. This paper deals with identification of availability issues occurring in the Internet. For example, a customer has registered with a cloud service and the customer is also having latest Internet facilities, still the services are not loaded quickly due to the network availability.

1.1 Cloud Computing

According to NIST, the frame work for enabling shared, continuous, easy access, scalable network access to a pool of configurable computing resources (e.g., Networks, Servers, Storage, Applications, and Services) that can be quickly provided and withdrawn with minimal management effort or service provider interaction [1].

I. Raman et al. (Eds.): ICC3 2021, CCIS 1631, pp. 76–90, 2022.
https://doi.org/10.1007/978-3-031-15556-7_6

1.2 Cloud Providers

The organization or enterprise, which provides cloud services as API (Application Program Interface) is known as cloud providers. The services are categorized based on their needs. These services are provided as pay for use model through the Internet [1, 2].

1.3 Cloud Customers

An organization or individuals who request for any category of services from the cloud providers are known as cloud customers.

1.4 Cloud Services

There are three main service delivery models in the cloud environment [2]. Software as a Service (SaaS) – The end user utilizes only the application provided by the cloud provider, the control of operating system, hardware, network infrastructure and servers are maintained by cloud providers. Platform as a Service (PaaS) - The end user controls and maintains the application layer to deploy their applications. The control of operating system, hardware, network infrastructure and servers are maintained by the cloud providers. The platform is an application control framework for end users. Infrastructure as a Service (IaaS) – End user can deploy their own platform over the cloud providers infrastructure. The end user can control the operating system, storage, deployed applications and networking components such as firewalls and load balancers. The cloud infrastructure is controlled by the cloud provider.

1.5 Availability

The term availability refers to the existence of service over 24/7. It is the probability of the service is working in the given moment of time t. The reliability of the service is the probability within the time interval 0 and t the service should not down [3].

1.6 Routing Information Protocol

This protocol is used to locate the shortest distance from the source node to the target node, while there are multiple paths between them. It updates the table of the routers whenever the packets flow through the network. The RIP protocol works under the principle of Distance Vector routing algorithm. The main drawback of RIP protocol is, if the hop count is greater than 15, the network is considered as unreachable, since the updated information reach every router in the network overloads the bandwidth [4, 5].

1.7 Open Shortest Path First (OSPF)

OSPF also finds the shortest path between the source node and all known targets. The Dijkstra's algorithm is used to find the shortest path for OSPF protocol. Once the shortest path is identified, all the packets are transferred in the shortest path [5]. In this work Ford Fulkerson algorithm is used for the calculation of availability in the network to reach the cloud services. Using this information the cloud customer can identify how the services respond in the Internet. This measurement methodology identifies the link failure, break downs, congestion in a network and outages caused in the cloud services. The exiting methodologies such as Trouble Ticketing, Device Reachability and Service Assurance (SA) agent can be applied to the specific segment of the network to save the money and time. The first chapter describes the availability calculation formulas, the second chapter deals with existing methods for availability calculation, the third chapter explains the proposed algorithm for availability calculations, forth chapter shows the results of the proposed method, fifth chapter describes future enhancement of this project and the last chapter specifies the conclusion of this paper.

2 Availability Calculation

Availability is defined as the capability of a service unit to be in active state to perform a required operation over the allotted time interval. The service unit can be an application/platform/storage/network. Availability of component can be written as follows

$$A = MTBF \div (MTBF + MTTR) \tag{1}$$

In Eq. (1), Mean Time Between Failure is represented as MTBF, and Mean Time to Repair is represented as MTTR.

2.1 Availability Calculation in Internet

Availability in Internet is measured as a actual amount of time the network is delivering services in percentage divided by the amount of time it is agreed to deliver services.

$$A = TTDS \div ETDS \tag{2}$$

where, TTDS is the Time Taken to Deliver the Services and ETDS is the Expected Time to Deliver the Services. For example the TTDS $= 59$ s and ETDS $= 60$ s the availability is measured as 98.33%. Availability calculation of the network using uptime and downtime of a service is shown below [6].

$$A = AUT \div TT = (TT - ADT) \div TT \tag{3}$$

where, AUT is the Actual up Time; TT is the Total Time and ADT is the Actual Down Time.

2.2 Need for Availability Calculation

When a customer selects a service from the cloud provider automatically the customer and the provider accepts the SLA (Service Level Agreement) [7]. It specifies the parameters that are needed to provide the service. Availability, reliability, risk of outage is the some of the parameters of the service. The paper focuses on calculating availability of the network. SLA consists of availability value similar to that of the Table 1. These down time values represents the service unavailable time for the customers. This down time is represented as scheduled unavailable time. Apart from this scheduled down time the customers suffer from 44% unscheduled down time according to cisco survey. That is out of 100%, 18% of cloud customers experiences 100 h of unscheduled downtime. Network outage is based on the following parameters. Congestive degradation - Occurs due to network peak flow [8], Change management - occurs when network configuration design changes [9], WAN failure (fiber cut/carrier failure) - occurs due to physical disaster of the network cables. This network outage affects the availability of the network.

Table 1. Down time based on availability value

Availability	Days	Hours	Minutes
99.9999	0	0	.5
99.999	0	0	5
99.99	0	0	53
99.95	0	4	23
99.9	0	8	46
99.5	1	19	4
99	3	15	36

2.3   Existing Methods

This chapter describes some of the exiting measurement methodologies for availability calculation.

Trouble Ticketing (TT). TT system helps to manage major of the problems, failures and breakdowns in the network [10].There are three states in the TT, and they are creation, open and close. Creation state - Once the problem in the network is identified a new ticket is created to represent that problem. Open State - Created TT is solved manually or automatically. Some problems need specifically trained technician, who have to travel to fix the problem. Some other can solve these problems remotely without human intervention [10]. Live TT before solving the issue will be in this state. Close state - Once the issue is addressed and solved the TT will be in this state.

Pros. Ticket creation is easy; TT won't introduce any overhead to the network; network outage can be categorized.

Cons. False positive (FP) and False Negative (FN) prediction may occur in TT. FP - Mis-prediction of network problems, FN - Not identifying network problems; More resources are needed for automatic recovery.

Device Reachability. There are two methods under this device reachability technique. They are ICMP ping and SNMP. ICMP ping method will send the ICMP echo request to the destination and get ICMP echo reply from the destination using TCP protocol. This ICMP echo request/reply used to identify the device reachability from the source. The source is the controller system which collects information of the network. ICMP ping messages are categorized into two types they are checking networking device reachability from the controller system and checking end device reachability from the controller system. In both the cases if the reply message won't reach the controller system, it is identified that some fault is there either in the link or in the network [11, 12].

Pros. Availability calculation is less accurate; able to identify routing problems; Individual devices/links can be analyzed in the network.

Cons. Since individual packets are send to check the device availability, it increases the network overhead; No multi point measurement from the controller system, only end to end measurement; Granularity of availability is proportional to the ping frequency; Requires database maintenance to store the ICMP ping messages.

SNMP method works based on voting and cut off on links, edge ports or edge devices. SNMP consists of one master and number of agents. The agent is configured such that to vote and organize the down times for the defined services or links. Database is maintained to store the down times and agreed service time. The voting interval is inversely proportional to the sampling rate. Less duration of voting interval increases the accuracy level of the data collected. Trap information increases the accuracy level of outage information. Polling will be conducted on the available agents, if any agent identifies the downtime immediately the information passed to the administrator module [13, 14].

Pros. Interval of Outage and its scope are less accurate; inherit the existing NMS (Network Management System), hence low network overhead.

Cons. Element service database maintenance requires outstanding change management and provisioning services; doesn't report for packet forwarding problems; it does not provide true point to point measure.

SA Agent. Service Assurance Agent is the embedded feature of Cisco IOS software. To operate this SA Agent, configuration of SA Agent features on router within the customer network is mandatory. A data collector creates the SA Agents on routers to monitor certain network services or performance. The SA Agent's monitored data are collected from the router and makes it available.

Pros. Accurate network availability is calculated for the defined paths; Identify routing problems; low network overhead.

Cons. Requires a system to collect the SA Agent data; Implementation of SA Agent should be in the router; Granularity of availability is limited by the polling frequency; Critical network paths to measure.

Other methods the following are some of the other methods used to measure the availability.

COOL Component. Outage Online Measurement which filters the event notification and store the outage information in the router.

Application Reachability this is similar to ICMP ping. In-spite of using network layer protocol, application layer protocol HTTP is used to check the application availability from the source.

Embedded RMON. Embedded Remote Monitoring is also Cisco component which generates alarm and event based on the network statistics. It sets thresholds in router configuration, SNMP trap to send when the network variable rises above and/or falls below a given threshold.

3 Availability Calculation

Ford Fulkerson algorithm is used to find the max flow of a unidirectional network [18]. This algorithm concept is applied to the existing real time networks to calculate the maximum bandwidth from the source to the destination nodes. Since the real time network is bidirectional, they are separated into two unidirectional graphs [18]. In the first graph the flow is from the source to the destination and it is represented as down-link bandwidth. Similarly in the second graph the flow is from the destination to the source and it is represented as up-link bandwidth. The max flow is calculated for the up-link and down-link of the network. If there is any outage in the network due to congestive degradation or change management or WAN failure (fiber cut/carrier failure) this will affect the max flow values of up-link and down-link. From this we can identify the availability of the network. This method is used to identify the unscheduled outages of a cloud provider. Scheduled outage will be available as availability information in SLA as in Table 1. Different quantifiable parameters are used for ranking the cloud providers based on the customers need [15–17]. In which availability is the most important parameter to rank the cloud providers. The algorithm process is shown below.

3.1 Availability Calculation in Internet

Step1 Identify the most common utilized path between the source and destination using RIP or OSPF.
Step2 Bidirectional graph is obtained between the source and destination.
Step3 Separate the bi-direction graph into two unidirectional graphs.
Step4 In the first unidirectional graph, the flow is taken from the source to destination which is represented as down-link (DL).

Step5 In the second unidirectional graph, the flow is taken from the destination to the source which is represented as up-link (UL).

Step6 Apply Ford Fulkerson algorithm to both DL and UL graphs and calculate the maximum flow as DLMF (Down-link Max Flow) or ULMF(Up-link Max-Flow).

Step7 DLMF or ULMF are kept as threshold values.

Step8 step 1 to 7 is executed when there is no network overhead to dynamically calculate the max flow of up-link and down-link.

Step9 Calculate DLMF and ULMF with network traffic and name it as NTDLMF and NTULMF. Such that,

$$NTDLMF < DLMF \tag{4}$$

$$NTULMF < ULMF \tag{5}$$

Step10 If the currently measured 'mDLMF' and 'mULMF' satisfies the following equation then there is no unscheduled outage.

$$NTDLMF < mDLMF < DLMF \tag{6}$$

$$NTULMF < mULMF < ULMF \tag{7}$$

Step11 else unscheduled outage is identified.

Step12 Use any one of the existing technique to solve the problem.

3.2 Path Identification Using RIP

Small amount of information can passed as RIP messages using Distance vector algorithms. Each router/host that participates in the routing will keep information of the destinations within the measurable network. All entities of path information will summarize by a single entry. This describes the route to all destinations on that network. Using IP protocol this summarization is possible, routing within a network is invisible. Each entry of the router table includes the next router to which datagrams destined for the entity should send. In addition to the routing information it includes a "metric" measuring the total distance to the entity. Figure 1 is an example of a network which consists of six routers. If the source and destination represented as A and B, by using RIP the path identified marked in red line. Router table updated information shown from Table 1, 2, 3 and 4. The path selected by RIP for sending the messages is alone shown in the table. Through which interface of the router the path identified. Identified path highlighted in the tables. Shortest path between the node Wired Node A => Switch C => Router 5 => Router 9 => Router 7 => Router 8 => Switch D => Wired Node B.

Table 2. Router 5 RIP table.

Destination IP	Subnet mask	NextHopIP	Interface	Metric	Timer (Micro sec)
11.1.0.0	255.255.0.0	11.1.1.1	1	0	3000000
11.3.0.0	255.255.0.0	11.3.1.1	2	0	3000000
11.6.0.0	255.255.0.0	11.6..1.1	3	0	3000000
11.4.0.0	255.255.0.0	11.3.1.2	2	1	48.2
11.7.0.0	255.255.0.0	11.6.1.2	3	1	48.2

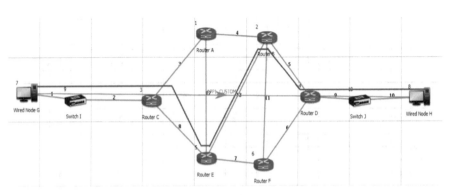

Fig. 1. Routing message packets using RIP/OSPF.

Table 3. Router 9 RIP table

Destination IP	Subnet mask	NextHopIP	Interface	Metric	Timer (Micro sec)
11.6.0.0	255.255.0.0	11.6.1.2	1	0	0
11.7.0.0	255.255.0.0	11.7.1.1	2	0	0
11.1.0.0	255.255.0.0	11.6.1.1	1	1	48.2
11.3.0.0	255.255.0.0	11.6.1.1	1	1	48.2
11.8.0.0	255.255.0.0	11.7.1.2	2	1	48.2

Table 4. Router7 RIP table

Destination IP	Subnet mask	NextHopIP	Interface	Metric	Timer (Micro sec)
11.4.0.0	255.255.0.0	11.4.1.2	1	0	0
11.5.0.0	255.255.0.0	11.5.1.1	2	0	0
11.3.0.0	255.255.0.0	11.4.1.1	1	1	48.2
11.8.0.0	255.255.0.0	11.5.1.2	2	1	48.2
11.2.0.0	255.255.0.0	11.5.1.2	2	1	48.2

Table 5. Router8 RIP table

Destination IP	Subnet mask	NextHopIP	Interface	Metric	Timer (Micro sec)
11.5.0.0	255.255.0.0	11.5.1.2	1	0	0
11.8.0.0	255.255.0.0	11.8.1.2	2	0	0
11.2.0.0	255.255.0.0	11.2.1.1	3	0	0
11.4.0.0	255.255.0.0	11.5.1.1	1	1	48.2
11.7.0.0	255.255.0.0	11.8.1.1	2	1	48.2

3.3   Path Identification Using OSPF

The Open Source shortest path algorithm works based on Link state routing (LSR).Link State router stores the database of all OSPF routers. Router exchange Link State. Advertisement within neighboring routers, each router knows its neighbor. When no node to explore in the Network, converged all routers have the appropriate entries in their router table. The shortest path from source to destination estimated by using Dijkstra's Algorithm. Each OSPF router performs a least cost path information available in the router tables. Create a minimum spanning tree of shortest path network with them as the root. OSPF algorithm applied on Fig. 1. Tables 5, 6, 7 and 8 represents the router information for the shortest path from source A to destination B. Shortest path from the node Wired Node A => Switch C => Router 5 => Router 9 => Router 7 => Router 8 => Switch D => Wired Node B (Table 9).

Table 6. Router5 OSPF table

Destination IP	NextHopIP	Subnet mask	Cost	AreaID	Pathtype
11.1.0.0	11.1.1.1	255.255.0.0	1	0	Intra_area
11.3.0.0	11.3.1.1	255.255.0.0	1	0	Intra_area
11.6.0.0	11.6..1.1	255.255.0.0	1	0	Intra_area
11.4.0.0	11.3.1.2	255.255.0.0	2	0	Intra_area
11.7.0.0	11.6.1.2	255.255.0.0	2	0	Intra_area

Table 7. Router7 OSPF table

Destination IP	NextHopIP	Subnet mask	Cost	AreaID	Pathtype
11.4.0.0	11.4.1.2	255.255.0.0	1	0	Intra_area
11.5.0.0	11.5.1.1	255.255.0.0	1	0	Intra_area
11.11.0.0	11.11.1.1	255.255.0.0	1	0	Intra_area
11.12.0.0	11.12.1.2	255.255.0.0	1	0	Intra_area
11.8.0.0	11.5.1.2	255.255.0.0	2	0	Intra_area

Table 8. Router8 OSPF table

Destination IP	NextHopIP	Subnet mask	Cost	AreaID	Pathtype
11.5.0.0	11.5.1.2	255.255.0.0	1	0	Intra_area
11.8.0.0	11.8.1.2	255.255.0.0	1	0	Intra_area
11.2.0.0	11.2.1.1	255.255.0.0	1	0	Intra_area
11.7.0.0	11.8.1.1	255.255.0.0	2	0	Intra_area
11.12.0.0	11.8.1.1	255.255.0.0	2	0	Intra_area

Table 9. Router9 OSPF table

Destination IP	NextHopIP	Subnet mask	Cost	AreaID	Pathtype
11.6.0.0	11.6.1.2	255.255.0.0	1	0	Intra_area
11.7.0.0	11.7.1.1	255.255.0.0	1	0	Intra_area
11.10.0.0	11.10.1.1	255.255.0.0	1	0	Intra_area
11.11.0.0	11.11.1.1	255.255.0.0	1	0	Intra_area
11.8.0.0	11.7.1.2	255.255.0.0	2	0	Intra_area

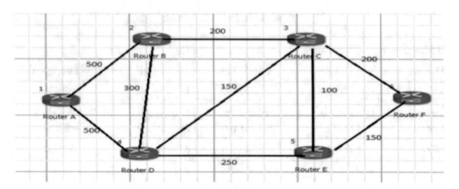

Fig. 2. Bidirectional graph.

3.4 Ford Fulkerson Algorithm

Algorithm for calculating Max Flow

Initial conditions
Flow on an edge doesn't exceed the given bandwidth of the edge. Incoming flow is equal to outgoing flow for every vertex except source and destination.

Step 1: Start with initial flow as 0.
Step 2: Input the bandwidth information of the network in a matrix form.
Step 3: Start the Breadth First Search from the source towards the sink.
Step 4: Mark the source node as visited and enqueue it to the queue.

BFS loop
Dequeue'u' from the queue and mark it as visited. Get all adjacent vertices of the vertex 'u'. If an adjacent node unvisited, mark it visited and enqueue it.

Step 5: If we reach sink in BFS starting from the source return true else false.
Step 6: Return the max flow from source to sink.

The above algorithm applied to the Fig. 1 network routers. Obtained bidirectional graph represented in the Fig. 2. Unidirectional graph derived from Fig. 2 represented in Fig. 3 and Fig. 4.

4   Results

In this example the bandwidth unit considered as Mbps. In Fig. 3, Router A is the source and Router F is the destination.

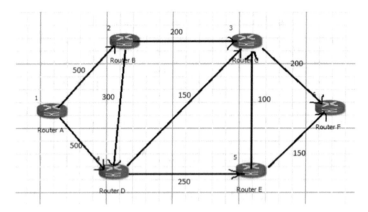

Fig. 3. Downlink unidirectional graph.

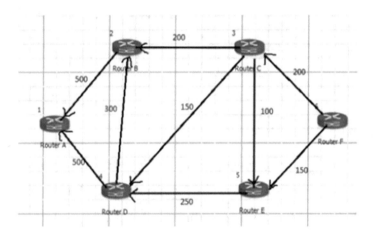

Fig. 4. Uplink unidirectional graph.

Downlink matrix representation shown in Table 10. The value of DLMF $= 350$ Mbps. In Fig. 4, Router F is the source and Router A is the destination. The matrix representation of UL directional graph given in the Table 11 the value of ULMF $= 350$ Mbps. Defects per Million (DPM) is the unit which used to measure the availability of the network device and the network links.

Table 10. Matrix representation of DLMF

-	1	2	3	4	5	6
1	0	500	500	0	0	0
2	0	0	300	200	0	0
3	0	0	0	150	250	0
4	0	0	0	0	0	200
5	0	0	0	100	0	150

Table 11. Matrix representation of ULMF

-	1	2	3	4	5	6
1	0	0	0	0	0	0
2	500	0	300	200	0	0
3	500	300	0	0	0	0
4	0	200	150	100	0	0
5	250	0	0	0	0	0

4.1   General DPM Calculation

$$DPM = \sum connection\, outage\, minutes \div \sum connection\, total\, minutes \quad (8)$$

In the point of customers who gets service from the provider, DPM represented as,

$$DPM = \sum End\, user\, outage\, minutes \div \sum End\, user\, total\, minutes \quad (9)$$

For example consider a network with 50 customers and the reporting period is one year. 5 customers have 24 h down time per year. The DPM represented in Eq. (10),

$$DPM = [(5 \times 24) \div (50 \times 24 \times 365)] \times 106 \quad (10)$$

From Eq. (10) we will get the value as 273.97. The availability calculation using DPM given in Eq. (11),

$$Availability = 1 - [(5 \times 24) \div (50 \times 24 \times 365)] \quad (11)$$

Availability is 0.997. Hence the availability percentage is 99.7%. Similarly the availability calculation using Ford Fulkerson algorithm described in Eq. (12),

$$DPM = ((DLMF - NTDLMF) \div DLMF \times 103) \times 106 \quad (12)$$

Consider NTDLMF value as 300, from the algorithm, the calculated the value of DLMF is 350. NTDLMF value is chosen such that it should satisfy the Eq. 4. Substitute these values in Eq. (12).

$$DPM = ((350 - 300) \div 350 \times 103) \times 106 \quad (13)$$

The value of Eq. 13 is 142.85.

$$Availability = 1 - (DLMF - NTDLMF) \div DLMF \times 103 \qquad (14)$$

By substituting the values in Eq. (14),

$$Availability = 1 - ((350 - 300) \div 350 \times 103) \qquad (15)$$

The value of Eq. (15) and availability percentage are 0.9985 and 99.85. MTBF calculated for one year shown in Eq. (16) and (17).

$$MTBF = 24 \times 365 \div (DLMF - NTDLMF) = 20\,hours \qquad (16)$$

$$MTTR = (20 \times (1 - 0.995)) \div 995 = 10\,hours \qquad (17)$$

where MTBF stands for Mean Time between Failure. MTTR stands for Mean Time to Repair. Hence proved that using Ford Fulkerson algorithm we can measure the availability of the network.

5 Conclusion

This paper proposes a new method of network availability calculation using Ford Fulkerson algorithm. The importance and measurement of availability in communication networks described in the papers [19–21]. Theoretical analysis and experimental results show that compared to traditional method the proposed method reflect the macro situation of availability and its evolution and trends over time. Netsim software simulator tool used to analyze the results. Based on this calculation method software has developed allowing the availability calculation of the network. MTBF and MTTR can calculated for the individual link of the network.

References

1. Mell, P., Grance, T.: NIST Definition of cloud computing, computer security division, Information Technology Laboratory, September 2011
2. Ahronovitz, M., Amrhein, D.: Cloud Computing Use Cases, version 4.0 A white paper produced by the Cloud Computing Use Case Discussion Group, July 2010
3. Cabarkapa, M., Mijatovic, D., Krajnovic, N.: Network topology availability analysis. Telfor J. **3**(1), 23–27 (2011)
4. Balchunas, A.: Routing Information Protocol, RIP v1.03 (2012)
5. CISCO Documentation OSPF Design Implementation Guide
6. Hwang, G.H., Yeh, S.Y.: Proof of violation for availability in cloud systems. In: IEEE-ICIS (2016)
7. Yadranjiaghdam, B., Hotwani, K., Tabrizi, N.: A risk evaluation framework for service level agreements. In: IEEE International Conference on Computer and Information Technology (2016)
8. Kalampoukas, L., Varma, A.: Explicit window adaptation: a method to enhance TCP performance. IEEE/ACM Trans. Netw. **10**(3), 338–350 (2002)

9. Kalampoukas, L., Varma, A.: Verification of configuration management changes in self-organizing networks. IEEE Trans. Netw. Serv. Manag. **13**(4) (2016)
10. Temprado, Y., Garca, C., Molinero, F.J., Gomez, J.: Knowledge discovery from trouble ticketing reports in a large telecommunication company. In: CIMCA 2008 and ISE 2008. IEEE Computer Society (2008)
11. Kaur, J., Wendzel, S., Meier, M.: Counter measures for convert channel-internal control protocols. In: 10th International Conference on Availability, Reliability and Security (2015)
12. Lampson, B.W.: A note on the confinement problem. Commun. ACM **16**(10), 613–615 (1973)
13. Affandi, A., Riyanto, D., Pratomo, I., Kusrahardjo, G.: Design and implementation fast response system monitoring server using Simple Network Management Protocol (SNMP). In: International Seminar on Intelligent Technology and its Applications (2015)
14. Hwang, K.C., Hong, J.J., Lee, K.H.: A SNMP group polling for the management traffic. TENCON (IEEE) J. **99** (1999). Department of Computer Science and Engineering
15. Devi, R., Dhivya, R., Shanmugalakshmi, R.: Secured service provider selection methods in cloud. In: 2016 3rd International Conference on Advanced Computing and Communication Systems, (ICACCS), vol. 1, pp. 1–5 (2016)
16. Dhivya, R., Devi, R., Shanmugalakshmi, R.: Parameters and methods used to evaluate cloud service providers: a survey. In: 2016 International Conference on Computer Communication and Informatics (ICCCI), pp. 1–5 (2016)
17. Devi, R., Shanmugalakshmi, R.: Design of frame work for cloud providers selection based on user requirement and trust. Int. J. Sci. Dev. Res. **1**(5), 313–317 (2016)
18. Devi, R., Shanmugalakshmi, R.: Distributed denial of service attacks identifying using Ford Fulkerson algorithm in cloud. Int. J. Adv. Technol. Eng. Sci. **5**(1), 48–57 (2017)
19. Berggren, G., Stromberg, M.: Availability calculation in communication networks. In: Reliability and Maintainability Symposium, pp. 452–457 (1984)
20. He, Y., Zhang, Y.: Network availability index and its flow-based quantitative calculation method. In: International Conference on Computer Engineering and Technology, vol. 1, no. 4, pp. 551–555 (2010)
21. Niemann, K.H.: Availability Calculation of Meshed, Ethernet based Automation Networks. IEEE (2011)

Machine Learning in Cancer Genomics

Hrushikesh Joshi[✉], Kannan Rajeswari, and Sneha Joshi

Pune, Maharashtra, India
hrushikeshrjoshi@gmail.com, kannan.rajeswari@pccoepune.org

Abstract. Genomics of cancer plays a very important role in the detection of tumour type, Treatment, involves analysis of genes that are causing cancer. DNA Microarray is used to measure the gene expression of particular tissue or cell. Data generated from DNA Microarrays is large. Machine learning can be well suited for genomics data. We used different cancer gene expression datasets such as leukaemia, Lung, Bladder, prostate, Liver and pancreas and used various Machine learning algorithms such as Decision tree, Naïve Bayes, Logistic Regression and SVM for classification of cancer types. We proposed a new classification method for gene expression dataset which can apply to any numeric dataset known as "Mean based Classification". Mean based classification considers the mean for each class and selects the features from datasets having maximum mean difference. Classification is given by minimum distance which is similar to Rocchio classification used for text classification. Mean based classification and its variant which uses standard deviation and mean performed well and obtained high accuracy for all cancer genomics datasets. Explainable AI methods like shapely value explanations are also used for explanations of results and to understand interactions among genes and also to understand which genes are causing cancer.

Keywords: Cancer genomics · Machine learning · Mean based classification · Explainable AI

1 Introduction

Cancer is an important cause of death worldwide. Cancer is excessive, abnormal, uncontrolled growth of cells losing normal function. Cancer occurs when the mechanism that maintains normal growth rates malfunction to cause excess cell division.

Digital pathology has revolutionized the field of pathology. Digital pathology involves histopathology i.e., viewing analysing histopathological slides digitally, Cancer genomics i.e., Analysis of abnormal expression of genes [1] Various machine learning methods can be applied to the approaches mentioned above.

Deep learning for histopathological whole slides has already succussed in the detection of various cancers [2]. Deep learning approach finds intricate features of the histopathological image and uses it for classification of cancer type. Cancer classification using histopathological images has limitations as cancers having similar morphological features might be having different molecular origin therefore, cancer therapy also differs.

I. Raman et al. (Eds.): ICC3 2021, CCIS 1631, pp. 91–105, 2022.
https://doi.org/10.1007/978-3-031-15556-7_7

Cancer genomics is the study of gene expression differences between tumour cells and normal cells, it deals with understanding the genetic basis of tumour cell proliferation, for example, Tumour suppressor genes normally restrain growth so mutations that inactivate them cause inappropriate cell division. Mutations in the tumour suppressor genes BRCA1 and BRCA2 have been linked to a much higher risk of breast, ovarian and prostate cancer.

Caretaker genes normally protect the integrity of genomes when they are inactivated cell acquires additional mutations that cause cancer. HER2 positive breast cancers involve a mutated HER2 Oncogene, which produces a protein that increases the growth of cells.

The most pathologist uses histopathological slides to classify cancer, however, in certain cases the only morphological analysis is not enough as cancer showing similar morphological origins might differ in genetical origin so cancer treatment also differs. Genomic study in such cases is important to find the root cause of cancer and to provide treatment. Cancer-causing genetic mutations can be discovered and to develop potential treatment [3]. For example, in chronic lymphocytic leukaemia, the presence of a mutation in the TP53 gene means that cancer won't respond to chemoimmunotherapy in such cases stem cell transplant might be needed. The potential personalized treatment plan for cancer by detecting mutations in the respective individual can be obtained through machine learning.

Machine learning can handle a massive amount of data. Cancer genomics contains a large amount of data on gene expression. Machine learning methods can be effectively applied to the Gene expression dataset, by applying machine learning on gene expression classification of tumour can be done [4].

Machine learning in genetic data possess a challenge as genetic data has many features also extracted genes from microarray has noise. Machine learning on DNA microarray data can be divided into four categories as Classification, Clustering, Gene identification, Gene network modelling [5]. Generally, Machine learning for DNA microarray data involves extraction of microarray data, Feature selection, Classification or clustering. Various feature selection techniques are partial least squares [6], PCA, Akaike information criterion and Bayesian information criterion [7] genetic algorithm [8] . We used the proposed method "mean based classification" for feature selection and classification.

Machine learning is a vital research tool to gain insights into cancer genomics. Interpretable AI methods can be applied to the cancer genomics problem, Genes that are most responsible for causing cancer can be studied in detail Further, how different genes interact with each other, a correlation between genes can be studied which is vital for bioinformatics research [9]. A variety of machine learning methods are well suited for genomics data.

DNA microarray is used to deduce gene expression [10]. DNA microarrays are used to analyse the genes which are expressed in tissue or cell. Mutations in genes lead to cancer, DNA microarray is a tool to detect which genes are mutating and causing cancer. DNA microarray works as follows. Figure 1 outlines the working of DNA microarray. The patients' tissue sample which is having a tumour is taken and DNA is cut into small pieces known as fragments which represent genes. The control sample which is having normal tissue is taken and it is cut into fragments. Both tissue samples are labelled with a fluorescent dye, Patients sample having red dye and the normal sample having green dye. Both sets of genes are inserted in the microarray chip and allowed to hybridize. Genes having mutation doesn't hybridize well to the normal sample which can be detected in a microarray chip.

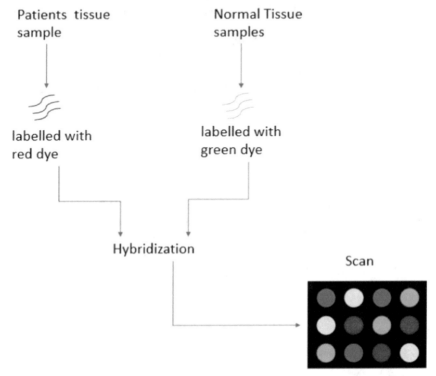

Fig. 1. 1) Patients and a normal tissue sample are taken. 2) Samples are labelled with different colours 3) Samples are allowed to hybridize 4) Microchip is scanned for mutations (Color figure online)

Machine learning methods such as SVM, Decision tree, naïve Bayes, Logistic regression are used for classification in the dataset used for this article. We proposed and used a novel classification approach known as "mean based classification" which considers the mean value of a specific feature for two classes present in the dataset. Here, all cancer gene expression datasets contain two class labels. Mean based classification algorithm takes consideration of the mean difference in classes. The main reason behind considering mean difference is when mean difference is maximum, feature shows distinct signature or range for different classes hence could be useful for classification. Classification in mean-based classification is done by finding difference from mean for respective classes and considering minimum among them, the class label will be assigned to the class which is having a minimum distance between the class mean and feature value which is similar to Rocchio classification [11]. We also proposed variant for mean based classification which uses standard deviation. Standard deviation for each class for a feature is calculated. Two values for each standard deviation is added known as sum of standard deviation. Algorithm aims to find feature which has maximum mean difference and minimum sum of standard deviation. Finding minimum of sum of standard deviation basically means that distributions for two classes are closer to mean and have less chance of overlapping values.

Explainable AI also has great potential in the field of genomics. The understanding black box of a particular model is essential as it could shed light on many important research questions such as which genes are contributing most to particular cancer, how different genes are interacting to affect the model's behaviour. Shapely value-based explainable ai methods are used.

2 Proposed Approach

2.1 Overview

The overview of the proposed method used in this article is shown in Fig. 2. Gene expression microarray data is used for classification. Classification methods such as SVM, Naïve Bayes, Decision tree, logistic regression and novel centroid classification is used for classification. Interpretation methods such as shapely value explanations are used to understand genes that are most important for the classification of cancer type.

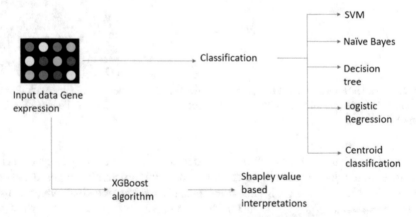

Fig. 2. Schematic diagram of the methodology used in this article. Input data for gene expression in microarray data. The different classification algorithm is used on cancer genomics dataset. XGBoost algorithm is used and a shapely value-based method is used for explainable AI.

2.2 Machine Learning Algorithms

Naïve bayes: Naïve bayes is supervised learning method. It is based on Bayes (Eq. 1). $P(C|x)$ is the probability of instance x belongs to class c which is known as posterior probability. $P(x|C)$ is the probability of having instance x given class c known as likelihood. P (C) is a number of instances of class C known as prior.

$P(C|x)=(P(x|C)P(C))/(P(x))$

Equation 1 – Bayes Theorem

Naïve Bayes algorithm assumes that the presence of a particular feature in a class is unrelated to the presence of any other feature [12].

Decision Tree:
Decision Tree uses a tree-like structure. Each node in the Decision tree indicates a test at that node, each branch represents an outcome of the test. A terminal node in the decision tree indicates the class label.

A tree can be "learned" by splitting the source set into subsets based on an attribute value test. This process is repeated on each derived subset in a recursive manner called recursive partitioning. The recursion is completed when the subset at a node all has the same value of the target variable, or when splitting no longer adds value to the predictions. The construction of a decision tree classifier does not require any domain knowledge or parameter setting, and therefore is appropriate for exploratory knowledge discovery. Entropy is used to measure homogeneity. If data is completely homogeneous then the entropy is 0, else if data is divided 50-50 entropy is 1.

Information gain is used for the splitting of the decision tree.

SVM
Support vector machine algorithm is linear classification. If some data points are given and the task is to classify them. Linear classifier approaches this problem by finding a hyperplane that divides the classes. However, there exists a set of hyperplanes that can classify the data. SVM not only finds a hyperplane that divides the classes but find the best hyperplane which is having a maximum margin from the classes, It takes the help of a support vector to achieve this [13].

Logistic regression
Logistic regression is an asymmetric statistical model used for mapping numerical value to probability. Logistic regression uses a logistic function to model a binary dependent model. The binary logistic model has two possible values. In binary logistic regression model, the dependent variable has two levels. Log odds are an alternate way of expressing probabilities. Odds are the ratio of something happening to something not happening [14].

Glossary of Terms

Class-wise Mean – Mean for feature value calculated across classes, i.e., for dataset having two classes benign and malignant for feature value average for values belonging to benign class is calculated and also for malignant class is calculated.

Mean difference- Mean difference is difference between class-wise mean i.e., for dataset having two classes benign and malignant for each class average is calculated for feature and difference between average is calculated. This value is indicative feature importance. Higher value of mean difference higher the feature importance.

Class-wise Standard deviation- Standard deviation for feature value is calculated across classes, i.e., for dataset having two classes benign and malignant for feature value standard deviation belonging to benign class is calculated and for malignant class is calculated.

Standard deviation sum- It is sum of class-wise standard deviation. Lower value of standard deviation sum indicates data spread for specific feature is less, and is highly preferable since there is lower chance of overlapping values across classes.

Box 1. Glossary ot terms used in proposed approach.

3   Mean Based Classification

Mean based classification is based on average, here mean is an average value for a particular feature. Mean based classification is an easily interpretable algorithm.

The best features are those which vary by different classes. Mean based classification selects the features which are varying across classes. The detailed procedure is shown in Fig. 4. In the first step i.e. Feature selection phase For the respective feature calculate average for respective classes i.e. if dataset is having two classes then for each class average for respective feature will be calculated so two averages per feature will be generated.

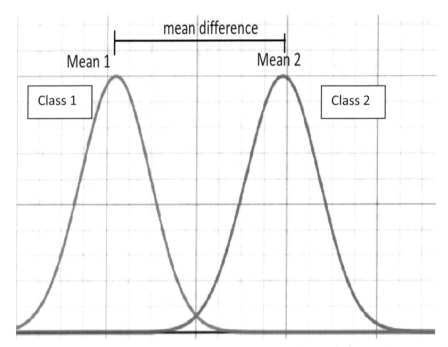

Fig. 3. Shows the distribution for each class i.e., class 1 and class 2. For each class mean is calculated i.e., mean 1 and mean 2 respectively. Mean difference is the absolute difference between two means. The Mean based classification algorithm aims to find out a feature which is having a maximum mean difference.

In the next step, the Difference between Averages is calculated for each feature. The feature having maximum difference is varying across classes thus it is most suitable for classification will be selected for classification.

In the classification step, the Feature which is selected from the feature selection phase is considered, for this feature difference from average to feature is calculated and the class is assigned to test instance according to minimum difference. The classification step of mean-based classification is similar to the Rocchio classifier which is used for text classification. Figure 5 shows, the concept of the Rocchio classification algorithm.

Figure 3 depicts the concept of the mean difference. Mean 1 and mean 2 are calculated for class 1 and class 2 respectively and the mean difference is an absolute difference between mean 1 and means 2. The feature which has the largest mean difference is selected for classification Classification is similar to Rocchio classification which is depicted in Fig. 5.

Algorithm

Step 1 and step 2 of the mean-based classifier algorithm are for feature selection. Step 3 and step 4 are for classification.

Step 1) For all features in Feature set F = {f1, f2, f3, f4—fn} is set of input features in dataset. Class set = {y1, y2 } is set of classes in dataset. $\mu(i, j)$ will be the mean for feature fi of all training instances having class yi. For each feature in the feature set, there will be two averages as mean based classification works for two classes i.e. $\mu(i, 1)$ and $\mu(i, 2)$. Mean difference of I'th feature is MD(i) = $|\mu(i, 1)-\mu(i, 2)|$ is calculated for each feature so Mean difference set MD={MD(1), MD(2), MD(n)} is obtained.

Step 2) For set MD max {MD(1), MD(2),...MD(n)} = MD(i) is obtained, where MD(i) is maximum element in set MD and i corresponds to fi feature will be selected for classification in set F.

Step 3) If X be instance to be classified and have feature X ={xf1, xf2,..xfn}. I'th feature selected from step 2 will be selected from set X i.e. xfi.

Step 4) class1 difference is cd1 = $|\mu(i, 1)-xfi|$ and class 2 difference is cd2 = $|\mu(i, 2)-xfi|$, X will be assigned to class by selecting minimum from cd1 and cd2 i.e., min {cd1, cd2} and respective class corresponding to that difference will be assigned.

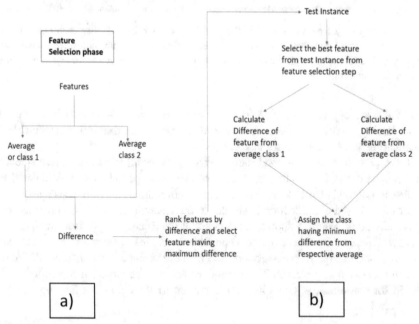

Fig. 4. Mean based classification algorithm. a) Feature selection phase. For every feature class-wise average (see Box 1) is calculated and mean difference is calculated. The feature which is having a maximum mean difference is selected. b) Classification phase. For novel instance select value of feature from feature selected in the feature selection phase. Calculate the difference of feature value of the novel subject average for each class. Assign the class having minimum difference from the respective average.

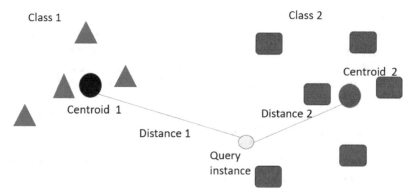

Fig. 5. Rocchio Classification. Blue triangles represent class 1 while red rectangles represent class 2. Query instance is shown in yellow. Distance 1 is the distance from centroid 1 to query instance while distance 2 is the distance between centroid 2 and query instance. Query instance will be assigned to class 2 since distance 2 is smaller than distance 1. (Color figure online)

4 Mean Based Classification (Standard Deviation Variant)

General Mean-based classification suffers from feature having maximum mean difference may not be best as there may be values in both classes that are overlapping, to minimize overlapping standard deviation variant is considered. Mean based classification using standard deviation considers standard deviation for each class. The Sum of standard deviation for classes is calculated. Standard variation-based variant of mean-based classification selects feature for classification which have maximum mean separation across classes and have minimum standard deviation across classes, these two characteristics refers to features will have minimum overlapping across classes will be given high priority.

A schematic diagram for mean based classification using standard deviation variant is shown in Fig. 6.

Algorithm

Step 1) For all features in Feature set $F = \{f1, f2, f3, f4\text{—}fn\}$ is set of input features in dataset where n is number of input features. Class set $= \{y1, y2\}$ is set of classes in dataset. $\mu(i,j)$ will be the mean for feature fi of all training instances having class yi. For each feature in the feature set, there will be two averages as mean based classification works for two classes i.e. $\mu(i, 1)$ and $\mu(i, 2)$. Mean difference of I'th feature is $MD(i) = |\mu(i, 1) - \mu(i, 2)|$ is calculated for each feature so Mean difference set $MD = \{MD(1), MD(2), MD(n)\}$ is obtained.

Step 2) For all features in Feature set F = {f1, f2, f3, f4—fn} is set of input features in dataset. Class set = {y1, y2 } is set of classes in dataset. σ (i, j) will be standard deviation for feature fi of all training instances having class yj. as mean based classification works for two classes i.e. σ (i, 1) and σ (i, 2) . Standard deviation sum will be given as SD(i) = σ (i, 1) + σ (i, 2) calculated for each feature so Set SD = {SD(1), SD(2),…SD(n)}
Step 3)
Find out feature from F which maximizes MD and minimizes SD will have corresponding mean difference as MD(i) and SD(i) so feature fi will be selected for classification.
Step 4)
If X be instance to be classified and have feature X = {xf1, xf2,..xfn}. I'th feature selected from step3 will be selected from set X i.e. xfi.
Step 5)
class1 difference is cd1 = |μ(i, 1)−xfi| and class 2 difference is cd2 = |μ(i, 2)−xfi| , X will be assigned to class by selecting minimum from cd1 and cd2 i.e., min {cd1, cd2} and respective class corresponding to that difference will be assigned.

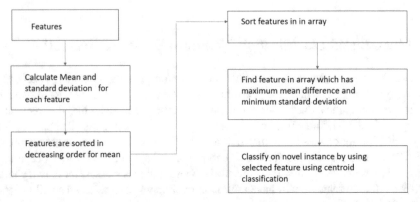

Fig. 6. Mean based classification using standard deviation. 1) For given features mean difference and standard deviation sum (see Box 1) are calculated. 2) Features are stored in the array and sorted for mean difference and sorted in decreasing order so that the first feature in the array will have maximum mean difference. Till this point steps are similar to the mean-based algorithm discussed in Fig. 1. 3) Feature which is having maximum mean difference and the minimum standard deviation is selected iteratively and used for classification discussed in Fig. 4b.

5 Shapely Value-Based Interpretation

For any model, certain numbers of features are involved in model prediction. The basic Intuition behind shape values is to consider each feature and to explain the model further by feature interaction and impact and explaining global model behaviour.

SHAP (Shapely Additive Explanation) by Lundberg and Lee (2016) [15] is a method to explain individual prediction. It is based on Shap values from game theory. This method can be used on Tabular data and also on unstructured data.

Shapely values are based on game theory. The goal of shapely value-based prediction is to computer contribution of each feature to the final prediction. It is based on coalition game theory. The feature values of a data instance act as players in a coalition. Shapely value tells us about how to fairly distribute the payout among features. The player can be individual feature value e.g., Tabular data. The player can also be a group of features. A group of features also can be regarded as a player.

6 Results and Discussions

6.1 Dataset Used

We have considered 5 different cancer genomic datasets. All dataset was obtained from SBCB (https://sbcb.inf.ufrgs.br/cumida). The genomic dataset consists of gene expression values for genes and corresponding cancer class labels.

Prostate Cancer gene dataset: is having 51 subjects having 54677 features i.e., genes, it has two classes tumoral and normal.

Pancreas Cancer gene dataset: is having 48 subjects having 54677 features i.e., genes, it has two classes tumoral and normal.

Liver Cancer gene dataset: is having 357 subjects having 22279 features i.e., genes, it has two classes HCC and normal.

Blood Cancer gene dataset: is having 52 subjects having 22647 features i.e., genes, it has two classes CLL and normal_B_Cell

6.2 Machine Learning Algorithms Results

We used various machine learning algorithms and also novel Mean based classification. Accuracies for all machine learning models are shown in Table 1. Mean based classification algorithm and centroid classification (Standard deviation variant) and logistic regression obtained high accuracy for all cancer datasets. Mean based classification with standard deviation obtained high accuracy almost for all datasets.

Figure 7 shows, comparison of accuracies between SVM, Logistic regression, mean based classification and mean based classification standard deviation variant. Mean based classification-std and Logistic regression obtained the highest accuracy among other classification algorithms.

Table 1. Machine learning models on different cancer datasets are used. Mean based classification (Standard deviation variant) and logistic regression are performing well for classification on all dataset.

ML model	Prostrate	Liver	Pancreas	Lung	Blood
SVM	100	98	96	100	93
Naïve Bayes	93	86	100	93	80
Decision tree	80	92	81	86	87
Mean based classification	86	86	84	88	90
Mean based classification (std variant)	100	98	99	100	100
Logistic regression	100	98	87	100	93

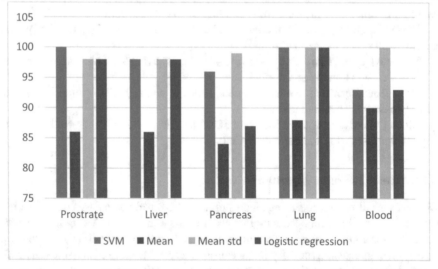

Fig. 7. Comparison of Machine learning models. Mean based classification -standard deviation colour-coded in grey and SVM and Logistic regression method is having highest accuracy for all datasets.

6.3 Shapely Value-Based Explanations on Pancreas Dataset

Shapely value-based explanations can be given on the pancreas dataset. Figure 8 shows a shap summary plot for the pancreas dataset. Gene 1552295_a_at is having the highest impact classification. Shap summary plot summarizes the impact of each feature on the overall classification.

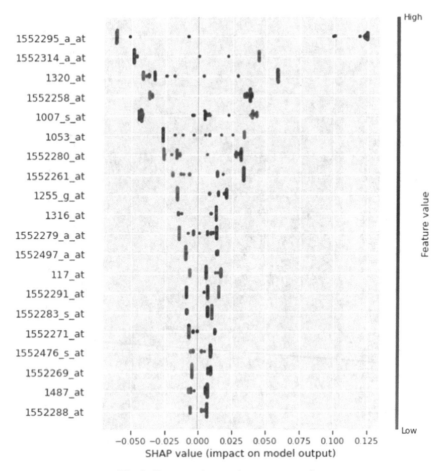

Fig. 8. Pancreas dataset shap summary plot.

Prostate cancer

An explainable AI approach is applied to the prostate cancer gene expression dataset. Gene 121_at is having the highest impact on the model. Higher the value of gene 121_at lowers its impact on the model while lower value has a higher impact on the model (Fig. 9).

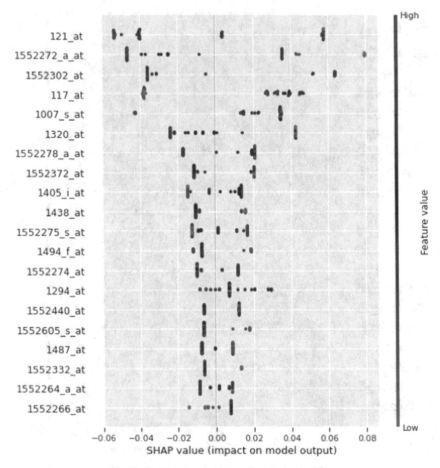

Fig. 9. Prostate cancer gene shap summary plot.

7   Conclusion and Future Scope

Machine learning algorithms applied successfully on various cancer genomics datasets. All machine learning algorithms performed better in terms of accuracy. The proposed method for classification "Mean based classification and its variant" obtained high accuracy for all dataset. Performance for Mean based classification for standard deviation is better than mean based classification. The shapely value-based interpretation method successfully applied to the dataset. The overall impact of an induvial gene can be predicted from shap interaction plots. Mean based classification can be extended to a multilabel dataset. The algorithm for finding the best feature in feature space in the case of mean-based classification-standard deviation is a linear optimised algorithm needed to be developed to further optimise this method. To conclude, Machine learning can be used in cancer genomics and interactable methods can be applied successfully to further understand results.

References

1. Jahn, S.W., Plass, M., Moinfar, F.: Digital pathology: advantages, limitations and emerging perspectives. J. Clin. Med. **9**, 3697 (2020)
2. LeCun, Y., Bengio, Y., Hinton, G.: Deep learning. Nature **521**, 436–444 (2015)
3. Nogrady, B.: How cancer genomics is transforming diagnosis and treatment. Nature **579**, S10 (2020)
4. Pirooznia, M., Yang, J.Y., Yang, M.Q., et al.: A comparative study of different machine learning methods on microarray gene expression data. BMC Genomics (2008). https://doi.org/10.1186/1471-2164-9-S1-S13
5. Cho, S.B., Won, H.H.: Machine learning in DNA microarray analysis for cancer classification. In: Proceedings of the First Asia-Pacific Bioinformatics Conference on Bioinformatics, vol. 19 (2003)
6. Nguyen, D.V., Rocke, D.M.: Tumor classification by partial least squares using microarray gene expression data. Bioinformatics **18**(1), 39–50 (2002)
7. Li, W., Yang, Y.: How many genes are needed for a discriminant microarray data analysis. In: Lin, S.M., Johnson, K.F. (eds.) Methods of Microarray Data Analysis, pp. 137–149. Springer, Boston (2002). https://doi.org/10.1007/978-1-4615-0873-1_11
8. Li, L., et al.: Gene selection for sample classification based on gene expression data: study of sensitivity to choice of parameters of the GA/KNN method. Bioinformatics **17**, 1131–1142 (2001)
9. Lundberg, S.M.: From local explanations to global understanding with explainable AI for trees. Nat. Mach. Intell. **2**, 56–67 (2020)
10. Heller, M.J.: DNA microarray technology: devices, systems, and applications. Annu. Rev. Biomed. Eng. **4**, 129–153 (2002)
11. Rocchio, J.J.: Relevance feedback in information retrieval (1965)
12. Bayes, P.: An essay towards solving a problem in the doctrine of chance. Philos. Trans. R. Soc. London **53**, 370–418 (1763)
13. Cortes, C., Vapnik, V.: Support-vector networks. Mach. Learn. **20**, 273–297 (1995). https://doi.org/10.1007/BF00994018
14. Walker, S.H., Duncan, D.B.: Estimation of the probability of an event as a function of several independent variables. Biometrika **54**(1–2), 167–179 (1967)
15. Lundberg, S.M., Lee, S.I.: A unified approach to interpreting model predictions. In: Advances in Neural Information Processing Systems (NIPS), vol. 17 (2017)

Cyber Security

Privacy-Preserving Blockchain-Based EHR Using ZK-Snarks

R. Anusuya(✉) , D. Karthika Renuka , S. Ghanasiyaa, K. Harshini,
K. Mounika, and K. S. Naveena

PSG College of Technology, Coimbatore 641004, TN, India
anusuya12@gmail.com

Abstract. The electronic health record (EHR) of a patient is a digital record of their health records, progress notes, problems, and medications. As with any online digital format, concerns of breach exist. Similarly, EHR data is susceptible to significant security and privacy concerns these days. This paper has designed a secure decentralized medical blockchain to address privacy and security concerns associated with the exchange of patient health care data across entities. Historically advanced methods for protecting EHRs have often rendered data unavailable to patients. These methods are always attempting to strike a balance between data confidentiality, patient request, and continuous engagement with provider data. The aforementioned difficulties are resolved by blockchain technology, which distributes information in a transactional and decentralised manner. This paper offers a blockchain-based security architecture for efficiently and securely storing and maintaining electronic health records. Moreover, the patients feel insecure about their data being shared so they do not prefer to choose EHR. Maintaining anonymity may facilitate more efficient dialogue between physician and patient, which is critical for ensuring the highest possible quality of treatment. To ensure this, We propose a non-interactive zero-knowledge proof-based authentication method that is lightweight enough to operate on medical heath devices with limited resources. The concept of Zero-Knowledge Proof refers to demonstrating anything without disclosing the facts on which the proof is based. It enables physicians, patients, and insurance agents to get medical information efficiently and securely. The goal of this research is to establish if our architecture complies with doctors', patients', and third-party security needs. The simulation results demonstrate that this architecture effectively safeguards EHR data.

Keywords: Blockchain · EHR · Zero knowledge proofs

1 Introduction

A digital health record (EHR) is a computer-based storage system for a patient's health information (history, physical examination, investigations, and treatment). Physicians and hospitals are adopting EHRs due to the many benefits

Supported by organization x.

they provide over paper records. The electronic health record (EHR) is the technology that has the potential to offer the foundation for new functionality and services for patients. They increase health-care access, improve care quality, and lower costs. However, when it comes to EHRs, health care practitioners are faced with ethical difficulties. Patients' autonomy is endangered when health data about them is shared or linked without their agreement. The patient may conceal information out of concern for the system that stores their data's security. As a consequence, the treatment of these patients may be jeopardised. There is a risk that the health data of thousands of patients may be disclosed as a consequence of human mistake or theft.

Additionally, patient access to EHRs is severely limited, with patients unable to share information with physicians or researchers. Conflicts between suppliers, research institutes, and hospitals, to name a few, also obstruct efficient information transfer. EHRs are fragmented rather than synchronised because of a lack of integrated information sharing with management. If a patient is able to keep his or her electronic health records, health departments may profit greatly since it may avoid the need for another doctor to re-diagnose the patient's previous medical history the next time the patient seeks treatment at another facility. By getting blockchain instances from the blockchain, the suggested method accomplishes the goal of increasing cooperation and dependability across all institutions.

To store EHRs, blockchain technology establishes a decentralized healthcare data management ledger [11–15]. When healthcare information is exchanged over peer-to-peer networks, it becomes impervious to modification. To preserve this immutability, the EHR data are connected to one another. Additionally, it protects the privacy of patient EHRs when they are shared and viewed by many users and physicians. The above-mentioned blockchain security architecture protects the integrity, confidentiality, interoperability, authenticity, and accountability of electronic health data shared between two organisations. Individual data is defined as data that will be utilised privately and to which only authorised parties will have access. Zero-knowledge proof is used to ensure privacy. Zero-Knowledge Proof is a relatively new yet very effective idea for establishing trust-based networks. In cryptography, a zero-knowledge proof or protocol is a mechanism for one party (the prover) to show to another party (the verifier) that they know a value x without revealing anything else. The zk-Snark is a kind of extremely secure cryptographic testing that use Zero-Knowledge Proof (ZKP) principles to generate encrypted data that can be readily confirmed without disclosing sensitive information. The inclusion of Zero-Knowledge Proofs in healthcare transactions will assist the sector in optimising its processes and moving toward seamless operations.

The primary benefit is the prevention of assaults from external devices that damage communication between Medical-Healthcare data and their official application. Our strategy is built on a non-interactive zero-knowledge proving method that is both lightweight and resource-efficient.

We suggest a blockchain-based method to solve the problems of storing, managing, and exchanging data. However, the typical blockchain ecosystem does not provide data privacy during transactions or storage. The patient establishes an access policy and distributes the decryption keys to authorised system users. This eliminates the possibility of healthcare professionals collecting or sharing data without permission. As a result, we have a system that ensures patient privacy and is completely self-managed by the patient.

Additionally, we propose a new national healthcare architecture built on the InterPlanetary File System (IPFS) and smart contracts for the storage and administration of electronic health records (EHRs) and other medical records.

2   Related Work

Numerous methods have been suggested to address the issue of interoperability and access control for EHR sharing and insurance claims separately, as well as to address the lack of privacy in EHRs. However, none of the options offered patients with access to their EHR.

Nguyen et al. [1] suggested a novel framework for distributing electronic health records (EHRs) that incorporates blockchain technology and a decentralised interplanetary file system (IPFS) on the mobile cloud. Notably, the authors developed a reliable access control technique based on smart contracts to ensure the secure transfer of electronic health records between different medical providers and patients. The authors concluded that their study demonstrated an efficient method for ensuring the integrity of information transfers on the mobile cloud, including the protection of critical medical data from potential threats.

Sharma et al. [2] has proposed a system for automated insurance claims, interoperability, and data interchange between diverse healthcare providers. They employed a smart card to validate beneficiaries' identities using zero-knowledge proofs and to delegate access to service providers using proxy re-encryption.

Antonio et al. [3] suggested a method for preventing extraneous devices from interfering with communication between medical health devices and their official application. Additionally, they suggested a blockchain-based method to solve the problems of storing, managing, and exchanging data. They proposed a method that utilises Attribute-Based Encryption for data transport, storage, and sharing. A system that ensures privacy and is completely controlled by the patient was suggested. It was constructed using an authentication method based on Non-Interactive Zero-Knowledge Proofs that is lightweight enough to operate on devices with low computing capabilities.

Wanxin Li et al. [4] have presented a new privacy-preserving identity verification method for ridesharing apps by extending zero-knowledge proof (ZKP) and blockchain. They've built a permissioned blockchain network for ZKP identity verification that also functions as an immutable record for ride logs and ZKP data. They develop a protocol for the ZKP module that enables user verification without needing the sharing of any sensitive information. They developed a prototype of the proposed system using the Hyperledger Fabric platform and the Hyperledger Ursa cryptography library, as well as considerable testing.

Adler et al. [5] explain the advantages of a paperless EHR system versus a paper-based one. It also examined the barriers to adoption of a new information technology-based healthcare system and found that a payment system reform was necessary to encourage improved healthcare. We were motivated to use smart cards and zero-knowledge proofs for authentication after reading [6], which used e-passport-based zero-knowledge proofs to establish pseudo-anonymous identities for Sybil-resistant blockchain mining. This approach is ideal for our later-explained verification of identification for healthcare.

Arun et al. [7] They have developed a secure decentralised cloud-based medical blockchain (CMBC) in this study to address privacy and security concerns associated with transferring patient health care data with various medical institutions. Ibrahim et al. [8] developed a blockchain security framework (BSF) for storing and maintaining EHRs efficiently and securely. It provides a secure and efficient method for physicians, patients, and insurance agents to get medical information while preserving the patient's data. Chen et al. [9] presented a blockchain-based concept in which the index for electronic health records is created using complicated logic expressions and maintained on the blockchain. Tanwar et al. [10] offered a strategy that makes use of blockchain technology to address concerns such as the loss of patient privacy, data accessibility, and so on.

3   Blockchain Concepts

A blockchain is a kind of data structure that executes and records transactions in blocks. Each block contains a timestamp and a hash link that connects it to the preceding block. Blocks preserve the integrity of data records and cannot be altered retroactively. It should be seen as a distributed database in which no entity trusts another, and no central point of control exists. Participants may fully depend on one another decentralised. To modify the current block, it is necessary to modify all preceding blocks. As a result, blockchain technology provides a very secure method of transmitting digital assets, money, and contracts without the need of third-party agents. Blockchain serves as a public record of all transactions between participating entities throughout digital activities. Mining is the process of generating a new block. Consensus is reached among all participants to validate each block, ensuring the integrity and trustworthiness of the system. Blockchain technology allows the creation of a decentralised platform amongst participating entities where agreement is reached democratically.

3.1   Ethereum

Ethereum is a public blockchain (all nodes are completely decentralised) in which transactions are sorted (through miners) and updated by individual nodes. Through a method known as Proof of Work, miners earn the privilege to update the blockchain. They enable virtually anybody to engage in the community in nearly any capacity due to their intrinsic architecture, thus boosting adoption rates. Many of the emerging initiatives want to offer decentralised usefulness to as many people as possible, but they are constrained by problems of scalability and trust.

3.2 Hyperledger Sawtooth

Hyperledger Sawtooth is a business-focused blockchain technology that allows the creation of distributed ledger applications and networks. The design philosophy emphasises the importance of distributed ledgers and the security of smart contracts, especially for business usage. Sawtooth facilitates the creation of blockchain applications by decoupling the core technology from the application domain. Application developers may define the business rules necessary for their application in the language of their choosing, without having to be familiar with the core system's underlying architecture.

3.3 Consensus

Although the primary security feature of blockchain is the use of hashes, attackers may still utilise very costly and very fast machines to recalculate all the hashes, breaching the security layer. To address this issue, the consensus mechanism between blockchain nodes is created. The most well-known consensus mechanisms in blockchain technology are as follows:

– Proof of Work
– Proof of Stake
– Delegated Proof of Stake
– Practical Byzantine Fault Tolerance.

3.4 Consensus Algorithms in Hyperledger Sawtooth

PoET Consensus

Proof of Elapsed Time is a consensus method in the Nakamoto style that is optimised for big networks. PoET is not definitive (can fork).

Sawtooth provides two distinct implementations of PoET consensus:

PoET-SGX implements a leader-election lottery system using a Trusted Execution Environment (TEE), such as Intel® Software Guard Extensions (SGX). PoET-SGX is sometimes referred to as PoET/BFT because to its Byzantine fault tolerance.

On systems lacking a Trusted Execution Environment, the PoET simulator implements the same consensus method. The PoET simulator is sometimes known as PoET/CFT because to the fact that it is crash-tolerant, not Byzantine-tolerant.

PBFT Consensus

Practical Byzantine Fault Tolerance is a finality-assured voting-based consensus method with Byzantine fault tolerance (BFT) (does not fork). Sawtooth PBFT adds features such as dynamic network membership, frequent view changes, and a block catch-up process to the original PBFT algorithm.

Devmode Consensus

A straightforward random-leader consensus method for testing a transaction processor on a single Sawtooth node. (Devmode is an abbreviation for "developer mode.") Devmode consensus is not advised for a network with many nodes and should not be utilised in production.

Raft Consensus

A straightforward random-leader consensus method for testing a transaction processor on a single Sawtooth node. (Devmode is an abbreviation for "developer mode.") Devmode consensus is not advised for a network with many nodes and should not be utilised in production.

3.5   Merkle Tree

A Merkle tree is a kind of data structure that is often used in computer science. Merkle trees are used in bitcoin and other cryptocurrencies to better effectively and securely encode blockchain data. Additionally, they are known as "binary hash trees." Data verification is critical in a variety of distributed and peer-to-peer systems. This is because the same data is stored in numerous places. Thus, if data is modified in one place, it must be modified elsewhere. Data verification is used to ensure that data is consistent throughout. However, checking the whole of each file anytime a system wishes to validate data is time consuming and computationally costly. As a result, Merkle trees are utilised. We wish to minimise the quantity of data transmitted across a network (such as the Internet). Thus, rather than transmitting a full file across the network, we just send a hash of the file to check for consistency.

4   Zero-Knowledge Proof (ZKP)

Zero-Knowledge Proof (ZKP) is a collection of techniques that enables the validation of a piece of information without exposing the underlying facts. These are probabilistic evaluations, which implies they do not establish anything as conclusively as just disclosing it would. Rather than that, they offer fragments of unconnected evidence that may collect to demonstrate that an assertion's validity is overwhelmingly likely. The principle behind zero-knowledge proofs is that it is easy to demonstrate possession of a piece of information simply by disclosing it; the challenge is to establish such ownership without releasing the piece of information or any other information. Each transaction is accompanied by a 'verifier' and a 'prover'. In a transaction using ZKPs, the prover tries to prove something to the verifier without disclosing any more information about the item being proved. By supplying the result, the prover establishes that they are capable of computing anything without disclosing the input or the calculation method. Meanwhile, the verifier gains knowledge about the output.

A genuine ZKP must satisfy three criteria:

1. Completeness: It should persuade the verifier that the prover is aware of what they claim to be aware of.
2. Soundness: If the information is incorrect, it cannot persuade the verifier that the information provided by the prover is genuine.
3. Zero-knowledge-ness: It should include no further information for the verifier.

Zero-Knowledge Proof for Privacy Preservation. A blockchain is a collection of records that are jointly maintained by a number of dispersed parties, with each party having a copy of the list. Because blockchains enable all participants to see all transactions, they lack privacy/anonymity. Zero-knowledge proofs enable the posting of private transactions to the blockchain while maintaining their privacy by proving that the transaction was completed properly without disclosing the secret information utilised in the transaction.

5 Proposed Methodology

The above framework illustrates the transactions involving blockchain-based Electronic Health Records. The patient may manage, download, and distribute his or her EHRs autonomously while using a blockchain-based EHR. Five entities comprise the proposed blockchain-based EHR framework: Doctor, Patient, Pharmacy, EHR server, and Insurance Agent. The patient visits the doctor under this method to be treated by doctor. Here, the EHR system server serves as a miner. Whenever an EHR is created for a patient, all the nodes in the blockchain receive it and verify its validity. Once the verification is done it waits inside the memory pool until the miner node takes it and inserts it inside a block. Then the miner starts to verify the information in the block. During verification, a unique hash value is created for that block. Hash is a numeric value that uniquely identifies a block. Once the creation of a block is completed, the miner node distributes it to all the available nodes. Now except for the patient, no one else in the blockchain can view the patient's details. Additionally, the doctor may examine the information of the patients he or she has treated. Because the patient has access to their information, they may share it with the insurance agent.

The insurance agent may see the EHRs of patients who have filed claims on his/her blockchain and, upon approval, can also give the patient with the insurance amount. While buying the medications the patient must disclose the prescription provided by their doctor. The pharmacist must check if the disclosed prescription is valid or not. The pharmacists must give the medicine only if the prescription is valid. If the patient wishes to consult another doctor, they can simply share the details that are stored in the blockchain with them. In blockchain-based EHR, the patient has exclusive access to his EHR information; no one else has access to the information. Additionally, the doctor has access to just the EHRs of patients he has treated. A physician and insurance agents may only see patient blocks that have been given authorization.

In today's healthcare industry, a lot of time-consuming due diligence is done based on a lack of trust. Insurance companies are always wary of fraudulent claims, hence a lot of documentation and details are obtained and analyzed. Doctors need to know more details about their patients such as their insurance status, payment options, etc., during the time of admission. Hence, they do detailed checks. Pharmacists want to verify if the patient was advised to take the medicine or not and then provide them the same. Patients want to ensure if that doctor has a legitimate license with no history of malpractice or any other wrongdoing. To help these entities in verifying their requirements without compromising the privacy of the other entities, the zero-knowledge proof is used. A zero-knowledge protocol is a mechanism for probabilistic verification that involves two parties: a prover and a verifier. The prover is considered to operate in an exponential time domain, while the verifier operates in a linear time domain. The prover's objective is to show that the verifier is aware of a witness, W, without revealing the witness. ZK-snark is the zero-knowledge proof that we will use in our solution. "SNARK stands for Succinct, Non-interactive, Arguments of Knowledge. zk SNARK enables the proof/verification of the correctness of computations without requiring the verifier to run them or divulge any secret information that may have been used in the calculations - the verifier just knows the computation was performed properly." In a healthcare scenario, either of the parties, i.e. patient, doctor, pharmacy, insurance agencies, can take on the role of a verifier, and typically patients and sometimes doctors are the provers. While the ZKP can be applied to any of the transactions involving the above parties, currently the research in the industry is mostly focused on patient privacy rights and ZKP initiatives target more on how much or less information a patient (prover) can share with a verifier before getting the required service based on the assertion of that proof. The above framework includes zero-knowledge proof which preserves the privacy of the patient.

6   Implementation

This paper aims to build a health care system using blockchain technology. We must write smart contracts according to the functions the system is supposed to achieve. First of all, we should design the functions that the system should implement and write corresponding functions in the smart contract for each function to implement it. Ethereum is a decentralised, distributed, and open-source computing tool for developing smart contracts and decentralised applications, or D-Apps. We use Ethereum for writing smart contracts. Primarily, doctors, patients, and pharmacies will be added to the blockchain network. Patients can choose their doctor and send their diagnosis history to the doctor. Once the patient has consulted the doctor, the doctor can update their medical records to the IPFS server.

We combine EHR and blockchain/IPFS architectures to create a distributed database where data may be handled solely by patients and physicians. The IPFS (InterPlanetary File System) provides a decentralized way of storing med-

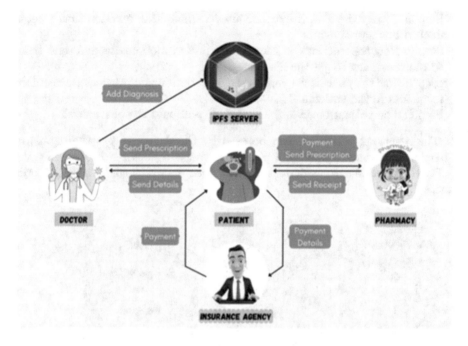

Fig. 1. Design flow of the proposed methodology

ical images, making the records more secure. The required medicines will be prescribed by the doctor and the prescription will also be added. The patient can view their EHRs as well as their prescription. Patients can send the prescription to pharmacies for purchasing the prescribed medications. So far, the contract has realized the basic functions of adding doctors, adding patients, inserting EHRs and prescriptions of the patients, viewing the EHRs by the patients, and sending the patient's prescription to pharmacies. All the above operations will be permanently recorded in the blockchain to ensure data security and transparency of healthcare records (Fig. 1).

Algorithm Design

- Step 1: The primary function is to add the doctor, the patient, and the pharmacy to the blockchain. The functions AddDoctor, AddPatient, and AddPharmacy help to add these details to the block.
- Step 2: If a patient wants to consult a particular doctor, they will send their details to the doctor through a function 'PatientdetailstoDoctor.'
- Step 3: The doctor analyses the patient and generates an EHR based on the patient's health condition.
- Step 4: Now the doctor uploads the EHR of the patient to the blockchain using the setRecord function and generates the prescription and uploads it to the blockchain with the help of the setPrescription function.

- Step 5: To pay the fees, the patient uses a transaction function that accepts doctorId as a parameter.
- Step 6: Now the Patient can access their prescription details and send them to the pharmacy to get the medicines.
- Step 7: Now the pharmacist verifies the prescription and provides the required medicines to the patients.
- Step 8: The patient receives the medicines and pays the pharmacist.

The functions getPatient can be used by the doctor to get the details of a particular patient. Similarly, a patient can view a doctor's details using the getDoctor function. Also, a patient can view their details by using the getRecords function.

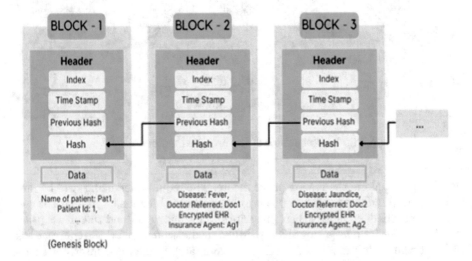

Fig. 2. Blocks storing patient records

Figure 2 depicts the patients' records stored into the block in the blockchain. These blocks will contain the disease information, the doctor they consulted, EHR data, and insurance agent details related to the patients.

Figure 3 depicts the doctor records stored into the block in the blockchain. These blocks will contain ID, the patient they treated, patient's disease information, and EHR data related to the patients.

Figure 4 depicts the insurance records stored into the block in the blockchain. These blocks will contain the medical and financial records of the patients.

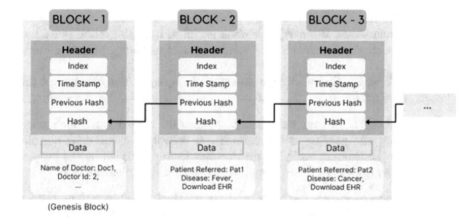

Fig. 3. Blocks storing doctor records

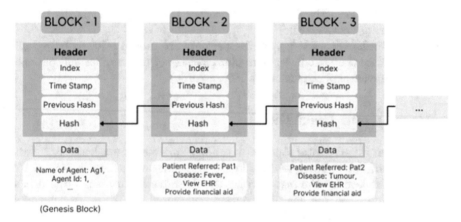

Fig. 4. Blocks storing insurance records

6.1   Zero-Knowledge Proof Algorithm

To achieve privacy in our blockchain network we use Zero-Knowledge Proof.

- **Input:** documents shared by the prover.
- **Output:** true for a valid proof and false for an invalid proof
- **Step 1:** Verifier compiles and runs the zok file, creating proving and verification keys. "proving.key" file is sent to the prover.
- **Step 2:** The prover compiles the zok file independently to make sure it doesn't disclose information they want to keep secret.
- **Step 3:** The prover creates a witness file with the values of all the parameters in the program. Using this witness, the pharmacy's proving.key and the compiled program generate the actual proof. It is created in the file "proof.json".
- **Step 4:** prover shares the "proof.json" file with the verifier. Verifier can verify the file.

– **Step 5:** So far, the prover and the verifier have validated the prescription between themselves. However, it is often useful to have the values published on the blockchain. To do this, the verifier creates a solidity program, "verifier.sol".
– **Step 6:** To verify, the verifier file is compiled, deployed, and checked for the result to be true.

Let the above algorithm be called as a function named zkp which takes verifier, prover, and zokFile as the parameters. ZokFile is a zok extension file that contains the logic for verifying the documentation provided by the prover. zkp(verifier, prover, zokFile) The above algorithm is implemented for

– Patients want to ensure that doctors have a legitimate license with no history of malpractices. Here the patient is the verifier and the doctor is the prover. zkp(patient, doctor, zokFile)
– Doctors need to obtain a lot of documentation from patients for verifying insurance. Here the doctor is the verifier and the patient is the prover. zkp(doctor, patient, zokFile)
– Pharmacists have to verify that the patients are indeed advised by a valid doctor to take the medicines. Here pharmacists act as a verifier and patients act as a prover. zkp(pharmacy, patient, zokFile).

7   Results and Discussions

We provide an experimental study of a solidity smart contract-based authentication method. For building and deploying our code, we utilised a 8GB RAM i5 CPU. As advised by the instructions, the Zokrates library was utilised in a docker container, and the health care data was stored via IPFS. To determine the scalability of our authentication strategy, we used Ganache to simulate a blockchain without requiring long block mining. A hyperledger caliper is used for the performance analysis of the smart contract implementation in hyperledger sawtooth and ethereum.

Ethereum. The below tabulation in Fig. 5 shows the performance analysis of deploying smart contracts in ethereum.

Graphical representation of performance analysis is shown in Fig. 6

Name	Success	Fail	Send Rate (TPS)	Max Latency (s)	Min Latency (s)	Avg Latency (s)	Throughput (TPS)
Fixed TxnCount-TxnPerBatch (16)	16	0	18.5	4	3.13	3.57	4
Fixed TxnCount-TxnPerBatch (120)	120	0	170.5	8.45	3.46	5.89	13.2
Fixed TxnCount-TxnPerBatch (225)	225	0	271.1	18.08	3.69	9.27	11.9
Fixed TxnCount-TxnPerBatch (560)	560	0	530.3	38.01	3.96	20.18	14.3

Fig. 5. Performance analysis of ethereum

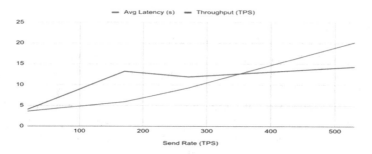

Fig. 6. Graphical representation of performance analysis of ethereum

7.1 Hyperledger Sawtooth

The below tabulation in shows the performance analysis of deploying smart contracts in hyperledger sawtooth (Fig. 7).

Name	Success	Fail	Send Rate (TPS)	Max Latency (s)	Min Latency (s)	Avg Latency (s)	Throughput (TPS)
Fixed TxnCount-TxnPerBatch (10)	16	0	19.8	0.49	0.45	0.47	12.3
Fixed TxnCount-TxnPerBatch (100)	120	0	198.3	2.84	1.72	2.28	34.8
Fixed TxnCount-TxnPerBatch (200)	225	0	351	6.14	2.16	4.12	33.2
Fixed TxnCount-TxnPerBatch (500)	560	0	598.3	16.16	2.39	8.94	32.8

Fig. 7. Performance analysis of hyperledger sawtooth

Performance analysis is shown in Fig. 8

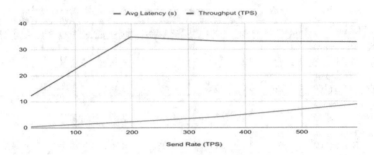

Fig. 8. Graphical representation of performance analysis of hyperledger sawtooth

From the performance analysis of ethereum and hyperledger sawtooth, we can observe that for a sending 560 successful transactions, in ethereum the TPS (Transactions Per Second) is 14.3 whereas in hyperledger sawtooth, the TPS is 32.8. Hyperledger sawtooth is faster than ethereum. We propose a decentralised healthcare system in this article to safeguard data integrity and privacy in a scenario involving several blockchain-based linked networks. Our technology integrates zero-knowledge proof into the healthcare system in a novel way, allowing us to validate a doctor's licence, a legitimate prescription, and a patient's insurance information without disclosing any sensitive information.

8   Conclusion

This article offers a security architecture utilizing blockchain for effectively and securely storing electronic health data. We highlighted the impediments to implementing a 'conventional' Blockchain-based EHR sharing architecture. This methodology ensures that patients have unrestricted access to EHRs while also protecting patients' privacy and maintaining EHR consistency. In our system, we employed zero-knowledge proofs for authentication, which allowed us to distribute EHR access swiftly and securely while respecting patient privacy. The patient may manage, download, and distribute his or her EHRs autonomously utilising this blockchain architecture. The testing findings demonstrate that our blockchain enables users to share data securely. Most significantly, the blockchain security framework access control system is capable of safeguarding critical electronic health records from external assaults. Investigating these advantages of our approach has the potential to revolutionise healthcare and accomplish the goal of privacy preserving EHRs. This research used the blockchain security architecture only in the healthcare sector. We want to apply this paradigm in the future to a variety of areas, including supply chain management, IoT, agriculture, finance, smart grid, education, logistics and finance.

References

1. Nguyen, D.C., Pathirana, P.N., Ding, M., Seneviratne, A.: Blockchain for secure EHR sharing of mobile cloud-based e-health systems. IEEE Access **7**, 66792–66806 (2019)
2. Sharma, B., Halder, R., Singh, J.: Blockchain-based interoperable healthcare using zero-knowledge proofs and proxy re-encryption. In: 2020 International Conference on COMmunication Systems & NETworkS (COMSNETS), pp. 1–6. IEEE, January 2020
3. Tomaz, A.E.B., Do Nascimento, J.C., Hafid, A.S., De Souza, J.N.: Preserving privacy in mobile health systems using non-interactive zero-knowledge proof and blockchain. IEEE Access **8**, 204441–204458 (2020)
4. Li, W., Meese, C., Guo, H., Nejad, M.: Blockchain-enabled identity verification for safe ridesharing leveraging zero-knowledge proof. In: 2020 3rd International Conference on Hot Information-Centric Networking (HotICN), pp. 18–24. IEEE, December 2020
5. Adler-Milstein, J., Bates, D.W.: Paperless healthcare: progress and challenges of an it-enabled healthcare system. Bus. Horiz. **53**(2), 119–130 (2010)
6. Kalaipriya, R., Devadharshini, S., Rajmohan, R., Pavithra, M., Ananthkumar, T.: Certain investigations on leveraging blockchain technology for developing electronic health records. In: 2020 International Conference on System, Computation, Automation, and Networking (ICSCAN), pp. 1–5. IEEE, July 2020
7. Arunkumar, B., Kousalya, G.: Blockchain-based decentralized and secure lightweight E-health system for electronic health records. In: Thampi, S.M., et al. (eds.) Intelligent Systems, Technologies and Applications. AISC, vol. 1148, pp. 273–289. Springer, Singapore (2020). https://doi.org/10.1007/978-981-15-3914-5_21
8. Abunadi, I., Kumar, R.L.: BSF-EHR: blockchain security framework for electronic health records of patients. Sensors **21**(8), 2865 (2021)
9. Chen, L., Lee, W.K., Chang, C.C., Choo, K.K.R., Zhang, N.: Blockchain-based searchable encryption for electronic health record sharing. Future Gener. Comput. Syst. **95**, 420–429 (2019)
10. Tanwar, S., Parekh, K., Evans, R.: Blockchain-based electronic healthcare record system for healthcare 4.0 applications. J. Inf. Secur. Appl. **50**, 102407 (2020)
11. Vora, J., et al.: BHEEM: a blockchain-based framework for securing electronic health records. In: 2018 IEEE Globecom Workshops (GC Wkshps), pp. 1–6. IEEE, December 2018
12. Yang, G., Li, C.: A design of blockchain-based architecture for the security of electronic health record (EHR) systems. In: 2018 IEEE International Conference on Cloud Computing Technology and Science (CloudCom), pp. 261–265. IEEE, December 2018
13. Shahnaz, A., Qamar, U., Khalid, A.: Using blockchain for electronic health records. IEEE Access **7**, 147782–147795 (2019)
14. Ivan, D.: Moving toward a blockchain-based method for the secure storage of patient records. In: ONC/NIST Use of Blockchain for Healthcare and Research Workshop. ONC/NIST, Gaithersburg, Maryland, United States, pp. 1–11. Sn, August 2016
15. Tang, F., Ma, S., Xiang, Y., Lin, C.: An efficient authentication scheme for blockchain-based electronic health records. IEEE Access **7**, 41678–41689 (2019)

Offensiveness Detection in Hinglish Code-Switched Language

Sri Harshini Vissamsetti⬤, K. S. S. Pravallika⬤, Shiva Charan Jadhav⬤, and Hima Bindu Kommanti[✉]⬤

National Institute of Technology Andhra Pradesh, Tadepalligudem, Andhra Pradesh, India
himabinduk@nitandhra.ac.in

Abstract. Detecting offensive content is one of the most sought-after tasks with the increased online presence. Though it is a challenging task on its own due to the short text, spell variations, and emojis, it is even more challenging for code-switched languages. Many Indian users are habituated to use Hinglish (Hindi and English) on almost all social media platforms. Hinglish has no grammar rules, it is very difficult to infer the meaning for the current machine translation tools. We have built an offensive language detection system that deals with code-switched languages, by fine-tuning the pre-trained BERT on the HOT (Hinglish Offensive Tweets) dataset with a fully connected network as a task-specific layer. We used sentiment score and the number of bad words as two additional features to build the classifier. By using weighted cross-entropy loss in our model, we could improve the F1 Score to 0.902 while the current state-of-the-art model on this dataset has only 0.895.

Keywords: Offensive language · Code-switched languages · Transliteration · BERT

1 History and Introduction

In this 21st century, the penetration of social media platforms and websites into the public has drastically increased and there are millions of active users per minute over various available platforms. All these platforms act as global communities and will connect people around the globe. Each user has freedom to post and comment whatever they wish, following the policies [1] and conditions that are imposed by the platform.

But some users may misuse their freedom of expression to spread hateness to threaten or abuse others. Hence, the administrators of these platforms must prevent users from adopting such inappropriate behaviours, by restricting the offensive language. In the initial stages, platforms have incorporated manual Report Content features to check, verify and remove hateful content. But as there is enormous big data that is being generated every second, it's highly impossible to manually check all the content that is being pushed onto the platform.

This difficulty has thrown a light on the problem of automatic detection of hateful content on social media. As per Schmidt and Wiegand(2017) [2] Hate Speech is defined

I. Raman et al. (Eds.): ICC3 2021, CCIS 1631, pp. 124–135, 2022.
https://doi.org/10.1007/978-3-031-15556-7_9

as a communication that abuses, offends or disparages a person or group of individuals, based on their nationality, race, caste, colour, religion, ethnicity, gender or sexual orientation. Both Hate speech and Abusive speech come under Offensive speech. In specific, offensive speech targeted to a single individual is termed as abusive, whereas offensive speech targeted to a group of people is termed as hate speech.

Many researchers have explored this new domain of study and proposed NLP and ML based models to automate the task and many tech giants have incorporated automatic detectors that alerts and prompts users if he/she attempts to post offensive content.

Even after diligent and enormous research, this problem didn't receive much classifying ability. Social media platforms revealed that they still receive millions of manual reports in the comments. This is due to an increase in usage of code-switched languages, which makes the task difficult for the classifiers that are trained only on English corpus.

It was observed that the current detectors are able to identify the text "You look so dirty" as hate speech, whereas they failed to detect the text "Tum bahut dirty ho", the Hinglish code-switched version of the same text.

The key characteristics of code-switched languages, that turned out as challenges for this task are:

1. Lack of proper grammatical rules and semantics
2. As in the real world, switching between keyboards and typing languages in their script consumes much time, users generally prefer typing their native languages in Roman script. This allows users to use spellings of their own. Absence of a fixed spelling for a word, makes the task even more difficult.

In this paper, we have proposed an approach to deal with the challenges of linguistic code- switching by devising a model based on BERT [3]. To implement this, we have chosen the Hinglish Offensive Tweets dataset and built a binary classifier to detect whether a given text is offensive or not.

Remaining sections of this paper are organized as follows. Section 2 presents the existing work in this domain. Section 3 describes the dataset we have used. Section 4 details our proposed approach and model architecture. In Sect. 5 we have mentioned the results and provided result analysis in Sect. 6. We have concluded in Sect. 7.

2 Related Work

Recognition of hostile messages was first studied in 1997 by Ellen Spertus [4], on 1222 handpicked email messages, using SMOKEY Architecture and Rule-Based Decision Tree Approach. Decision tree was used as the classifier and content was captured through occurrence order of predefined flame words. Though it was built on a very small dataset, this became the base reference for many of the later researches in this domain.

Lexical Syntactic Feature (LSF) based framework was published by Ying Chen et al. (2012) [5] in their work. Data was retrieved from YouTube comment boards of top videos in various categories such as Music, Comedies, Entertainment, Education, Sports and News. Along with sentence level offensiveness prediction, their work also incorporated user offensiveness estimation based on profile history.

With the emergence of powerful deep-learning models, many attempts were made to increase the classification ability of the task by using them. Later, in 2016, Nobata C et al. [6] have built a supervised model that surpasses performance of existing deep learning models, with a feature set derived from NLP based features such as N-Grams, Linguistic, Syntactic and distributional semantic techniques.

Davidson et al. [7] have proposed a model to differentiate hate speech from other forms of offensive speech. They also have developed a Hate Speech Offensive Language dataset (HSOL) with a corpus of 25k tweets categorized as hate speech, offensive speech and neither. This stood out as a benchmark dataset for many of the further researches. Zampeiri et al. [8] explored a way to identify the target of offense i.e.,whether it is targeting an individual (or) a group. They proposed a novel 3-level hierarchical annotation schema and evaluated it with SVM, CNN and BiLSTM models and also presented their annotated Offensive Language Identification Dataset (OLID).

Although there are many prominent works that are being published in detecting offensiveness, the exploration of code-switching in this domain was first done by Mathur et al. 2018 [9], by effectively employing a transfer learning based model.

The use of transfer learning had enabled the model to learn the knowledge derived from large English based corpus, to understand the offensive context and transference of the knowledge on small Hinglish code-switched data. Another interesting attempt in the same direction was proposed by Raghav Kapoor [10] et al. through a model based on Long Short Term Memory (LSTM) classifier. Development of Indic transliterators by Khapra et al. [11] and introduction of Hindi to English dictionaries by Pushpak Bhattacharyya et al. [12] have significantly contributed to deal with researches that rely on code-mixed Hinglish language.

3   Dataset

For our work, we used the Hinglish Offensive Tweet (HOT) dataset which was released by Mathur et al. 2018 [13]. HOT dataset contains tweets that are collected using twitter streaming API containing Hinglish words, in November 2017. The authors have extracted tweets by imposing geo-location restriction in order to fetch tweets from India. HOT is a ternary annotated dataset, containing a total of 3189 tweets belonging to 3 categories (Non-offensive, Abusive and Hate-inducing).

However, as our model's main objective is to predict whether a given text is offensive or not, we have formulated it to be a binary classifier. So, we have combined hate-speech and abusive tweets under the same category. Table 1 represents the distribution of our dataset.

There is a clear class imbalance in the dataset i.e., offensive and non-offensive tweets are in ratio 1:0.54, which we have scrutinized as one of the challenges to build an efficient model.

Table 1. Distribution of actual HOT dataset

Label	Number of tweets
Non-offensive (0)	1121
Offensive (1)	2068
Total	3189

4 Proposed Approach

Our methodology primarily consists of 3 modules.

1. Tweet pre-processing
2. Dealing with Code-switching
3. Building our BERT based classifier and then evaluating it on the dataset

4.1 Pre-processing

Table 2 represents some tweet instances from the dataset. Most of the tweets have unnecessary data such as user mentions, URLs which are of no use as we cannot infer any information from such data.

Table 2. Noisy tweet instances from HOT dataset

Label	Tweet
0	*@guptatripti37 @MohdSha88 @suyyashrai:-)*
1	*RT @soitbedone:* https://t.co/MgWnknCkYA
1	*@priya_hhh Saali lund khao chinaal...hehe*
1	*@myvotetoday Is chinaal ko italy bhejo*

We have incorporated the below mentioned steps to convert this noisy data into a clean dataset.

i. The retweet indication tag 'RT' was removed.
ii. Whole tweet text was converted into lower case, for ease of use.
iii. All the user mentions, URLs and links were removed.
iv. All the digits, escape characters such as '\n' and '\x' were removed.
v. **Negation tagging:** In the sentences that contain negative words (such as not, n't), all the words that are present in between the negative word and the next punctuation mark are appended with the negation tag 'not_'. For example, consider the sentence –

"They are not to be treated equally."

After negation tagging, the text gets converted to: "they are not not_to not_be not_treated not_equally."

Negation tagging was done to preserve and carry the negative context throughout the sentence.

vi. **Emoticon conversion:** The text had emoticons, which are shorter ways of expressing emotions. For example, emotion ':(' represents sadness. So, we have used the emoji library [14] and converted all the existing emoticons into their corresponding textual representations.

vii. All the punctuation marks except hash '#' were removed. Hash was preserved as it acts as a prefix for hashtags that are usually used to express context.

viii. All the words were converted into their root words using Wordnet Lemmatizer [15].

ix. After the pre-processing the null data was removed and Table 3. Shows the description of training and test sets after pre-processing.

Table 3. Distribution of training and testing sets

	Number of tweets
Null data	67
Total (after removing null data)	3122
Training set	2159
Training set	963

4.2 Dealing with Code-Switching

Dealing with Hinglish code-mixing in our data is one of the most concerning and challenging aspects of this task. Many ways were proposed to deal with it over various text classification tasks. D. Stiraram et al. [16] used language identifiers and bifurcated sentences into two groups containing words of corresponding language. They invoked language-specific models on respective groups to implement the task of sentiment classification.

Vilares et al. [17] presented the usage of Multilingual models. These are language-independent models that are trained using a large language corpus. Sentence level Machine-Translation can also be used to translate Hinglish text into corresponding English text. Mathur et al. [13] introduced another way of dealing with linguistic code switching by performing transliteration and word-level translation.

Transliteration is the process of producing the text in another script. This can be done by changing alphabets corresponding to the same phonetics in other scripts. Khapra et al. [11] have contributed and published their Hindi-English Transliterator model. This is a deep learning model that can deal with spelling variations in roman scripted Hinglish and can convert to respective actual Hindi words, in Devanagari script.

Pushpak Bhattacharyya et al. [12] have released a Hindi-English dictionary, which contains nearly 133012 Hindi words in Devanagari script and their corresponding English words in roman script.

Text bifurcation into groups based on language can break the context and may not always preserve it. Vilares et al. [17] model achieved very less accuracy (55%) by using multilingual models. We observed that existing sentence level machine translation models are performing well at translating sentences by preserving context but they are not able to efficiently handle spell mistakes in text.

But code-switched languages contain many spell variations. Hence, in our model, we have incorporated transliteration and word-level translation as a step to convert Hinglish text to English text.

1. For Hinglish -> Hindi, we have used transliteration pairs provided by Xlit-Crowd conversion dictionary [18].
2. For Hindi -> English, we have used a Hindi-English translation dictionary sourced from CFILT, IIT Bombay [12].

By combining the above steps, we have built a Hinglish -> English dictionary for words contained in our dataset. The dictionary contains 5063 Hinglish-English word pairs. By using this dictionary, we have converted Hinglish tweets in our dataset to English. Table 4 illustrates some word pair examples from this dictionary.

Table 4. Word pair examples from Hinglish-English dictionary

Word in Hinglish	Word in English
badan	Body
mera	Mine
meraaa	Mine
hawa	air
hava	air
havaa	air
ke	from
kae	from

4.3 BERT - Based Model Architecture

Jacob Devlin and co-researchers at Google AI Language, published BERT (Bidirectional Encoder Representations from transformers) [3], a powerful language representation model. This is a multi-tasking model that has achieved state-of-the-art results in many NLP based tasks such as classification, question and answering systems, text summarisation etc.

BERT is pre-trained on large language corpus and its parameters can be finetuned by adding a task-specific layer, so that it adapts itself to fit best on smaller datasets for downstream tasks.

In our work, we proposed a model architecture by fine-tuning BERT with a fully connected neural network as a task specific layer and Sentiment score, Number of bad words as additional features. Figure 1 represents our proposed model architecture.

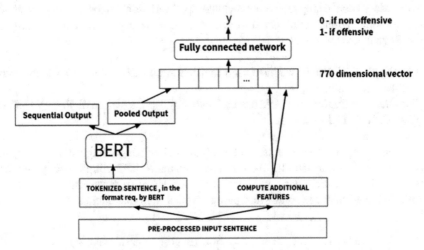

Fig. 1. Proposed BERT-based model for offensiveness detection in Hinglish tweets

There are many variants of BERT, but we have used a BERT-base model in which the number of encoder layers 'l' is set to 12, the hidden size 'h' is set to 768 and the number of attention heads 'a' is set to 12.

Use of Additional Features:

1. *Number of bad words* - By analysing our dataset, we have observed that the users who intend to spread offense are using loopholes of these models in order to mask themselves from automatic detectors, by inclusion of character '*' in bad words. The data contains words like f**k, bas**rd. Hence, we included an additional feature to count such bad words and keep track of them.
2. *Sentiment Score* - We have used the TextBlob library to get the sentiment score of each tweet and added it as another additional feature to the data. This is done to differentiate sarcasm from offense. Offensive tweets with positive sentiment are most likely to be sarcastic. Sentiment score of ' + 1' represents positive, '0' represents neutral and '−1' represents negative sentiment.

Implementation Steps:

1. All the clean tweets obtained after the pre-processing step are fed to the BERT model after input formatting.
2. Pooled output of BERT is a 768-dimensional representational vector.
3. After adding the 2 additional features, the resultant 770-dimensional feature space is fed to the BERT architecture with the fully-connected neural network as a task specific layer.
4. This whole architecture is fine-tuned to fit best on the training data.

Model Parameters:
All the BERT layers are kept active for fine-tuning. We have performed hyper parameter tuning to obtain a good combination of hidden layers in a fully connected network and learning rate of the model. Figure 2 represents the structure of the fully connected network.

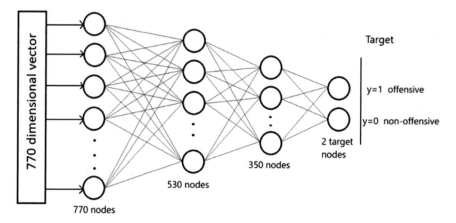

Fig. 2. Structure of fully connected network in proposed model architecture

Parameters: BERT-base → Dense Layer (770 units, activation = 'relu') → Dropout (0.2) → Dense Layer (530 units, activation = 'relu') → Dropout (0.2) → Dense Layer (350 units, activation = 'relu') → Dropout (0.2) → Dense Layer (2 units, activation = 'softmax').

Model comprises 11,00,76,540 (≈110 million) trainable parameters in total. The final compile layer of architecture comprises weighted categorical cross-entropy loss function with Adam optimizer. As a result of hyper-parameter tuning, the learning rate of the task is fixed at 0.006. Weighted cross entropy loss deals with the problem of class imbalance present in the data.

5 Model Evaluation and Results

The proposed model was trained on our dataset and the learned model weights were used to predict the class labels of tweets belonging to the evaluation dataset.

We also have performed the same task with sentence - level machine translation step instead of transliteration and word - level translation step. We have translated Hinglish sentences into meaningful English sentences with the help of the public Google Cloud Translate API. The obtained datasets are trained and evaluated on proposed model architecture with and without the presence of additional features to compare the results.

Table 5 illustrates the results we have obtained by the proposed model with Cross Entropy as loss function.

Table 6 illustrates the results we have obtained by the proposed model with Weighted Cross Entropy as loss function.

Table 5. Results obtained with cross entropy as loss function

Step to deal with code-switching	Precision	Recall	F1-score	Accuracy
Sentence level machine translation	0.831	0.522	0.641	0.599
Transliteration and word level translation	0.877	0.861	0.869	0.823
Sentence level machine translation + additional features	0.687	0.995	0.813	0.686
Transliteration and word level translation + additional features	0.859	0.887	0.873	0.824

Table 6. Results obtained with weighted cross entropy as loss function

Step to deal with code-switching	Precision	Recall	F1-score	Accuracy
Sentence level machine translation	0.864	0.866	0.865	0.816
Transliteration and word level translation	0.875	0.783	0.827	0.776
Sentence level machine translation + additional features	0.884	0.852	0.868	0.823
Transliteration and word level translation + additional features	0.900	0.904	0.902	0.866

6 Result Analysis

As presented in Table 6, our model has obtained the best results in the case of transliteration and word-level translation as a step to deal with code-switching, in presence of additional features by using Weighted Cross Entropy as loss function. Table 7 illustrates the confusion matrix of the obtained results in this case.

Table 7. Confusion matrix in the case of transliteration and word-level translation as a step to deal with code-switching

	Actual Label 0	1
Predicted Label		
0	240 (True negatives)	63 (False negatives)
1	66 (False positives)	594 (True positives)

* 0 - represents non-offensive tweet label, 1 - represents offensive tweet label

The model tagged 21.5% of non-offensive tweets as offensive, which counts as false positive rate. We found that the reason behind the exhibition of high false positive rate by our model is due to lack of semantic ordering in training data.

We observed that, after transliteration and word-level translation steps, the obtained English text lost its semantics. Due to this reason and the small size of the dataset, the model failed to grab the exact context in the text that contained religion-specific words and tagged them as offensive.

7 Conclusions and Future Work

We have proposed a novel model that surpasses the state-of-the-art models which are existing in detection of offensive language on HOT dataset. We have tried various cases as presented and obtained best results in the case of Transliteration and Word-level translation as a step to deal with code switching in presence of additional features and weighted cross entropy as loss function.

Table 8 presents the comparison of various models with respect to results in this domain. By our model, the outstanding abilities of BERT in NLP tasks are proven again. Weighted cross entropy loss function has efficiently dealt with the class imbalance in the dataset.

Table 8. Comparison of our model results against various proposed models on HOT dataset

Model	Precision	Recall	F1-score	Accuracy
Mathur et al. [9]	0.802	0.698	0.714	0.839
Mathur et al. [13]	0.816	**0.928**	0.895	–
Raghav Kapoor et al. [10]	–	–	–	**0.87**
Our Proposed model	**0.900**	0.904	**0.902**	0.866

* -(hyphen) denotes the absence of performance metric in the corresponding paper, highlighted values indicate the highest performance value among others

Although our work has improvised performance with respect to HOT dataset, we would also like to standardize and revamp our model by comparing against large English datasets such as OffensEval 2019 OLID dataset. In the data, we also observed that many users used intentional spelling mistakes in order to fool the machines. So, as an extension to our approach, we would like to build a revised version of our model with an objective to obtain significant reduction in false positive rate, standardizing against large English datasets and also to incorporate methods that deal with intentional spelling mistakes. We will extend our work in light of low resource language models.

References

1. Facebook Hate Speech Policy. www.facebook.com/communitystandards#hate-speech. Twitter's policy, https://support.twitter.com/articles/20175050
2. Schmidt, A., Wiegand, M.: A survey on hate speech detection using natural language processing. In: Proceedings of the Fifth International Workshop on Natural Language Processing for Social Media (2017)
3. Devlin, J., Chang, M.W., Lee, K., Toutanova, K.: BERT: pre-training of deep bidirectional transformers for language understanding. CoRR, abs/1810.04805 https://arxiv.org/abs/1810.04805 (2019)
4. Spertus, E.: Smokey: automatic recognition of hostile messages. In: AAAI/IAAI-1997, pp. 1058–1065 (1997)
5. Chen, Y., Zhou, Y., Xu, H., Zhu, S.: Detecting offensive language in social media to protect adolescent online safety. In: International Conference of Privacy, Security and Trust (2012)
6. Nobata, C., Tetreault, J., Thomas, A., Mehdad, Y., Chang, Y.: Abusive language detection in online user content. In: International Conference on World Wide Web, WWW 2016 (2016)
7. Davidson, T., Warmsley, D., Macy, M., Weber, I.: Automated hate speech detection and the problem of offensive language. arXiv preprint https://arxiv.org/abs/1703.04009 (2017)
8. Zampieri, M., Malmasi, S., Nakov, P., Rosenthal, S., Farra, N., Kumar, R.: Predicting the type and target of offensive posts in social media. In: Proceedings of the 2019 Conference of the North American Chapter of the Association for Computational Linguistics: Human Language Technologies (2019)
9. Mathur, P., Shah, R., Sawhney, R., Mahata, D.: Detecting offensive tweets in Hindi-English code-switched language. In: Proceedings of the Sixth International Workshop on Natural Language Processing for Social Media (2018)
10. Kapoor, R., Kumar, Y., Rajput, K., Shah, R.R., Kumaraguru, P., Zimmermann, R.: Mind your language: abuse and offense detection for code-switched languages. arXiv preprinthttps://arxiv.org/abs/1809.08652 (2018)
11. Khapra, M.M., Ramanathan, A., Kunchukuttan, A., Visweswariah, K., Bhattacharyya, P.: When transliteration met crowdsourcing: an empirical study of transliteration via crowdsourcing using efficient, non-redundant and fair quality control. In: LREC, pp. 196–202 (2014)
12. Bhattacharyya, P., et al.: Hindi-English dictionary. IIT, Bombay. https://www.cfilt.iitb.ac.in/~hdict/webinterface_user/
13. Mathur, P., Sawhney, R., Ayyar, M., Shah, R.: Did you offend me? Classification of offensive tweets in Hinglish language. In: Proceedings of the 2nd Workshop on Abusive Language Online (ALW2) (2018)
14. Emoji library. https://pypi.org/project/emoji/
15. Wordnet Lemmatizer. https://www.nltk.org/_modules/nltk/stem/wordnet.html
16. Sitaram, D., Murthy, S., Ray, D., Sharma, D., Dhar, K.: Sentiment analysis of mixed language employing Hindi-English code switching. In: International Conference on Machine Learning and Cybernetics (ICMLC) (2015). https://doi.org/10.1109/icmlc.2015.7340934

17. Vilares, D., Alonso, M.A., Gómez-Rodríguez, C.: Sentiment analysis on monolingual, multilingual and code-switching Twitter corpora. In: Proceedings of the 6th Workshop on Computational Approaches to Subjectivity, Sentiment and Social Media Analysis (2015)
18. Khapra, M.: Xlit-Crowd: Hindi-English Transliteration Corpus. https://github.com/chsasank/indic-transliteration

Computational Models

Modelling RNA Motifs Using Matrix Insertion-Deletion System

Anand Mahendran[✉]

Laboratory of Theoretical Computer Science, HSE University, Moscow, Russia
amahendran@hse.ru

Abstract. In RNA editing, insertion and deletion are recognized to be fundamental operations. Many investigations have been carried out in the literature to identify the relationship between the formal language theory and gene (biological) sequences. The output of such investigation is to represent the bio-molecular structures of gene sequences in terms of formal languages. In the literature, Matrix insertion-deletion system (MIDS) has been introduced to capture bio-molecular structures that are often noticed at various levels. As an extension, in this paper, we model (some more) RNA motifs using MIDS by giving a suitable formal language representation.

Keywords: Insertion-deletion systems · RNA · Bio-inspired computing · Secondary structures · Motif

1 Introduction

In the recent decades, the usage of computer has been increased enormously starting from storing and retrieving data, manipulating scientific computations and performing other complex operations. To nab the needs of the fast growing world, a constant research has been there in the domain of computer science. Due to the need of increase in computation speed and storage of data, the computing models used for computation, the technologies used for storage medium have to be changed rapidly. As nature is always more faster than human brains and the computing devices, researchers felt that the nature would play a critical role while framing the computing model. More specifically, biology can inspire to model the computing devices. This introduced the notion of *natural computing* which bridged the gap between nature and computer science. Such computing can be performed as a fundamental research and as well as a computing model to solve the problems in computer science and information technology.

In the last few decades, researchers have mainly concentrated on the domain of natural computing in particular, to DNA computing as it has potential (theoretical) applications in the field of computer science. Such a tremendous development in DNA computing has kindled the researchers to introduce various (theoretical) computing models like *sticker systems, splicing systems, Watson-Crick*

The article was prepared within the framework of the HSE University Basic Research Program.

automata, finite H systems, distributed H systems, insertion-deletion systems
[2,18] to study the theoretical behaviour of the DNA computing in terms of
operations. Insertion operation in DNA computing was mainly studied in [7],
where as both insertion and deletions were introduced and studied in [9]. Insertion of a string β between two substrings is called *insertion* operation. Deletion
of a string α between two substrings is called *deletion* operation.

RNA molecules are formed over the basic four chemical bases, namely *ade-
nine (a), uracil (u), guamine (g), cytosine (c)*. Such RNA molecules are represented by Σ_{RNA}. The RNA structures are formed over the gene sequence based
on the complementary pairs. The complementary pairs of RNA are denoted as
$\bar{a} = u$, $\bar{u} = a$, $\bar{g} = c$, $\bar{c} = g$. The structures can be classified as *intramcolecular,
intermolecular* in DNA computing and *secondary structures* in RNA editing.
In [8], the relationship between formal language theory, DNA computing and its
generative capacity were analyzed. In [22–24], the connection between the formal language theory and biological sequences were investigated. In the literature
survey, there exists different grammar formalisms to model the structures that
are normally detected in DNA and RNA molecules. However, there is no single
grammar formalism to enclose the (commonly noticed) bio-molecular structures
in DNA and RNA molecules. To overcome this, in [10] a new bio-inspired computing model was introduced namely MIDS by stitching the idea of insertion-
deletion system and matrix grammars. In the same paper, using the defined
bio-inspired model various structures that are perceived at intermolecular levels
were studied. In [11], the structures that are often observed in intramolecular
level were investigated using the bio-inspired computing model.

In the domain of computational biology, RNA molecules deserve a special
attention because they act as messengers mainly in protein structures. In particular, the RNA structures are formed by folding back of the complementary
pairs on itself. Such RNA motifs are broadly classified as primary, secondary
and tertiary structures. If the structure is based on the complete sequence of
the molecule it is primary. If the structures are represented in 2D format, then
the structures are known to be secondary. If a 3D representation is given then
the RNA structures are termed to be tertiary. Many attempts have been made
to theoretically study about the RNA structure modelling, prediction by defining new (theoretical) grammar formalisms. For more details on such grammar
formalisms, we refer to [4,21,25]. A RNA motif is a discrete sequence of base
paired molecules that occur frequently in a RNA sequence. As RNA motifs perform some functions they are found (frequently) almost in modern organisms
as a mutative products. In general, the RNA motifs are classified as terminal
loop and internal loop. The study of such RNA motifs will help to identify the
interaction between RNA and Protein. For more details on the RNA motifs, we
refer to [1,5,6,13,14,17,19]. In [12], a formal language representation has been
given to various RNA secondary structures and the corresponding structures are
modelled by MIDS. Several attempts have been made in [3,15,16,20] to study
about the basic RNA structures and motifs. In this paper, we further encom-
pass the work conceded on modelling RNA secondary structures by identifying

some more complicated RNA motifs. In this regard, a structural representation is given to the recognized motifs and design them using MIDS by means of formal language. The paper is organized as follows: Sect. 2 mainly deals with preliminaries, Sect. 3 deals with the modelling of RNA motifs using MIDS by giving an appropriate formal language representation. Finally, Sect. 4 deals with conclusion and future work.

2   Preliminaries

We start with discussing about the fundamental notations used in formal language theory. V (or Σ) is called an alphabet set. The free monoid generated by V (or Σ) is represented as V^* (or Σ^*). The null string is denoted by Λ. By eliminating Λ from V^* (and Σ^*), we can obtain V^+ (and Σ^+). *Strings* or *words* are the elements from V^* (or Σ^*). A language L is represented as $L \subseteq \Sigma^*$. A MIDS is defined as: $\Upsilon = (V, T, A, R)$ where V represents an alphabet, $T \subseteq V$, A is a finite language over the alphabet, R is defined as a set of finite insertion-deletion rules in a matrix format: (i) R_{I_i}, (ii) R_{D_j}, and (iii) R_{I_i/D_j}. The following represents $[(u_1, \Lambda/\beta_1, v_1), ..., (u_n, \Lambda/\beta_n, v_n)]$ the matrix insertion rule. In the matrix rule β_1 is inserted between (u_1, v_1) followed by the insertion of β_2 between (u_2, v_2) and continued up to the insertion of β_n between (u_n, v_n). The matrix insertion rule is represented as R_{I_i}. The following denotes $[(u_1, \alpha_1/\Lambda, v_1), ..., (u_n, \alpha_n/\Lambda, v_n)]$ the matrix deletion rule. In the matrix rule α_1 is deleted between (u_1, v_1) followed by the deletion of α_2 between (u_2, v_2) and continued up to the deletion of α_n between (u_n, v_n). The matrix deletion rule is represented as R_{D_j}. The matrix which has the combination of insertion, deletion rules are denoted as R_{I_i/D_j}.

Any derivation in MIDS is derived by applying a matrix insertion rule or a matrix deletion rule or a matrix which has the combination of insertion, deletion rules. In the derivation step of a MIDS, the rules are applied in a sequential manner (no appearance checking is allowed). Parallel application of rules in a matrix is not permitted. The language produced by MIDS, Υ is given as

$$L(\Upsilon) = \{w \in T^* \mid x \Longrightarrow^*_{R_\Psi} w, \text{ for some } x \in A, \ \Psi \in \{I_i, D_j, I_i/D_j\}\}$$

$\Longrightarrow^*$ is the transitive and reflexive closure of the defined relation $\Longrightarrow$. All rules in a matrix should be applied in order and string over T^* are collected for the language.

3   RNA Motifs Structural Illustration and Generation by MIDS

In this section, given a RNA sequence or RNA motif, we design a MIDS which generates it by giving a pertinent formal language depiction. In the derivation steps ↓ marks the location of the string to be inserted, the inserted string is represented by a underline, ⇓ represents the position of the deleted string and the rule which is present at the bottom of $\Longrightarrow$ represents the application of a particular matrix rule. The arrowed line in the diagrams denotes the direction of the language to be identified.

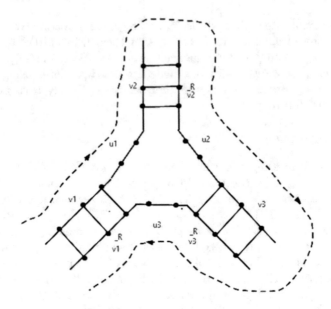

Fig. 1. 3-way junction structure

Theorem 1. *The 3-Way Junction structure (3WJ) (see Fig. 1)* $L_{3WJ} = \{v_1 u_1 v_2 \bar{v}_2{}^R u_2 \ v_3 \bar{v}_3{}^R u_3 \bar{v}_1{}^R \mid u_1, u_2, u_3, v_1, v_2, v_3 \in \Sigma_{RNA}^*\}$ *can be modelled by MIDS.*

Proof. The language L_{3WJ} can be modelled by the MIDS $\Upsilon_{3WJ} = (\{x, \bar{x}, \triangledown_1, \triangledown_2, \triangledown_3, \triangledown_4, \triangledown_5\}, \{x, \bar{x}\}, \{\triangledown_1 \triangledown_2 \triangledown_3 \triangledown_4 \triangledown_5\}, R)$, where $x \in \Sigma_{RNA}$, the counterpart of x is $\bar{x}$ and the insertion, deletion rules R are given below:

$R_{I_1} = [(\Lambda, \Lambda/x, \triangledown_1), (\triangledown_5, \Lambda/\bar{x}, \Lambda)]$, $R_{I_2} = [(\triangledown_1, \Lambda/x, \Lambda)]$, $R_{I_3} = [(\Lambda, \Lambda/x, \triangledown_2), (\triangledown_2, \Lambda/\bar{x}, \Lambda)]$, $R_{I_4} = [(\Lambda, \Lambda/x, \triangledown_3)]$, $R_{I_5} = [(\triangledown_3, \Lambda/x, \Lambda), (\Lambda, \Lambda/\bar{x}, \triangledown_4)]$, $R_{I_6} = [(\Lambda, \Lambda/x, \triangledown_5)]$, $R_{D_1} = [(\Lambda, \triangledown_1/\Lambda, \Lambda)]$, $R_{D_2} = [(\Lambda, \triangledown_2/\Lambda, \Lambda)]$, $R_{D_3} = [(\Lambda, \triangledown_3/\Lambda, \Lambda)]$, $R_{D_4} = [(\Lambda, \triangledown_4/\Lambda, \Lambda)]$, $R_{D_5} = [(\Lambda, \triangledown_5/\Lambda, \Lambda)]$.

The below steps depict a sample derivation for a string from the language L_{3WJ}:

$$^{\downarrow}\triangledown_1 \triangledown_2 \triangledown_3 \triangledown_4 \triangledown_5^{\downarrow} \Longrightarrow_{R_{I_1}} \underline{a} \triangledown_1^{\downarrow} \triangledown_2 \triangledown_3 \triangledown_4 \triangledown_5 \underline{u} \Longrightarrow_{R_{I_2}} a \triangledown_1 \underline{u}^{\downarrow} \triangledown_2^{\downarrow} \triangledown_3 \triangledown_4 \triangledown_5 u$$

$$\Longrightarrow_{R_{I_3}} a \triangledown_1 u\underline{a} \triangledown_2 \underline{u}^{\downarrow} \triangledown_3 \triangledown_4 \triangledown_5 u \Longrightarrow_{R_{I_4}} a \triangledown_1 ua \triangledown_2 u\underline{g} \triangledown_3^{\downarrow\,\downarrow} \triangledown_4 \triangledown_5 u$$

$$\Longrightarrow_{R_{I_5}} a \triangledown_1 ua \triangledown_2 ug \triangledown_3 \underline{cg} \triangledown_4 \triangledown_5 u \Longrightarrow_{R_{I_6}} a \triangledown_1 ua \triangledown_2 ug \triangledown_3 cg \triangledown_4 \underline{a} \triangledown_5 u$$

$$\Longrightarrow_{R_{D_1}} a^{\Downarrow} ua \triangledown_2 ug \triangledown_3 cg \triangledown_4 a \triangledown_5 u \Longrightarrow_{R_{D_2}} aua^{\Downarrow} ug \triangledown_3 cg \triangledown_4 a \triangledown_5 u$$

$$\Longrightarrow_{R_{D_3}} auaug^{\Downarrow} cg \triangledown_4 a \triangledown_5 u \Longrightarrow_{R_{D_4}} auaugcg^{\Downarrow} a \triangledown_5 u \Longrightarrow_{R_{D_5}} auaugcga^{\Downarrow} u.$$

$\triangledown_1$, $\triangledown_2$, $\triangledown_3$, $\triangledown_4$ and $\triangledown_5$ are used as markers in generating the language. In particular, $v_1 \bar{v}_1{}^R$ part of the language is generated by the markers $\triangledown_1$ and $\triangledown_5$. By using such markers a proper synchronization is achieved by having both the insertion rules in a single matrix. The synchronization is achieved in such a way that when x is inserted to the left of the marker $\triangledown_1$, simultaneously its complementary $\bar{x}$ is inserted to the right of the marker $\triangledown_5$. The marker $\triangledown_2$ is used to guide in generating the $v_2\bar{v}_2{}^R$ part of the language. The $v_3\bar{v}_3{}^R$ part of the language is generated by the markers $\triangledown_3$ and $\triangledown_4$. The u_1, u_2 and u_3 part of the language is generated by the markers $\triangledown_1, \triangledown_3$ and $\triangledown_5$ respectively. As the u_1, u_2 and u_3 is only dependent on inserting x alone, synchronization is not required. Using R_{D_j}, $\triangledown$'s can be eliminated. The left and right context of the deletion rules are Λ. □

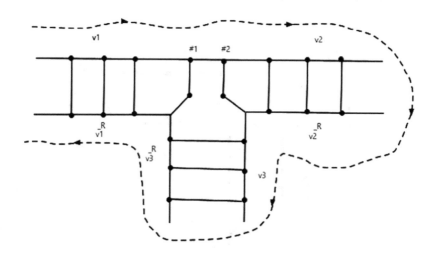

Fig. 2. Clocked 3-way junction structure

Theorem 2. *The Clocked 3-Way Junction structure (C3WJ) (see Fig. 2)*
$L_{C3WJ} = \{v_1\#_1\#_2 v_2\bar{v}_2{}^R v_3\bar{v}_3{}^R\bar{v}_1{}^R \mid v_1, v_2, v_3 \in \Sigma_{RNA}^*, \#_1, \#_2 \in \Sigma_{RNA}\}$ *can be modelled by MIDS.*

Proof. The language L_{C3WJ} can be modelled by MIDS $\Upsilon_{C3WJ} = (\{x, \bar{x}, \triangledown_1, \triangledown_2, \triangledown_3, \triangledown_4\}, \{x, \bar{x}\}, \{\triangledown_1\#_1\#_2 \triangledown_2 \triangledown_3\triangledown_4\}, R)$, where $\#_1, \#_2, x \in \Sigma_{RNA}$, the counterpart of x is $\bar{x}$ and the insertion, deletion rules R are given below:

$R_{I_1} = [(\Lambda, \Lambda/x, \triangledown_1), (\triangledown_4, \Lambda/\bar{x}, \Lambda)], R_{I_2} = [(\Lambda, \Lambda/x, \triangledown_2), (\triangledown_2, \Lambda/\bar{x}, \Lambda)], R_{I_3} = [(\Lambda, \Lambda/x, \triangledown_3), (\triangledown_3, \Lambda/\bar{x}, \Lambda)], R_{D_1} = [(\Lambda, \triangledown_1/\Lambda, \Lambda)], R_{D_2} = [(\Lambda, \triangledown_2/\Lambda, \Lambda)], R_{D_3} = [(\Lambda, \triangledown_3/\Lambda, \Lambda)], R_{D_4} = [(\Lambda, \triangledown_4/\Lambda, \Lambda)].$

The below steps depict a sample derivation for a string from the language L_{C3WJ}:

$$\overset{\downarrow}{\triangledown_1} au \triangledown_2 \triangledown_3\overset{\downarrow}{\triangledown_4} \Longrightarrow_{R_{I_1}} \underline{c} \triangledown_1 au^{\downarrow} \overset{\downarrow}{\triangledown_2} \triangledown_3 \triangledown_4 \underline{g} \Longrightarrow_{R_{I_2}} c \triangledown_1 au\underline{c} \triangledown_2 \underline{g}^{\downarrow} \overset{\downarrow}{\triangledown_3} \triangledown_4 g$$

$$\Longrightarrow_{R_{I_3}} c \triangledown_1 auc \triangledown_2 g\underline{c} \triangledown_3 \underline{g} \triangledown_4 g \Longrightarrow_{R_{D_1}} c^{\Downarrow} auc \triangledown_2 gc \triangledown_3 g \triangledown_4 g$$

$$\Longrightarrow_{R_{D_2}} cauc^{\Downarrow} gc \triangledown_3 g \triangledown_4 g \Longrightarrow_{R_{D_3}} caucgc^{\Downarrow} g \triangledown_4 g \Longrightarrow_{R_{D_4}} caucgcg^{\Downarrow} g.$$

$\triangledown_1, \triangledown_2, \triangledown_3$, and $\triangledown_4$ are used as markers in generating the language. In particular, $v_1\bar{v}_1{}^R$ part of the language is generated by the markers $\triangledown_1$ and $\triangledown_4$. By using such markers a proper synchronization is achieved by having both the insertion rules in a single matrix. The synchronization is achieved in such a way that when x is inserted to the left of the marker ∇_1, simultaneously its complementary $\bar{x}$ is inserted to the right of the marker ∇_4. The marker ∇_2 is used to guide in generating $v_2\bar{v}_2{}^R$ part of the language. The $v_3\bar{v}_3{}^R$ part of the language is generated by the marker ∇_3. As the axiom already contains $\#_1$ and $\#_2$ the need of markers to generate it are not required. Using R_{D_j}, ∇'s can be eliminated. The left and right context of the deletion rules are Λ.   □

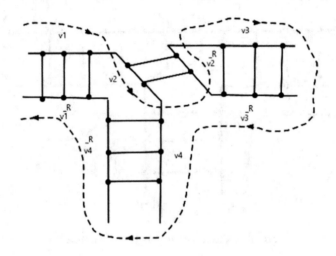

Fig. 3. 3-way loop structure

Theorem 3. *The 3-Way Loop structure (3WL) (see Fig. 3)* $L_{3WL} = \{v_1v_2\bar{v}_2{}^R v_3\bar{v}_3{}^R\ v_4\bar{v}_4{}^R\bar{v}_1{}^R \mid v_1, v_2, v_3, v_4 \in \Sigma_{RNA}^*\}$ *can be modelled by MIDS.*

Proof. The language L_{3WL} can be modelled by MIDS $\Upsilon_{3WL} = (\{x, \bar{x}, \nabla_1, \nabla_2, \nabla_3, \nabla_4\}, \{x, \bar{x}\}, \{\nabla_1\nabla_2\nabla_3\nabla_4\}, R)$, where $x \in \Sigma_{RNA}$, the counterpart of x is $\bar{x}$ and the insertion, deletion rules R are given below:

$R_{I_1} = [(\Lambda, \Lambda/x, \nabla_1), (\nabla_4, \Lambda/\bar{x}, \Lambda)], R_{I_2} = [(\nabla_1, \Lambda/x, \Lambda), (\Lambda, \Lambda/\bar{x}, \nabla_3)], R_{I_3} = [(\nabla_2, \Lambda/x, \Lambda), (\Lambda, \Lambda/\bar{x}, \nabla_3)], R_{I_4} = [(\nabla_3, \Lambda/x, \Lambda), (\Lambda, \Lambda/\bar{x}, \nabla_4)], R_{D_1} = [(\Lambda, \nabla_1/\Lambda, \Lambda)], R_{D_2} = [(\Lambda, \nabla_2/\Lambda, \Lambda)], R_{D_3} = [(\Lambda, \nabla_3/\Lambda, \Lambda)], R_{D_4} = [(\Lambda, \nabla_4/\Lambda, \Lambda)].$

The below steps depict a sample derivation for a string from the language L_{3WL}:

$${}^{\downarrow}\nabla_1 \nabla_2 \nabla_3 \nabla_4^{\downarrow} \Longrightarrow_{R_{I_1}} \underline{a}\nabla_1^{\downarrow}{}^{\downarrow} \nabla_2 \nabla_3 \nabla_4 \underline{u} \Longrightarrow_{R_{I_2}} a \nabla_1 \underline{au} \nabla_2^{\downarrow}{}^{\downarrow} \nabla_3 \nabla_4 u \Longrightarrow_{R_{I_3}}$$

$$a \nabla_1 au \nabla_2 \underline{cg} \nabla_3^{\downarrow}{}^{\downarrow} \nabla_4 u \Longrightarrow_{R_{I_3}} a \nabla_1 au \nabla_2 cg \nabla_3 \underline{gc} \nabla_4 u \Longrightarrow_{R_{D_1}} a^{\Downarrow}au \nabla_2$$

$$cg \nabla_3 gc \nabla_4 u \Longrightarrow_{R_{D_2}} aau^{\Downarrow}cg \nabla_3 gc \nabla_4 u \Longrightarrow_{R_{D_3}} aaucg^{\Downarrow}gc \nabla_4 u$$

$$\Longrightarrow_{R_{D_4}} aaucggc^{\Downarrow}u.$$

$\bigtriangledown_1, \bigtriangledown_2, \bigtriangledown_3$ and $\bigtriangledown_4$ are used as markers in generating the language. In particular, $v_1\bar{v}_1{}^R$ part of the language is generated by the markers $\bigtriangledown_1$ and $\bigtriangledown_4$. By using such markers a proper synchronization is achieved by having both the insertion rules in a single matrix. The synchronization is achieved in such a way that when x is inserted to the left of the marker $\bigtriangledown_1$, simultaneously its complementary $\bar{x}$ is inserted to the right of the marker $\bigtriangledown_4$. The markers $\bigtriangledown_1$ and $\bigtriangledown_2$ is used to guide in generating $v_2\bar{v}_2{}^R$ part of the language. The $v_3\bar{v}_3{}^R$ part of the language is generated by the markers $\bigtriangledown_2$ and $\bigtriangledown_3$. The markers $\bigtriangledown_3$ and $\bigtriangledown_4$ is used to guide in generating $v_4\bar{v}_4{}^R$ part of the language. Using R_{D_j}, $\bigtriangledown$'s can be eliminated. The left and right context of the deletion rules are Λ.   □

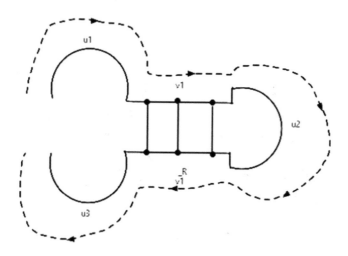

Fig. 4. RNA motif structure-1

Theorem 4. *The RNA Motif Structure 1 (RNAMS1) (see Fig. 4)* $L_{RNAMS1} = \{u_1v_1u_2\bar{v}_1{}^R u_3 \mid u_1, u_2, u_3, v_1 \in \Sigma^*_{RNA}\}$ *can be modelled by MIDS.*

Proof. The language L_{RNAMS1} can be modelled by MIDS $\Upsilon_{RNAMS1} = (\{x, \bar{x}, \bigtriangledown_1, \bigtriangledown_2, \bigtriangledown_3\}, \{x, \bar{x}\}, \{\bigtriangledown_1 \bigtriangledown_2 \bigtriangledown_3\}, R)$, where $x \in \Sigma_{RNA}$, the counterpart of x is $\bar{x}$ and the insertion, deletion rules R are given below:

$$R_{I_1} = [(\Lambda, \Lambda/x, \bigtriangledown_1)], R_{I_2} = [(\bigtriangledown_1, \Lambda/x, \Lambda), (\Lambda, \Lambda/\bar{x}, \bigtriangledown_3)], R_{I_3} = [(\bigtriangledown_2, \Lambda/x, \Lambda)],$$

$$R_{I_4} = [(\bigtriangledown_3, \Lambda/x, \Lambda)], \ R_{D_1} = [(\Lambda, \bigtriangledown_1/\Lambda, \Lambda)], \ R_{D_2} = [(\Lambda, \bigtriangledown_2/\Lambda, \Lambda)], \ R_{D_3} = [(\Lambda, \bigtriangledown_3/\Lambda, \Lambda)].$$

The below steps depict a sample derivation for a string from the language L_{RNAMS1}:

$$^\downarrow \bigtriangledown_1 \bigtriangledown_2 \bigtriangledown_3 \Longrightarrow_{R_{I_1}} \underline{a} \bigtriangledown_1^\downarrow \bigtriangledown_2^\downarrow \bigtriangledown_3 \Longrightarrow_{R_{I_2}} a \bigtriangledown_1 \underline{a} \bigtriangledown_2^\downarrow \underline{u} \bigtriangledown_3 \Longrightarrow_{R_{I_3}} a \bigtriangledown_1 a \bigtriangledown_2^\downarrow \underline{a}u \bigtriangledown_3$$

$$\Longrightarrow_{R_{I_3}} a \bigtriangledown_1 a \bigtriangledown_2 \underline{a}au \bigtriangledown_3 \Longrightarrow_{R_{D_1}} a^\Downarrow a \bigtriangledown_2 aau \bigtriangledown_3 \Longrightarrow_{R_{D_2}} aa^\Downarrow aau \bigtriangledown_3$$

$$\Longrightarrow_{R_{D_3}} aaaau^\Downarrow.$$

∇_1, ∇_2 and ∇_3 are used as markers in generating the language. In particular, $v_1\bar{v}_1{}^R$ part of the language is generated by the markers ∇_1 and ∇_3. By using such markers a proper synchronization is achieved by having both the insertion rules in a single matrix. The synchronization is achieved in such a way that when x is inserted to the right of the marker ∇_1, simultaneously its complementary $\bar{x}$ is inserted to the left of the marker ∇_3. The u_1, u_2 and u_3 part of the language is guided by the markers ∇_1,∇_2 and ∇_3 respectively. As the u_1, u_2 and u_3 is only dependent on inserting x alone, synchronization is not required. Using R_{D_j}, ∇'s can be eliminated. The left and right context of the deletion rules are Λ. □

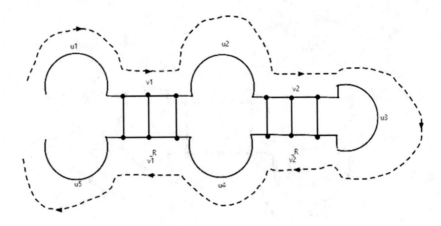

Fig. 5. RNA motif structure-2

Theorem 5. *The RNA Motif Structure 2 (RNAMS2) (see Fig. 5)* $L_{RNAMS2} = \{u_1v_1u_2v_2u_3\bar{v}_2{}^Ru_4\bar{v}_1{}^Ru_5 \mid u_1,u_2,u_3,u_4,u_5,v_1,v_2 \in \Sigma^*_{RNA}\}$ *can be modelled by MIDS.*

Proof. The language L_{RNAMS2} can be modelled by MIDS $\Upsilon_{RNAMS2} = (\{x,\bar{x},\nabla_1, \nabla_2,\nabla_3,\nabla_4,\nabla_5\},\{x,\bar{x}\},\{\nabla_1 \nabla_2 \nabla_3 \nabla_4 \nabla_5\},R)$, where $x \in \Sigma_{RNA}$, the counterpart of x is $\bar{x}$ and the insertion, deletion rules R are given below:

$R_{I_1} = [(\Lambda,\Lambda/x,\nabla_1)], R_{I_2} = [(\Lambda,\Lambda/x,\nabla_2)], R_{I_3} = [(\Lambda,\Lambda/x,\nabla_3)]$,

$R_{I_4} = [(\Lambda,\Lambda/x,\nabla_4)], R_{I_5} = [(\nabla_5,\Lambda/x,\Lambda)], R_{I_6} = [(\nabla_1,\Lambda/x,\nabla_4),(\Lambda,\Lambda/\bar{x},\nabla_5)]$,

$R_{I_7} = [(\nabla_2,\Lambda/x,\Lambda),(\nabla_3,\Lambda/\bar{x},\Lambda)], R_{D_1} = [(\Lambda,\nabla_1/\Lambda,\Lambda)], R_{D_2} = [(\Lambda,\nabla_2/\Lambda,\Lambda)]$,

$R_{D_3} = [(\Lambda,\nabla_3/\Lambda,\Lambda)], R_{D_4} = [(\Lambda,\nabla_4/\Lambda,\Lambda)], R_{D_5} = [(\Lambda,\nabla_5/\Lambda,\Lambda)]$.

The below steps depict a sample derivation for a string from the language L_{RNAMS2}:

$$^{\downarrow}\bigtriangledown_1 \bigtriangledown_2 \bigtriangledown_3 \bigtriangledown_4 \bigtriangledown_5 \Longrightarrow_{R_{I_1}} \underline{a}\,\bigtriangledown_1^{\downarrow} \bigtriangledown_2 \bigtriangledown_3 \bigtriangledown_4 \bigtriangledown_5 \Longrightarrow_{R_{I_2}} a\,\bigtriangledown_1 \underline{c}\,\bigtriangledown_2^{\downarrow} \bigtriangledown_3 \bigtriangledown_4 \bigtriangledown_5$$

$$\Longrightarrow_{R_{I_3}} a\,\bigtriangledown_1 c\,\bigtriangledown_2 \underline{a}\,\bigtriangledown_3^{\downarrow} \bigtriangledown_4 \bigtriangledown_5 \Longrightarrow_{R_{I_4}} a\,\bigtriangledown_1 c\,\bigtriangledown_2 a\,\bigtriangledown_3 \underline{c}\,\bigtriangledown_4 \bigtriangledown_5^{\downarrow} \Longrightarrow_{R_{I_5}} a\,\bigtriangledown_1^{\downarrow} c$$

$$\bigtriangledown_2 a\,\bigtriangledown_3 c\,\bigtriangledown_4^{\downarrow} \bigtriangledown_5 \underline{a} \Longrightarrow_{R_{I_6}} a\,\bigtriangledown_1 \underline{cc}\,\bigtriangledown_2^{\downarrow} a\,\bigtriangledown_3^{\downarrow} c\,\bigtriangledown_4 \underline{g}\,\bigtriangledown_5 a \Longrightarrow_{R_{I_7}} a\,\bigtriangledown_1 cc\,\bigtriangledown_2 \underline{ga}$$

$$\bigtriangledown_3 \underline{cc}\,\bigtriangledown_4 g\,\bigtriangledown_5 a \Longrightarrow_{R_{D_1}} a^{\Downarrow} cc\,\bigtriangledown_2 ga\,\bigtriangledown_3 cc\,\bigtriangledown_4 g\,\bigtriangledown_5 a \Longrightarrow_{R_{D_2}} acc^{\Downarrow} ga\,\bigtriangledown_3 cc\,\bigtriangledown_4 g$$

$$\bigtriangledown_5 a \Longrightarrow_{R_{D_3}} accga^{\Downarrow} cc\,\bigtriangledown_4 g\,\bigtriangledown_5 a \Longrightarrow_{R_{D_4}} accgacc^{\Downarrow} g\,\bigtriangledown_5 a \Longrightarrow_{R_{D_5}} accgaccg^{\Downarrow} a.$$

$\bigtriangledown_1$, $\bigtriangledown_2$, $\bigtriangledown_3$, $\bigtriangledown_4$ and $\bigtriangledown_5$ are used as markers in generating the language. In particular, $v_1\bar{v}_1^{\,R}$ part of the language is generated by the markers $\bigtriangledown_1$ and $\bigtriangledown_5$. By using such markers a proper synchronization is achieved by having both the insertion rules in a single matrix. The synchronization is achieved in such a way that when x is inserted to the right of the marker $\bigtriangledown_1$, simultaneously its complementary $\bar{x}$ is inserted to the left of the marker $\bigtriangledown_5$. The u_1, u_2, u_3, u_4 and u_5 part of the language is guided by the markers $\bigtriangledown_1, \bigtriangledown_2$, $\bigtriangledown_3, \bigtriangledown_4$ and $\bigtriangledown_5$ respectively. As the u_1, u_2, u_3, u_4 and u_5 is only dependent on inserting x alone, synchronization is not required. Using R_{D_j}, $\bigtriangledown$'s can be eliminated. The left and right context of the deletion rules are Λ.   □

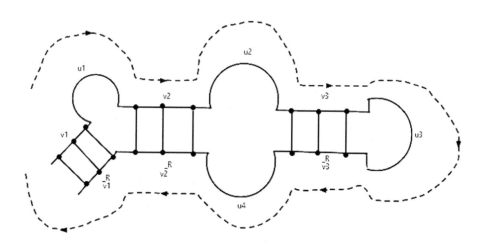

Fig. 6. RNA motif structure-3

Theorem 6. *The RNA Motif Structure 3 (RNAMS3) (see Fig. 6) $L_{RNAMS3} = \{v_1 u_1 v_2 u_2 v_3 u_3 \bar{v}_3^{\,R} u_4 \bar{v}_2^{\,R} \bar{v}_1^{\,R} \mid u_1, u_2, u_3, u_4, v_1, v_2, v_3 \in \Sigma_{RNA}^*\}$ can be modelled by MIDS.*

Proof. The language L_{RNAMS3} can be modelled by MIDS $\Upsilon_{RNAM3} = (\{x, \bar{x}, \nabla_1, \nabla_2, \nabla_3, \nabla_4, \nabla_5\}, \{x, \bar{x}\}, \{\nabla_1 \nabla_2 \nabla_3 \nabla_4 \nabla_5\}, R)$, where $x \in \Sigma_{RNA}$, the counterpart of x is $\bar{x}$ and the insertion, deletion rules R are given below:

$R_{I_1} = [(\nabla_1, \Lambda/x, \Lambda)], R_{I_2} = [(\nabla_2, \Lambda/x, \Lambda)], R_{I_3} = [(\nabla_3, \Lambda/x, \Lambda)], R_{I_4} = [(\nabla_4, \Lambda/x, \Lambda)], R_{I_5} = [(\Lambda, \Lambda/x, \nabla_1), (\nabla_5, \Lambda/\bar{x}, \Lambda)], R_{I_6} = [(\Lambda, \Lambda/x, \nabla_2), (\Lambda, \Lambda/\bar{x}, \nabla_5)], R_{I_7} = [(\Lambda, \Lambda/x, \nabla_3), (\Lambda, \Lambda/\bar{x}, \nabla_4)], R_{D_1} = [(\Lambda, \nabla_1/\Lambda, \Lambda)], R_{D_2} = [(\Lambda, \nabla_2/\Lambda, \Lambda)], R_{D_3} = [(\Lambda, \nabla_3/\Lambda, \Lambda)], R_{D_4} = [(\Lambda, \nabla_4/\Lambda, \Lambda)], R_{D_5} = [(\Lambda, \nabla_5/\Lambda, \Lambda)].$

The below steps depict a sample derivation for a string from the language L_{RNAMS3}:

$$\nabla_1^{\downarrow} \nabla_2 \nabla_3 \nabla_4 \nabla_5 \Longrightarrow_{R_{I_1}} \nabla_1 \underline{a} \nabla_2^{\downarrow} \nabla_3 \nabla_4 \nabla_5 \Longrightarrow_{R_{I_2}} \nabla_1 a \nabla_2 \underline{g} \nabla_3^{\downarrow} \nabla_4 \nabla_5$$

$$\Longrightarrow_{R_{I_3}} \nabla_1 a \nabla_2 g \nabla_3 \underline{u} \nabla_4 \nabla_5 \Longrightarrow_{R_{I_4}} \nabla_1 a \nabla_2 g \nabla_3 u \nabla_4 \underline{u} \nabla_5^{\downarrow}$$

$$\Longrightarrow_{R_{I_5}} \underline{c} \nabla_1 a^{\downarrow} \nabla_2 g \nabla_3 u \nabla_4 u^{\downarrow} \nabla_5 \underline{g} \Longrightarrow_{R_{I_6}} c \nabla_1 a\underline{c} \nabla_2 g^{\downarrow} \nabla_3 u^{\downarrow} \nabla_4 u\underline{g} \nabla_5 g$$

$$\Longrightarrow_{R_{I_7}} c \nabla_1 ac \nabla_2 g\underline{u} \nabla_3 u\underline{a} \nabla_4 ug \nabla_5 g \Longrightarrow_{R_{D_1}} c^{\Downarrow}ac \nabla_2 gu \nabla_3 ua \nabla_4 ug \nabla_5 g$$

$$\Longrightarrow_{R_{D_2}} cac^{\Downarrow}gu \nabla_3 ua \nabla_4 ug \nabla_5 g \Longrightarrow_{R_{D_3}} cacgu^{\Downarrow}ua \nabla_4 ug \nabla_5 g \Longrightarrow_{R_{D_4}} cacg$$

$$uua^{\Downarrow}ug \nabla_5 g \Longrightarrow_{R_{D_5}} cacguuaug^{\Downarrow}g.$$

∇_1, ∇_2, ∇_3, ∇_4 and ∇_5 are used as markers in generating the language. In particular, $v_1\bar{v}_1^R$ part of the language is generated by the markers ∇_1 and ∇_5. By using such markers a proper synchronization is achieved by having both the insertion rules in a single matrix. The synchronization is achieved in such a way that when x is inserted to the right of the marker ∇_1, simultaneously its complementary $\bar{x}$ is inserted to the left of the marker ∇_5. The markers ∇_2 and ∇_5 are used to guide the $v_2\bar{v}_2^R$ part of the language. The $v_3\bar{v}_3^R$ part of the language is guided by the markers ∇_3 and ∇_4. The u_1, u_2, u_3 and u_4 part of the language is guided by the markers ∇_1, ∇_2, ∇_3 and ∇_4 respectively. As the u_1, u_2, u_3 and u_4 is only dependent on inserting x alone, synchronization is not required. Using R_{D_j}, ∇'s can be eliminated. The left and right context of the deletion rules are Λ. $\qquad\square$

Theorem 7. *The RNA Motif Structure 4 (RNAMS4) (see Fig. 7)* $L_{RNAMS4} = \{u_1v_1\#_1v_2u_2\bar{v}_2^R\#_2\bar{v}_1^Ru_3v_3u_4\bar{v}_3^Ru_5v_4u_6\bar{v}_4^Ru_7 \mid u_1, u_2, u_3, u_4, u_5, u_6, u_7, v_1, v_2, v_3, v_4 \in \Sigma_{RNA}^*, \#_1, \#_2 \in \Sigma_{RNA}\}$ *can be modelled by MIDS.*

Proof. The language L_{RNAMS4} can be modelled by MIDS $\Upsilon_{RNAM4} = (\{x, \bar{x}, \nabla_1, \nabla_2, \nabla_3, \nabla_4, \nabla_5, \nabla_6, \nabla_7, \nabla_8\}, \{x, \bar{x}\}, \{\nabla_1\#_1 \nabla_2 \nabla_3\#_2 \nabla_4 \nabla_5 \nabla_6 \nabla_7\nabla_8\}, R)$, where $\#_1, \#_2, x \in \Sigma_{RNA}$, the counterpart of x is $\bar{x}$ and the insertion, deletion rules R are given below:

$R_{I_1} = [(\Lambda, \Lambda/x, \nabla_1)], R_{I_2} = [(\nabla_2, \Lambda/x, \Lambda)], R_{I_3} = [(\nabla_4, \Lambda/x, \Lambda)],$
$R_{I_4} = [(\nabla_5, \Lambda/x, \Lambda)], R_{I_5} = [(\nabla_6, \Lambda/x, \Lambda)], R_{I_6} = [(\nabla_7, \Lambda/x, \Lambda)], R_{I_7} = [(\nabla_8, \Lambda/x, \Lambda)], R_{I_8} = [(\nabla_1, \Lambda/x, \Lambda), (\Lambda, \Lambda/\bar{x}, \nabla_4)], R_{I_9} = [(\Lambda, \Lambda/x, \nabla_5), (\Lambda, \Lambda/\bar{x}, \nabla_6)], R_{I_{10}} = [(\Lambda, \Lambda/x, \nabla_2), (\Lambda, \Lambda/\bar{x}, \nabla_3)], R_{I_{11}} = [(\Lambda, \Lambda/x, \nabla_7), (\Lambda, \Lambda/\bar{x}, \nabla_8)], R_{D_1} = [(\Lambda, \nabla_1/\Lambda, \Lambda)], R_{D_2} = [(\Lambda, \nabla_2/\Lambda, \Lambda)], R_{D_3} = [(\Lambda, \nabla_3/\Lambda, \Lambda)], R_{D_4} =$

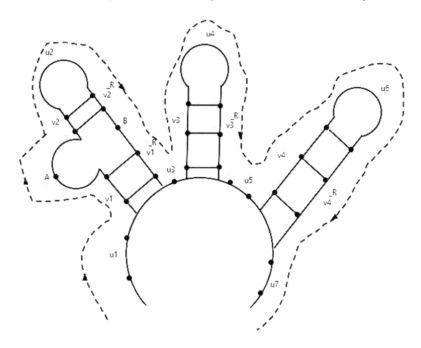

Fig. 7. RNA motif structure-4

$[(\Lambda, \triangledown_4/\Lambda, \Lambda)]$, $R_{D_5} = [(\Lambda, \triangledown_5/\Lambda, \Lambda)]$, $R_{D_6} = [(\Lambda, \triangledown_6/\Lambda, \Lambda)]$, $R_{D_7} = [(\Lambda, \triangledown_7/\Lambda, \Lambda)]$, $R_{D_8} = [(\Lambda, \triangledown_8/\Lambda, \Lambda)]$.

$\triangledown_1$, $\triangledown_2$, $\triangledown_3$, $\triangledown_4$, $\triangledown_5$, $\triangledown_6$, $\triangledown_7$ and $\triangledown_8$ are used as markers in generating the language L_{RNAMS4}. In particular, $v_1\bar{v}_1{}^R$ part of the language is generated by the markers $\triangledown_1$ and $\triangledown_4$. By using such markers a proper synchronization is achieved by having both the insertion rules in a single matrix. The synchronization is achieved in such a way that when x is inserted to the right of the marker $\triangledown_1$, simultaneously its complementary $\bar{x}$ is inserted to the left of the marker $\triangledown_4$. The marker $\triangledown_5$ and $\triangledown_6$ is used to guide the $v_2\bar{v}_2{}^R$ part of the language. The $v_3\bar{v}_3{}^R$ part of the language is guided by the markers $\triangledown_2$ and $\triangledown_3$. The $v_4\bar{v}_4{}^R$ part of the language is guided by the markers $\triangledown_7$ and $\triangledown_8$. The u_1, u_2, u_3, u_4, u_5, u_6 and u_7 part of the language is generated by the markers $\triangledown_1, \triangledown_2, \triangledown_4, \triangledown_5$, $\triangledown_6$, $\triangledown_7$ and $\triangledown_8$respectively. As the u_1, u_2, u_3, u_4, u_5, u_6 and u_7 is only dependent on inserting x alone, synchronization is not required. As the axiom already contains $\#_1$ and $\#_2$ the need of markers to generate it are not required. Using R_{D_j}, $\triangledown$'s can be eliminated. The left and right context of the deletion rules are Λ.   □

Theorem 8. *The RNA Motif Structure 5 (RNAMS5) (see Fig. 8)* $L_{RNAMS5} = \{u_1v_1u_2\bar{v}_1{}^Rv_2u_3v_3u_4\bar{v}_3{}^Ru_5\bar{v}_2{}^Rv_4u_6v_5u_7\bar{v}_5{}^Ru_8\bar{v}_4{}^Ru_9 \mid u_1, u_2, u_3, u_4, u_5, u_6, u_7, u_8,$ $u_9, v_1, v_2, v_3, v_4, v_5 \in \Sigma^*_{RNA}\}$ *can be modelled by MIDS.*

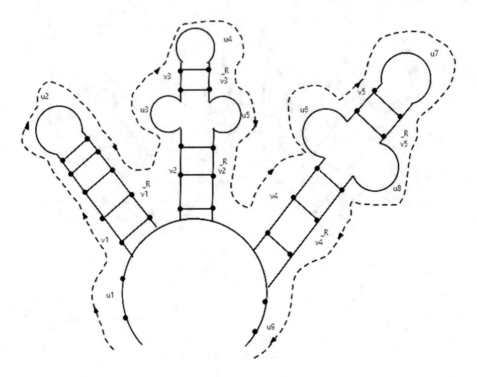

Fig. 8. RNA motif structure-5

Proof. The language L_{RNAMS5} can be modelled by MIDS $\Upsilon_{RNAM5} = (\{x, \bar{x}, \nabla_1, \nabla_2, \nabla_3, \nabla_4, \nabla_5, \nabla_6, \nabla_7, \nabla_8, \nabla_9, \nabla_{10}\}, \{x, \bar{x}\}, \{\nabla_1 \nabla_2 \nabla_3 \nabla_4 \nabla_5 \nabla_6 \nabla_7 \nabla_8 \nabla_9 \nabla_{10}\}, R)$, where $x \in \Sigma_{RNA}$, the counterpart of x is $\bar{x}$ and the insertion, deletion rules R are given below:

$R_{I_1} = [(\Lambda, \Lambda/x, \nabla_1)], R_{I_2} = [(\Lambda, \Lambda/x, \nabla_2)], R_{I_3} = [(\nabla_3, \Lambda/x, \Lambda)],$
$R_{I_4} = [(\nabla_4, \Lambda/x, \Lambda)], R_{I_5} = [(\nabla_5, \Lambda/x, \Lambda)], R_{I_6} = [(\Lambda, \Lambda/x, \nabla_7)],$
$R_{I_7} = [(\Lambda, \Lambda/x, \nabla_8)], R_{I_8} = [(\Lambda, \Lambda/x, \nabla_9)], R_{I_9} = [(\nabla_{10}, \Lambda/x, \Lambda)],$
$R_{I_{10}} = [(\nabla_1, \Lambda/x, \Lambda), (\nabla_2, \Lambda/\bar{x}, \Lambda)], R_{I_{11}} = [(\Lambda, \Lambda/x, \nabla_3), (\Lambda, \Lambda/\bar{x}, \nabla_6)],$
$R_{I_{12}} = [(\Lambda, \Lambda/x, \nabla_4), (\Lambda, \Lambda/\bar{x}, \nabla_5)], R_{I_{13}} = [(\nabla_6, \Lambda/x, \Lambda), (\nabla_9, \Lambda/\bar{x}, \Lambda)],$
$R_{I_{14}} = [(\nabla_7, \Lambda/x, \Lambda), (\nabla_8, \Lambda/\bar{x}, \Lambda)], R_{D_1} = [(\Lambda, \nabla_1/\Lambda, \Lambda)], R_{D_2} = [(\Lambda, \nabla_2/\Lambda, \Lambda)],$
$R_{D_3} = [(\Lambda, \nabla_3/\Lambda, \Lambda)], R_{D_4} = [(\Lambda, \nabla_4/\Lambda, \Lambda)], R_{D_5} = [(\Lambda, \nabla_5/\Lambda, \Lambda)],$
$R_{D_6} = [(\Lambda, \nabla_6/\Lambda, \Lambda)], R_{D_7} = [(\Lambda, \nabla_7/\Lambda, \Lambda)], R_{D_8} = [(\Lambda, \nabla_8/\Lambda, \Lambda)],$
$R_{D_9} = [(\Lambda, \nabla_9/\Lambda, \Lambda)], R_{D_{10}} = [(\Lambda, \nabla_{10}/\Lambda, \Lambda)].$

$\nabla_1, \nabla_2, \nabla_3, \nabla_4, \nabla_5, \nabla_6, \nabla_7, \nabla_8, \nabla_9$ and ∇_{10} are used as markers in generating the language L_{RNAMS5}. In particular, $v_1\bar{v_1}^R$ part of the language is generated by the markers ∇_1 and ∇_2. By using such markers a proper synchronization is achieved by having both the insertion rules in a single matrix. The synchronization is achieved in such a way that when x is inserted to the right of the marker ∇_1, simultaneously its complementary $\bar{x}$ is inserted to the left of the marker $\triangledown_2$. The marker $\triangledown_3$ and $\triangledown_6$ is used to guide the $v_2\bar{v}_2{}^R$ part of the language. The $v_3\bar{v}_3{}^R$ part of the language is guided by the markers $\triangledown_4$ and $\triangledown_5$. The $v_4\bar{v}_4{}^R$ part of the language is guided by the markers $\triangledown_6$ and $\triangledown_9$. The $v_5\bar{v}_5{}^R$ part of the language is guided by the markers $\triangledown_7$ and $\triangledown_8$. The u_1, u_2, u_3, u_4, u_5, u_6, u_7, u_8 and u_9 part of the language is generated by the markers $\triangledown_1, \triangledown_2, \triangledown_3, \triangledown_4$, $\triangledown_5$, $\triangledown_7$, $\triangledown_8$, $\triangledown_9$ and $\triangledown_{10}$ respectively. As the u_1, u_2, u_3, u_4, u_5, u_6, u_7, u_8 and u_9 is only dependent on inserting x alone, synchronization is not required. Using R_{D_j}, $\triangledown$'s can be eliminated. The left and right context of the deletion rules are Λ. □

4   Conclusion

In this paper, we have modelled (some) complicated RNA motifs using MIDS by giving a relevant formal language description. Modelling of complicated structures like α-helix, β-helix, $3D$-structures using MIDS can be considered as a future work.

References

1. Achar, A., Saetrom, P.: RNA motif discovery: a computational overview. Biol. Direct **10**(1), 1–22 (2015)
2. Calude, C.S., Paŭn, Gh.: Computing with Cells and Atoms, An Introduction to Quantum. DNA and Membrane Computing. Taylor and Francis, London (2001)
3. Durbin, R., Eddy, S., Krogh, A., Mitchison, G.: Biological Sequence Analysis. Cambridge Press, Cambridge (1998)
4. Eddy, S.R., Durbin, R.: RNA sequence analysis using covariance models. Nucleic Acids Res. **22**(11), 2079–2088 (1994)
5. Gandhi, M., Caudron-Herger, M., Sven, D.: RNA motifs and combinatorial prediction of interactions, stability and localization of noncoding RNAs. Nat. Struct. Mol. Biol. **25**(12), 1070–1076 (2018)
6. Gardner, P., Eldai, H.: Annotating RNA motifs in sequences and alignments. Nucleic Acids Res. **43**(2), 691–698 (2015)
7. Haussler, D.: Insertion languages. Inf. Sci. **131**(1), 77–89 (1983)
8. Head, T.: Formal language theory and DNA: an analysis of the generative capacity of specific recombinant behaviors. Bull. Math. Biol. **49**, 737–750 (1987)
9. Kari, L., Thierrin, G.: Contextual insertions/deletions and computability. Inf. Comput. **131**(1), 47–61 (1996)
10. Kuppusamy, L., Mahendran, A., Krishna, S.N.: Matrix insertion-deletion systems for bio-molecular structures. In: Natarajan, R., Ojo, A. (eds.) ICDCIT 2011. LNCS, vol. 6536, pp. 301–312. Springer, Heidelberg (2011). https://doi.org/10.1007/978-3-642-19056-8_23
11. Lakshmanan, K., Anand, M., Clergerie, E.V.: Modelling intermolecular structures and defining ambiguity in gene sequences using matrix insertion-deletion systems. In: Biology, Computation and Linguistics, New Interdisciplinary Paradigms, vol. 228, pp. 71–85. IOS Press (2011)
12. Lakshmanan, K., Anand, M.: Modelling DNA and RNA secondary structures using matrix insertion-deletion systems. Int. J. Appl. Math. Comput. Sci. **26**(1), 245–258 (2016)

13. Leontis, N.B., Westhof, E.: Analysis of RNA motifs. Curr. Opin. Struct. Biol. **13**(3), 300–308 (2003)
14. Leontis, N.B., Lescoute, A., Westhof, E.: The building blocks and motifs of RNA architecture. Curr. Opin. Struct. Biol. **16**(3), 279–287 (2006)
15. Lyngso, R.B., Zuker, M., Pedersen, C.N.S.: Internal loops in RNA secondary structure prediction. In: RECOMB99 Proceedings of the 3rd International Conference on Computational Molecular Biology, France, pp. 260–267 (1999)
16. Lyngso, R.B., Pedersen, C.N.S.: Pseudoknots in RNA secondary structure. In: RECOMB00 Proceedings of the 4th Annual International Conference on Computational Molecular Biology, Tokyo, Japan (2000)
17. Onge, S., Thibault, K., Hamel, P., Major, F.: Modeling RNA tertiary structure motifs by graph-grammars. Nucleic Acids Res. **35**(5), 1726–1736 (2007)
18. Păun, Gh., Rozenberg, G., Salomaa, A.: DNA Computing, New Computing Paradigms. Springer, Heidelberg (1998). https://doi.org/10.1007/978-3-662-03563-4
19. Quadrini, M., Merelli, E., Piergallini, R.: Loop grammars to identify RNA structural patterns. Bioinformatics 302–309 (2019)
20. Rivas, E., Eddy, S.R.: The language of RNA: a formal grammar that includes pseudoknots. Bioinformatics **16**, 334–340 (2000)
21. Sakakibara, Y., et al.: Stochastic context-free grammars for tRNA modelling. Nucleic Acids Res. **22**, 5112–5120 (1996)
22. Searls, D.B.: The linguistics of DNA. Am. Sci. 579–591 (1992)
23. Searls, D.B.: The computational linguistics of biological sequences. In: Hunter, L. (ed.) Artificial Intelligence and Molecular Biology, pp. 47–120. AAAI Press (1993)
24. Searls, D.B.: Formal grammars for intermolecular structures. In: First International IEEE Symposium on Intelligence and Biological Systems, pp. 30–37 (1995)
25. Yuki, S., Kasami, T.: RNA pseudoknotted structure prediction using stochastic multiple context-free grammar. IPSJ Trans. Bioinform. **47**, 12–21 (2006)

Pupil Segmentation Using Stirling's Interpolation Based Fractional Differential Mask

A. R. Kiruthiga[1]([✉]) and R. Arumuganathan[2]

[1] Researcher, Coimbatore, Tamil Nadu, India
kiruthi_am07@yahoo.co.in
[2] Department of Mathematics, PSG College of Technology, Coimbatore, India
ran.maths@psgtech.ac.in

Abstract. Pupil localization is one of the significant pre-processing steps in iris recognition system, which plays a vital role in human authentication system. This paper proposes a novel approach for computerized pupil segmentation. A new fractional differential mask based on Stirling's interpolation, has been employed to snip the pupil efficiently from the iris image. The pupil is segmented based on the dynamic threshold. The new mask and the dynamic threshold are the key factors in segmenting the pupil region. The proposed algorithm is implemented using MATLAB and tested on two public iris databases such as CASIA V1.0 and MMU2. Experimental results clearly indicate that the proposed method is comparably accurate in segmenting pupil with existing methods irrespective of its shape; the proposed method is also capable of handling low contrast images, specular reflections or images occluded by eyelids and eyelashes.

Keywords: Pupil segmentation · Fractional differential mask · Interpolation

1 Introduction

Recent developments in science and technology emphasize on biometric based security systems for personal verification and identification, owing to high reliability and accuracy. Biometric technology has a wide range of applications including unique identity detection, computer network log on, electronic data security, ATMs, credit card purchases, mobile phones, medical records management, airport and border security, crime control etc.,

With the increasing demands for safety and security, it is necessary to have secured identification systems. Amid the biometric traits available, we focus on the most accurate, reliable, stable and unique characteristic – iris, which remains unchanged for the entire lifetime of a person. It is also observed that the irises of twins are completely different; similarly, the two irises of same person are also not identical. The iris is a thin, circular shaped area in between the pupil and the sclera, containing many features like freckles, stripes, corneas, arching ligaments, zigzag collarette area etc., as shown in the following eye image (Fig. 1). The pupil is the central transparent area, surrounded by the iris; it

I. Raman et al. (Eds.): ICC3 2021, CCIS 1631, pp. 153–166, 2022.
https://doi.org/10.1007/978-3-031-15556-7_11

appears black in colour, as light rays entering the eye through the pupil are absorbed by the tissues inside the eye. The search space for finding the center of the iris is minimized if the pupil is localized accurately as the center of the iris lies inside the pupil. In general, the behaviour of an iris recognition system is mainly based on iris localization and segmentation.

The most intensive task in iris recognition is isolating iris from pupil, sclera, eyelashes and eyebrows, which is called iris segmentation. We need to accurately determine the inner and outer boundaries of the iris, which forms the basis for normalization, feature extraction, code generation and matching.

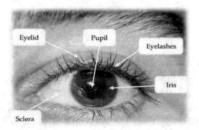

Fig. 1. Eye image for iris recognition

2   Related Works

Most of the algorithms assume the shape of the pupil as a circle. A denoising mask using improved fractional differentiation [19] preserves edges better than the existing methods, which require more iteration to ensure the stability and convergence. Medical images are enhanced adaptively based on the dynamic gradient feature of the image [3, 10]. Local descriptors named as principal patterns of fractional-order differential gradients [14] are designed for face recognition. Though, the local shape information and spatial information are preserved for face images, still the computational complexity of the method needs to be improved. The images enhanced by fractional differential mask using Newton's interpolation [6] retain more textural information in the enhanced images, compared to the traditional fractional differential operator. But the results are based only on few gray scale images chosen for experimentation.

An edge gradient algorithm combined with improved Hough transform is used to locate the pupil center [9] based on the assumption that the pupil is circular, which may not be practical in all situations. Six fractional differential masks [27] were defined, which has constant values for fractional orders that may change, if area features of the image are altered. Automatic pupil segmentation based on threshold, area and eccentricity of local histogram is implemented on FPGA using a non-iterative scheme [22]. But when the eccentricity values are equal- this approach fails to locate the pupil region. A multiscale approach for edge detection [7] is extended to locate the pupil center, the length of the semi-axes and its orientation. The drawback of this method is the assumption, which is the shape of the pupil is elliptic and the image is blurred by a Gaussian kernel, which may not be conventional in all situations.

The pupil is localized automatically using histogram thresholding and mask filter from the region with highest probability [18], where the technique for choosing the value of structuring element and constructing the region may be optimized. Fuzzy linear discriminant analysis with wavelet transforms [4, 25] is used to extract the iris features. The pupil is then recognized based on a pixel unit by measuring its area and diameter. Another solution to localize the pupil using eccentricity along with gray levels is developed [23]. The iris is then localized by finding the gradient of gray level profile extracted from directional decomposition of the eye image. Though it addresses the problem of eyelids and eyelashes, it fails to detect the pupil region in the presence of specular reflections. Another drawback is that, this method is computationally hard because of its iterative nature. A Graph cut method to segment the pupil region for iris recognition [15] considers only the gray level information whose performance may be deteriorated when the noises in the image are present with the same gray level.

Most of the techniques reported in literature for locating the boundary of the pupil are circular-edge based and histogram-based techniques. Circular-edge based techniques like Hough transform are sensitive to noise and have high computational complexity. Also, these methods show poor performance in case of low contrast images and specular reflections. While, the histogram-based techniques fails when the other parts of the eye have the same gray level as pupil region or when the eyes are partially opened and have dense eyelashes. The fractional differential masks obtained using Gauss and Lagrange interpolation formulas are found to be more suitable for image enhancement rather than segmentation.

In this paper, a new mathematical approach for automatic pupil segmentation using the newly derived fractional differential mask, based on the technique of Stirling's interpolation is proposed. Stirling's formula gives more accurate results than other interpolation formula, considering few terms of the function values. This is a non-iterative method and the pupil region are segmented based on the dynamic threshold; this approach works well in the presence of specular reflections, partially opened eyes and also, when the eyes are occluded by the eyelashes and eyelids or even in the presence of spectacles.

3   Theoretical Background of Fractional Differentials

Recent researches on engineering applications are concentrating on fractional calculus. Fractional derivative plays an important role in various fields such as solid mechanics, astro physics, nano plasmonics, biology, electricity, modeling, visco elasticity, robotics etc. Most of the edge detection operators such as Sobel, Prewitt and Roberts, in image processing are based on integer-order differentiation; the concept of non-integer differentiation or fractional differentiation which is the generalization of integer-order differentiation is currently employed in the fields of signal and image analysis. Fractional differentials are the best descriptors of natural phenomena [27] as they non-linearly enhance the complex texture features. They also preserve the low frequency details in smooth areas and high-frequency marginal details in the region. The traditional fractional differential operators usually not successful in processing pixels corrupted by noise and with small correlations.

3.1 Definition

The definition for fractional derivative given by Grunwald-Letnikov (G-L), Riemann Liouville (R-L) and Caputo [21] are most popular in Euclidean space. The R-L definition is for analytical purpose; G-L based derivative is used mainly for discrete computation in digital image processing applications. The G-L based v-order differential [20, 21] of a signal F(t) is,

$$D^v F(t) = \lim_{h \to 0} \frac{F^{(v)}(t)}{} = \lim_{h \to 0} \frac{h^{-v}}{\Gamma(-v)} \sum_{m=0}^{n-1} (-1)^m \frac{\Gamma(v+1)}{m!\Gamma(v-m+1)} F(t-mh) \quad (1)$$

where n = (t−a)/h, is the step size and $\Gamma(t) = (t-1)!$ is the gamma function of t. For all $v \in R$ (R represents the real set and [v] is its integral part), the duration of the signal F(t) is [a, t], where $a < t$, $a \in R$, $t \in R$, has m^{th} (m ∈ Z, Z represents integer set) order continuous differentiation. When $v > 0$, m is not less than [v]. The geometric meaning of fractional derivative of the signal f(t) is the fractional slope and its physical meaning is the fractional flow or speed, while the fractional order v is the fractional equilibrium coefficient. It is also the generalized amplitude modulation and phase modulation of the signal [3, 27].

Grunwald-Letnikov based fractional differential mask has been used for enhancing retinal images [12]. The degree of texture enhancement and effect of noise is controlled by the use of fractional differential. G-L fractional differential mask is also used to smoothen the iris images, which plays a key role in highlighting the essential features of the iris image for segmentation. The pupil is then segmented using wavelet transforms [13]. This method is efficient in segmenting the pupil regardless of its shape and noise in the image.

3.2 Fractional Differential Filter

For a two dimensional signal f(x, y), the v-order differentiation along the x and y direction of the signal will be

$$\frac{\partial^v f(x, y)}{\partial x^v} \cong f(x, y) + (-v)f(x-1, y) + \frac{(-v)(-v+1)}{2} f(x-2, y) + \ldots$$

$$+ \frac{\Gamma(n-v-1)}{(n-1)!\Gamma(-v)} f(x-n+1, y) \quad (2)$$

$$\frac{\partial^v f(x, y)}{\partial y^v} \cong f(x, y) + (-v)f(x, y-1) + \frac{(-v)(-v+1)}{2} f(x, y-2) + \ldots$$

$$+ \frac{\Gamma(n-v-1)}{(n-1)!\Gamma(-v)} f(x-n+1, y) \quad (3)$$

We observe that the sum of non-zero coefficients 1, $-v$, $(-v(-v+1)/2)$,..... $(\Gamma(-v+1)/(n-1)! \ \Gamma(-v+n))$ is not zero, which is the explicit difference between fractional differential and integer based differentials. In other words, the low-frequency component of signal is zero in integer differential, but it is non-zero, in the case of fractional differentials. This is the motivation for using fractional differentiation in the field of image processing.

Any $k \times k$ sized mask with fractional order is known as the fractional differential mask (filter). Figure 2 shows 3×3 fractional differential mask along the x and y directions from Eqs. (2) and (3).

$$
(a) \begin{bmatrix} 0 & 0 & 0 \\ \dfrac{v^2 - v}{2} & -v & 1 \\ 0 & 0 & 0 \end{bmatrix} \qquad (b) \begin{bmatrix} 0 & \dfrac{v^2 - v}{2} & 0 \\ 0 & -v & 0 \\ 0 & 1 & 0 \end{bmatrix}
$$

Fig. 2. Fractional differential mask in (a) x direction and (b) y direction

4   Formulation of New Segmentation Mask

The pursuance of the existing fractional differential operators needs to be improved for image processing applications. So, we use the approach of Stirling's interpolation to shape the fractional differential operator for image segmentation. Define any point between $t - mh - h$ and $t - mh + h$. When $v \in [-1, 1]$, let $\xi = t - mh + (v/2)h$. Then, the signal $F(t)$ in (1) using the Stirling interpolation becomes,

$$
F(\xi) = F(x_0) + \left[\frac{\xi - x_0}{h}\right]\left[\frac{F(x_1) - F(x_{-1})}{2}\right] + \frac{1}{2!}\left[\frac{\xi - x_0}{h}\right]^2 [F(x_1) - 2F(x_0) + F(x_{-1})]
$$

$$
+ \frac{1}{3!}\left[\frac{\xi - x_0}{h}\right]\left[\left(\frac{\xi - x_0}{h}\right)^2 - 1\right]\left[\frac{F(x_2) - 2F(x_1) + 2F(x_{-1}) - F(x_{-2})}{2}\right]
$$

$$
+ \dots \tag{4}
$$

where $x_0 = t - mh$, $x_1 = t - mh - h$, $x_{-1} = t - mh + h$, $x_2 = t - mh - 2h$ and $x_{-2} = t - mh + 2h$, substituting these values and ξ in the above Eq. (4) and simplifying we get,

$$
F(\xi) = \left(1 - \frac{v^2}{4}\right)F(t - mh) + \left(\frac{16v + 6v^2 - v^3}{48}\right)[F(t - mh - h)]
$$

$$
+ \left(\frac{v^3 - 4v}{96}\right)[F(t - mh - 2h)] + \left(\frac{6v^2 - 16v + v^3}{48}\right)[F(t - mh + h)]
$$

$$
- \left(\frac{v^3 - 4v}{96}\right)[F(t - mh + 2h)] + \dots\dots\dots \tag{5}
$$

The above Eq. (5), gives a signal value $F(\xi)$ for any new point. It can be noted that the new signal $F(\xi)$ is a linear combination of the points, $F(x_{-2})$, $F(x_{-1})$, $F(x_0)$, $F(x_1)$ and $F(x_2)$, thus $F(\xi)$ will contain more information from its neighborhood points. Since the shortest changing distance of gray-level is one pixel (i.e., h = 1), when we replace F(t) in (1) by F(ξ), from (5), the new approximation on expanding would be as follows:

$$
\frac{d^v F(t)}{dt^v} = \left(-\frac{v}{3} + \frac{v^2}{12} + \frac{v^3}{48} + \frac{v^4}{96}\right) F(t+h) + \left(1 + \frac{17v^2}{48} - \frac{7v^3}{48} - \frac{5v^4}{192} + \frac{v^5}{192}\right) F(t)
$$

$$
+ \left(-\frac{2v}{3} + \frac{14v^2}{48} + \frac{5v^4}{96} + \frac{v^5}{96}\right) F(t-h) + \left(\frac{v}{24} - \frac{v^3}{96}\right) F(t+2h) + \ldots +
$$

$$
\frac{\Gamma(m-v)}{\Gamma(-v)\Gamma(m+1)}
\begin{bmatrix}
\left(1 - \frac{v^2}{4}\right) F(t-mh) + \left(\frac{16v + 6v^2 - v^3}{48}\right)[F(t-mh-h)] + \\
\left(\frac{v^3 - 4v}{96}\right)[F(t-mh-2h)] + \\
\left(\frac{6v^2 - 16v + v^3}{48}\right)[F(t-mh+h)] \\
- \left(\frac{v^3 - 4v}{96}\right)[F(t-mh+2h)]
\end{bmatrix} + \ldots
$$

(6)

The above Eq. (6) is the new fractional differentiation of F(t) based on Stirling's interpolation. This expression actually gives an approximated value as it simplifies fractional differentiation. The coefficients of F(t + h), F(t), F(t−h).. F(t−nh) in the above Eq. (6) be denoted as,

$$
a_{-2} = \left(\frac{v}{24} - \frac{v^3}{96}\right)
$$

$$
a_{-1} = \left(-\frac{v}{3} + \frac{v^2}{12} + \frac{v^3}{48} + \frac{v^4}{96}\right)
$$

$$
a_0 = \left(1 + \frac{17v^2}{48} - \frac{7v^3}{48} - \frac{5v^4}{192} + \frac{v^5}{192}\right)
$$

$$
a_1 = \left(-\frac{2v}{3} + \frac{14v^2}{48} + \frac{5v^4}{96} + \frac{v^5}{96}\right)
$$

....

$$
a_n = \left(\frac{v}{24} - \frac{v^3}{96}\right) \frac{\Gamma(n-v-3)}{\Gamma(-v)\Gamma(n-2)} + \left(-\frac{v}{3} + \frac{v^2}{12} + \frac{v^3}{48} + \frac{v^4}{96}\right) \frac{\Gamma(n-v-2)}{\Gamma(-v)\Gamma(n-1)} +
$$
$$
\left(1 + \frac{17v^2}{48} - \frac{7v^3}{48} - \frac{5v^4}{192} + \frac{v^5}{192}\right) \frac{\Gamma(n-v-1)}{\Gamma(-v)\Gamma(n)} +
$$
$$
\left(-\frac{2v}{3} + \frac{14v^2}{48} + \frac{5v^4}{96} + \frac{v^5}{96}\right) \frac{\Gamma(n-v)}{\Gamma(-v)\Gamma(n+1)}
$$

Using the above values, Eq. (6) becomes,

$$
\frac{d^v F(t)}{dt^v} \cong a_{-2} F(t+2h) + a_{-1} F(t+h) + a_0 F(t) + a_1 F(t-h) +
$$

$$
a_2 F(t-2h) + \ldots + a_n F(t-nh) \tag{7}
$$

In order to ensure that the fractional differential masks are rotation invariant (isotropic), the proposed improved differential, 3×3 masks are constructed in eight symmetric directions (e.g. 0°, 45°, 90°, 135°, 180°, 225°, 270°, 315°) namely (i) negative y-coordinate, (ii) positive y-coordinate (iii) positive x-coordinate, (iv) negative x-coordinate, (v) left upper diagonal, (vi) left lower diagonal, (vii) right upper diagonal (viii) and right lower diagonal respectively as shown in the Fig. 3 below:

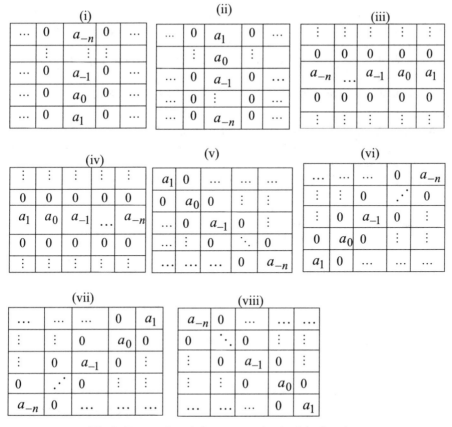

Fig. 3. Proposed mask for segmentation in eight directions

5 Proposed Method

The pupil is the large dark region, which differs from other parts of the eye not only with their physical characteristics, but also on the gray levels. This difference in the gray level motivated to segment the pupil from other parts of the eye. In this paper, we have used a newly designed fractional differential mask to locate the pupil. The true pupil region is isolated from the iris images by means of correlation in linear filtering - the Stirling's interpolation based fractional differential mask with the iris image. The threshold used to detect the pupil region is estimated dynamically from the gradient magnitude. These are the two factors, which play a key role for accurate pupil segmentation. The algorithm of the new fractional differential based Stirling's interpolation approach for pupil segmentation is described below:

New Pupil Segmentation Algorithm

Step 1: Input a gray scale image f. If it is a colour image, convert it to gray scale.

Step 2: Input the fractional differential order ν for the 3×3 sized differential mask,w.
Step 3: Calculate the values of coefficients a_0, a_1 and a_{-1} and define the mask, w in x and y directions.
Step 4: Calculate the gradients in x and y direction based on the defined mask using correlation in linear filtering.
Step 5: Calculate the magnitude of the gradient G_m using the formula,
$$G_m = \sqrt{g_x^2 + g_y^2}$$
Step 6: Compute the minimum value for each column of G_m.
Step 7: Compute the threshold T which is the average of all values computed in Step 6.
//dynamic threshold
Step 8: Check whether the gradient magnitude is greater than the given threshold, T.

    i.e., for each row r_i in G_m
        for each column c_i in G_m
           if $(G_m (r_i , c_i) > T)$
              seg $(r_i , c_i) = 1$ // seg is the segmented region
        else
           seg $(r_i , c_i) = 0$
        end if
        end for
    end for

Step 9: Display the segmented pupil region.
Step 10: Display the pupil boundary in the original image using the segmented region.

Here, the fractional differential order of 0.3 is chosen experimentally for pupil segmentation and the corresponding 3×3 masks are given below:

(a)				(b)		
0	0	0		0	-0.1733	0
-0.1733	1.0277	-0.0919		0	1.0277	0
0	0	0		0	-0.0919	0

Fig. 4. Fractional differential mask for $\nu = 0.3$ in positive (a) x direction and (b) y direction

6 Results and Discussion

We have evaluated the legitimacy of the proposed method on two public databases: CASIA Version 1.0 [5] and MMU version 2 database [16]. The proposed algorithm is implemented in MATLAB 7.50 on a computer with E5 2670v2 processor, 64 GB RAM and 8 TB Hard disk. The output images by the proposed method are obtained by using the proposed masks shown in Fig. 4. It is also evident from the Fig. 5 that the proposed method outperforms in segmenting the pupil region, compared to the well-known segmentation algorithms [7] like Canny, Sobel and Laplacian of Gaussian. These existing methods identify the pupil region together with more noises, which makes them unsuitable for pupil segmentation.

The performance of the proposed method is measured using the accuracy rate (AC_{rate}) [17] which is based on the accuracy error (A_{err}), defined as

$$A_{err} = \frac{|N_{pact} - N_{pdet}|}{N_{pact}} x100 \qquad (8)$$

where N_{pact} and N_{pdet} are the number of actual and detected pupil pixels, respectively. The actual and detected pupil pixels are obtained using functions in the image processing tool ImageJ [11]. If A_{err} is less than 10%, then the detected pupil is marked as the true pupil. AC_{rate} is defined as follows:

$$AC_{rate} = \frac{N_{success}}{N_{total}} \times 100 \qquad (9)$$

where $N_{success}$ is the total number of eye images in which the pupil has been localized successfully and N_{total} is the total number of images in the database. The detailed descriptions of the experimental results are as follows:

6.1 Experimental Setup1

In the first setup, results are obtained by testing the proposed algorithm on CASIA Version 1.0 Iris database. It contains 756 eye images of 108 persons, 7 images of each person, with a resolution of 320×280 pixels. Table 1 and 2 show the accuracy rates and accuracy error values of pupil segmentation by the proposed method for sample images from CASIA V1 database.

Table 1. Pupil segmentation comparison with existing methods on CASIA Version 1.0 (the results given by respective authors)

Author	Accuracy (%)
Daugman [8]	98.60
Basit [2]	99.60
Wildes [26]	99.90
Proposed method	99.98

Table 2. Accuracy error values of the proposed method for sample images from CASIA Version 1.0 database

S. No	Images	Area of pupil region (in pixels)		Accuracy error, A_{err}
		Original image	Segmented image	
1	051_1_1	6917	6861	0.008
2	051_1_3	6416	6414	0.0003
3	051_2_1	5739	5651	0.0002
4	051_2_4	5981	5894	0.0145
5	052_1_2	5442	5351	0.016
6	052_2_2	5701	5689	0.002
7	053_1_3	7847	7825	0.0028
8	054_1_2	5252	5138	0.02
9	054_1_3	6004	5890	0.019
10	055_1_1	4088	3978	0.027
11	055_1_3	3675	3666	0.0025
12	055_2_2	4204	4035	0.04
13	056_1_3	5402	5345	0.01
14	061_2_4	12365	12242	0.0099
15	062_2_1	3955	3756	0.05

The numbers quoted under images in the Table 2 and 3 are the names of images given in the databases.

Each image in MMU database contains a white spot in the pupil region due to specular reflection. Therefore, it is necessary to reduce the effect of this white spot, by means of filters. It is also noted that few images in this database are occluded by eyelashes or has dense eyebrows. In order to remove these noises, most of the existing methods have used separate filters or have pre-processed the images before applying their technique. But, the greatest advantage of the proposed method is that this newly defined fractional differential mask acts as a filter in removing these noises, even in the presence of spectacles and segments the pupil region more accurately. The computational time for the proposed method is 1.037 s on an average. A comparative analysis of the proposed method with few existing methods is shown in Table 1 and 4 for the two databases.

6.2 Experimental Setup2

In the next setup, results are obtained by testing the proposed algorithm on MMU 2.0 Iris database. It contains 995 contributed by 100 persons, 5 images per person, with a resolution of 320 × 240 pixels. Table 3 and 4 show the accuracy error values and accuracy rates of pupil segmentation by the proposed method for sample images from MMU 2 database.

Table 3. Accuracy error values of the proposed method for sample images from MMU 2.0 database

S. No	Images	Area of pupil region (in pixels)		Accuracy error, A_{err}
		Original image	Segmented image	
1	010101	773	778	0.006
2	010102	828	841	0.01
3	010105	1024	1030	0.005
4	020101	1359	1274	0.06
5	020105	763	720	0.056
6	020201	1339	1294	0.03
7	010202	749	682	0.089
8	010204	633	630	0.0047
9	030103	905	882	0.025
10	040104	1260	1256	0.003
11	040204	909	892	0.018
12	050105	1010	1011	0.00099
13	060203	776	767	0.01
14	080104	1214	1203	0.009
15	080202	829	909	0.096

Table 4. Pupil segmentation comparison with existing methods on MMU 2.0 (the results given by respective authors)

Author	Accuracy (%)
Wildes [26]	96.8
Teo [24]	98.4
Abdullah [1]	93.7
Proposed method	99.99

The results in Tables 1 and 4 show that the proposed algorithm has higher accuracy than the existing techniques for both the databases. The values of statistical measures computed based on the accuracy error is listed in Table 5. The accuracy error values listed in the Tables 2 and 3 are calculated based on the Eq. (8). These values indicate that the accuracy error of the entire images in the databases falls below 10%. Hence, an accuracy rate of 99.98% is achieved for CASIA V1 database images and 99.99% of accuracy is obtained for MMU2 database images, based on the average accuracy error, shown in the Table 5.

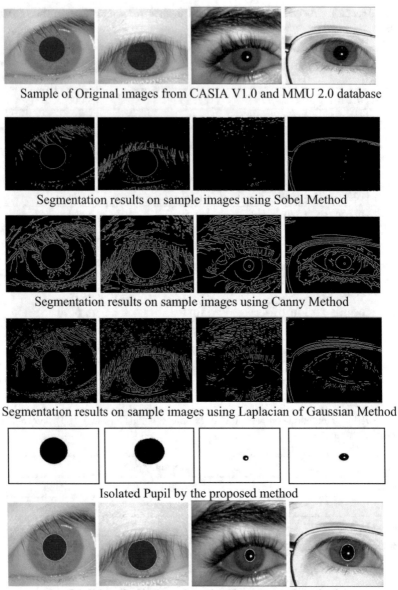

Sample of Original images from CASIA V1.0 and MMU 2.0 database

Segmentation results on sample images using Sobel Method

Segmentation results on sample images using Canny Method

Segmentation results on sample images using Laplacian of Gaussian Method

Isolated Pupil by the proposed method

Pupil localization results using the proposed method

Fig. 5. Segmentation results of the existing and proposed method from CASIAV1.0 and MMU2 database

Table 5. Statistical measures to evaluate the proposed method

Measure	CASIA V1 database	MMU2 database
Total number of images	756	995
Minimum AC_{error}	0.00039	0
Maximum AC_{error}	0.05	0.096
Standard deviation	0.007995	0.008523
Average AC_{error}	0.0176	0.01209

7 Conclusion

In this paper, a new method for segmenting the pupil region from iris images using the concept of Stirling's interpolation on fractional derivative is proposed. This paper presents an innovative view of using fractional derivative together with Stirling's interpolation for segmenting the pupil from the eye image. The pupil region is segmented from the eye image based on the dynamic threshold. This threshold overcomes the drawbacks of histogram-based thresholding. The performance of the proposed method is not deteriorated even in the presence of dense eyelashes, eyelids and spectacles. The research also reveals that the proposed mask acts as a filter or preprocessor to remove the noises. Experimental results, proves that the proposed method is highly accurate, compared to the reported ones. Hence, the proposed method can be chosen for iris recognition-based security applications and also in the fields of Ophthalmology.

Future work will involve extending this method for a complete iris recognition system.

Acknowledgements. The authors wish to thank the Chinese Academy of Science-Institute of Automation (CASIA) for providing CASIA Version 1.0 iris database and Multimedia University for providing MMU2 iris database.

References

1. Abdullah, M.A.M., Dlay, S.S., Woo, W.L., Chambers, J.A.: Robust iris segmentation method based on a new active contour force with a noncircular normalization. IEEE Trans. Syst. Man Cybern. **99**, 1–14 (2016)
2. Basit, A., Javed, M.: Localization of iris in grayscale image using intensity gradient. Opt. Lasers Eng. **45**, 1107–1114 (2007)
3. Li, B., Xie, W.: Adaptive fractional differential approach and its application to medical image enhancement. Comput. Electr. Eng. **45**, 324–335 (2015)
4. Boyina, S.R., Anu, H., Moneca, K., Mahalakshmi, G.M., Priyadharshini, R.: Pupil recognition using wavelet and fuzzy linear discriminant analysis for authentication. Int. J. Adv. Eng. Technol. (2012)
5. CASIA iris image database (Ver 1.0). http://biometrics.idealtest.org/
6. Gao, C., Zhou, J., Lang, F., Liu, C.: A new fractional differential mask for image enhancement. J. Convergence Inf. Technol. **8**(4), (2013)

7. Lacoviello, D., Lucchetti, M.: Parametric characterization of the form of the human pupil from blurred noisy images. Comput. Methods Programs Biomed. **77**, 39–48 (2005)
8. Daugman, J.G.: High confidence visual recognition of person by a test of statistical independence. IEEE Trans. Pattern Anal. Mach. Intell. **15**, 1148–1161 (1993)
9. Chen, D., Bai, J., Qu, Z.: Research on pupil center location based on improved Hough transform and edge gradient algorithm. In: National Conference on Information Technology and Computer Science, pp. 47–51 (2012)
10. Hu, F., Si, S., Wong, H.S., Fu, B., Si, M.X., H. Luo: An adaptive approach for texture enhancement based on a fractional differential operator with non-integer step and order. Neurocomputing **158**, 295–306 (2015)
11. ImageJ software. https://imagej.nih.gov/ij/index.html
12. Kiruthiga, A.R., Arumuganathan, R.: Fractional differential mask based retinal image enhancement – a new approach. Transylvanian Rev. **XXIV**(10), 1647–1659 (2016)
13. Kiruthiga, A.R., Arumuganathan, R.: Smoothening of iris images and pupil segmentation using fractional derivative and wavelet transform. In: 4th International Conference on Signal Processing, Communications and Networking (ICSCN), pp. 1–6. IEEE (2017). https://doi.org/10.1109/ICSCN.2017.8085713
14. Yu, L., Cao, Q., Zhao, A.: Principal patterns of fractional-order differential gradients for face recognition. J. Electr. Imaging **24**(1), 013021 (2015)
15. Mehrabian, H., Hashemi-Tari, P.: Pupil boundary detection for Iris recognition using Graph cuts. In: Proceedings of Image and Vision Computing, pp. 77–82. New Zealand (2007)
16. MMU 2 Iris Image Database. http://pesona.mmu.edu.my/~ccteo/
17. Ibrahim, M.T., Khan, T.M., Khan, S.A., Khan, M.A., Guan, L.: Iris localization using local histogram and other image statistics. Opt. Lasers Eng. **50**, 645–654 (2012)
18. Sahoo, N., Padhy, G., Bhoi, N., Rautaray, P.: Automatic localization of pupil using Histogram thresholding and region mask filter. Soft Comput. Tech. Vis. Sci. SCI **395**, 55–62 (2012)
19. He, N., Wang, J.-B., Zhang, L.-L., Lu, K.: An improved fractional-order differentiation model for image denoising. Sig. Process. **112**, 180–188 (2015)
20. Oldham, K.B., Spanier: The Fractional Calculus: Integrations and Differentiations of Arbitrary Order. Academic, New York (1974)
21. Samko, S.G., Kilbas, A.A., Marichev, O.I.: Fractional integrals and derivatives: theory and applications. Yverdon, Swizterland. Gordon and Breach (1993)
22. Khan, T.M., Kong, Y., Khan, M.A.U.: Hardware implementation of fast pupil segmentation using region properties. In: 12th International Conference on Quality Control by Artificial Vision. Proceedings of SPIE 9534 (2015)
23. Khan, T.M., Khan, M.A., Malik, S.A., Khan, S.A., Bashir, T., Dar, A.H.: Automatic localization of pupil using eccentricity and iris using gradient based method. Opt. Lasers Eng. **49**, 177–187 (2011)
24. Teo, C.C., Neo, H.F., Michael, G.K.O., Tee, C., Sim, K.S.: A robust iris segmentation with fuzzy supports. In: Wong, K.W., Mendis, B.S.U., Bouzerdoum, A. (eds.) Proceedings of ICONIP 2010. LNCS, vol. 6443, pp. 532–539. Springer, Heidelberg (2010). https://doi.org/10.1007/978-3-642-17537-4_65
25. Roselin, V., Waghmare, L.M.: Pupil detection and feature extraction algorithm for Iris recognition. Adv. Model. Optim. **15**(2) (2013)
26. Wildes, R.P.: Iris Recognition: an emerging biometric technology. Proc. IEEE **85**, 1348–1363 (1997)
27. Pu, Y.-F., Zhou, J.-L., Yuan, X.: Fractional differential mask: a fractional differential-based approach for multiscale texture enhancement. IEEE Trans. Image Process. **19**(2), 491–511 (2010)

EPAS: An Ergonomic Posture Analysis System

S. M. Vaishale⬤, B. Junaita Davakumar$^{(\boxtimes)}$ ⬤, V. Leelavathy ⬤, and A. P. Shanthi

College of Engineering Guindy, Anna University, Chennai, India
junaitadavakumar@gmail.com

Abstract. Ergonomics aims at creating a safe, productive and comfortable workspace by incorporating human abilities and limitations into the design of a workspace. A workplace ergonomics improvement process removes potential factors of risk that can lead to musculoskeletal injuries and enables enhanced human performance and productivity. Regular computer usage can lead to neck strain, typically due to improper posture. Periodic alerts and suggestions provided to users to correct their postures will result in better health and work experience for them. This paper proposes a system that analyzes the actual ergonomic rules with respect to the individual as well as their working environment and provides suggestions to improve their workplace posture.

Keywords: Posture · Ergonomic rules · Skeletonization

1 Introduction

Ergonomics is the study of the interaction between people and the surrounding environment and the factors that affect the interaction. Ergonomics reduces discomfort in the workplace and increases the efficiency of the workers. An ergonomic improvement procedure can contribute to the betterment of work experience for the employees as well as reduce the risk of health issues.

In the recent times, IT sector has become the fundamental stream with rapid evolution, changing the shape of business standards. The productivity and efficiency of the work delivered can be greatly affected if the workspace ergonomics are not taken into consideration. An IT based environment consists of several ergonomic factors to consider such as the sitting posture, height and position of monitor, position of keyboard and mouse etc. If these factors are left unnoticed, it can greatly affect the productivity and efficiency of the work being done. It also causes long term health issues in the workers.

The Ergonomic Posture Analysis System proposed in this work aims to analyze the work-space posture of a person based on the images that the user feeds into the system, ideally, as a side profile. All the key posture points from the user's posture as well as external physical factors such as chair height, and angle between the seat and the back rest are identified and then analyzed and scored against a set of test criteria. Based on the test results, improvements and suggestions are provided to the user in order to improve workplace posture for an overall better work experience.

The paper is organized as follows. Section 2 briefs the prior work related to this area. Section 3 explains the materials and methods of the work. Section 4 analyzes the performance and Sect. 5 concludes the work.

I. Raman et al. (Eds.): ICC3 2021, CCIS 1631, pp. 167–178, 2022.
https://doi.org/10.1007/978-3-031-15556-7_12

2   Related Work

Throughout the world, people spend a lot of money in treating pain in the body caused mainly due to bad posture. Many office jobs require long hours of sitting and most of the people lean forward and do not maintain proper posture. Maintaining good posture and changing the position from time to time can improve and maintain personal health. Many researchers have contributed to posture correction and maintenance in various ways. Ergonomic posture analysis methods include Owako working position analysis system (OWAS), Rapid Entire Body Assessment (REBA) and Rapid Upper Limbs Assessment (RULA). Many researchers have contributed in developing applications for posture correction and estimation.

2.1   Mobile Apps and Wearable Devices for Posture Correction

Many mobile apps have been developed that use different measurements to provide therapy/diagnosis assistance to people exhibiting bad posture. Puian et al. [1] use medical assistance software that uses the 3D-orientation received from measurement units worn at the head and the torso, to provide therapy/diagnosis assistance to people with neck problems. Hernan et al. [2] use measurements of the distance to face, orientation of the computing device, viewing angle of the individual and the amount of time the individual for posture recommendation.

Zhuqi et al. [3] utilize the front camera and inertial accelerometer of the smart phone to estimate the face-screen distance. Jinxing et al. [4] use a method that acquires an image containing the user's eyes, obtains a number of pixels between the user's eyes from the image, compares the number of pixels between the user's eyes with a preset (predetermined) value and warns the user if the number of pixels between the user's eyes is larger than the preset (predetermined) value.

Wearable devices/sensors have also been developed to assist users in maintaining proper posture [5–11]. Chu [12] has proposed a novel framework that analyzes ergonomic posture from the body joint angles by reconstructing the 3D worker body with the 2D videos recorded from a camera. Heidari et al. [13] assessed the various postures of laptop users in non-official places, and its effects on musculoskeletal disorders (MSDs). Li et al. [14] present an automated ergonomic risk assessment framework based on 3D modelling with the support of a user-friendly interface for data-post processing.

2.2   Posture Estimation Using Machine Learning and Deep Learning Methods

Maryam et al. [15] estimate and classify sleep postures of a person by extracting features using a frequency-based feature selection and classifying using a support vector machine (SVM). Santosh Kumar et al. [16] have proposed a hybrid deep learning model using convolutional neural network (CNN) and long short-term memory (LSTM) for Yoga recognition on real-time videos.

Konar et al. [17] provide a fuzzy logic based approach to recognize Ballet dance postures. Chin et al. [18] detect sitting postures from Kinect sensors and use Support Vector Machine (SVM) and Artificial Neural Network (ANN) for differentiating proper and improper postures. Liaqat et al. [19] propose a hybrid approach based on machine learning and deep learning classifiers to identify postures such as sitting, walking and standing. Ren et al. [20] use a hybrid fuzzy logic and machine learning approach to classify human postures when lying in a bed.

2.3 Observations

When compared with the existing work, the work presented in this paper differs as follows: Many of the systems that have been developed earlier need the use of external devices and sensors connected or attached to the human body. Wearable devices cause discomfort and are expensive in most of the cases. Our work is advantageous since it does not require a wearable device. There is not much of prior work done related to ergonomics. Our work can be used in an office kind of setup where images of people working can be taken using fixed cameras and suggestions can be provided to the working employees.

3   Materials and Methods

The input image is first pre-processed and is fed to a human figure analyzer. The human figure analyzer generates a skeleton of the human and also generates a score for the human posture. The input image and the human posture score are fed to the object analyzer. The object analysis subsystem analyzes the image and gives suggestions for the efficient placement of the object with respect to the human. Figure 1 depicts the block diagram of the proposed EPAS.

The human figure analysis phase consists of the following subphases: pose estimator, skeleton generator, ergonomic rule engine for human and scoring engine. The object analysis phase consists of the following subphases: object segmentation, object skeletonizer, graph processor and ergonomic rule engine for object.

3.1   Image Pre-processing

Image pre-processing is mainly done to improve the image data by suppressing unwanted distortions or enhancing some important features. Noise reduction is done using the Gaussian blur after reading and resizing the image. The orientation of the image is then checked. The image is checked to be left or right profiled. In order to do this, the module checks if the nose key point is to the left of that of the ear. If it is, the module concludes that it is left profiled else, the module is classified as right profiled. If the image is right profiled, the image is flipped.

3.2   Human Figure Analysis

Pose Estimator. The Pose Estimator takes the pre-processed image as input. It uses the PoseNet library which does the process of pose estimation. The library is pre-trained over various images of the human figure with the help of the TensorFlow package (TensorFlow.js).

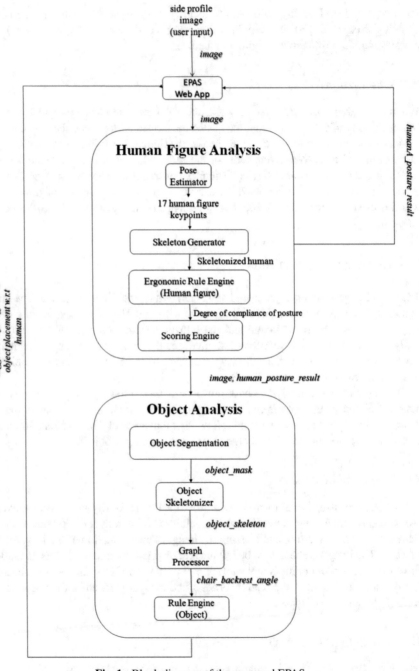

Fig. 1. Block diagram of the proposed EPAS

The pose estimator detects 17 key points. A key point is a part of a person's estimated pose, such as the right ear, nose, right foot, left knee, etc. The keypoint produced by the pose estimator contains a position and also a key point confidence score. The key point confidence score denotes the confidence that the estimated keypoint position is accurate. It ranges between 0.0 and 1.0. This score can be used to abstract keypoints that are not considered strong enough. The keypoint position contains the two-dimensional X and Y coordinates in the input image where a keypoint is detected.

Skeleton Generator. The keypoints returned from the pose estimator are in the form of coordinates with respect to the dimensions of the web application's screen. These co-ordinates are passed as input to the skeleton generator. The skeleton generator takes as parameters the pose keypoints, confidence and the context of the canvas. The skeleton generator uses the primitive logic of joining a pair of adjacent keypoints by examining their coordinates with respect to the canvas. Segments, native to JavaScript, are used to join a pair of points on a canvas. The skeleton is built and is then rendered.

Ergonomic Rule Engine. The pose keypoint coordinates of the estimated pose, along with the skeleton segments are fed into the Ergonomic Rule Engine. The ergonomic rule engine consists of a pre-determined set of rules that target various key posture points that ultimately determine the ergonomic comfort of a position. The rules are primarily focused on the angle subtended by one segment link on another. Thresholds compliant with existing ergonomic research data are set for all the major posture areas. Based on the degree of compliance to standards, the ergonomic efficiency is determined.

The ergonomic rules considered are Angle of the spine with respect to the horizontal (85–110°), Proximity of the backrest and the lumbar region, Equality of seat height and popliteal height, Optimal thigh-knee angle (95–130°), Optimal ankle angle (95–130°), Optimal forearm angle (approximately horizontal), Optimal wrist angle (160–190°), Angle between the neck and the spine (160–180°).

The output of the ergonomic rule engine is the degree of compliance of the posture to the standard. In this work, three degrees of compliance have been considered for the output: efficient, mediocre, inefficient.

Scoring Engine. The degrees of compliance of all the considered key posture points are fed as input to the Scoring Engine. The Scoring Engine performs a straightforward linear arithmetic function over all the degrees of compliance and outputs a cumulative posture score. This is done by assigning pre-determined values to the degrees of compliance such as 1 for efficient posture, 0 for mediocre posture and −1 for inefficient posture. Therefore, the ergonomic posture score is simply a sum of all the values of degrees of compliance. Higher the value of the ergonomic posture score, the better the posture. The ergonomic posture score is then normalized to a range of 0–10. The Ergonomic Posture Score thus obtained is used to calculate the final score and give the overall posture decision to the user.

3.3 Object Analysis

Object Segmentation. Mask Region-based convolutional neural network (mask R-CNN) is used in this step to segment the objects (that is, chair) from the input image.

The input to the object segmentation module is the user supplied side profile image and the output is an object mask of the detected chair. Mask RCNN, a deep neural network, is used to solve instance segmentation problems. In order to extract features from the images, ResNet 101 architecture had been used. The feature maps obtained from the ResNet backbone are chosen and a region proposal network (RPN) is applied. The outputs obtained denote the feature maps or regions which are predicted to contain some object. Application of a pooling layer converts all the regions to the same shape. The Intersection over Union (IoU) is calculated with the ground truth boxes. Regions with IoU is greater than or equal to 0.5, are considered a region of interest. Other regions are neglected. A mask branch is added. A mask of size 28 X 28 is returned for each region, and is then scaled up for inference. We have trained the neural network using a custom side-profiled chair dataset.

Object Skeletonizer. The input to the object skeletonizer is the object mask of the detected chair. The object skeletonizer is implemented in Python. The skeleton consists of the top-most point of the chair's backrest, bottom-most point of the chair's backrest and the endpoint of the chair's seat. The mask of the image is traversed and the topmost pixel that is marked as true is selected to be the first keypoint of the chair's skeleton: $x1$, $y1$. The leftmost as well as topmost point (for left-profiled images) in the mask when traversed bottom-up is elected to be the endpoint of the chair's seat: $x3$, $y3$.

The point $(x3, y1)$ is chosen. If the mask indicates a False value at this point, then we traverse diagonally upwards until we reach a point that is marked as True in the Mask (let this be P1). If such a value is found, we then traverse diagonally downwards until we reach the point marked False in the Mask (let this be P2). The midpoint of P1 and P2 is chosen as the bottom-most point of the chair's backrest.

If the point P1 could not be found as mentioned above, we traverse diagonally downwards until we reach the point marked True in the Mask (let this be P1). We again traverse diagonally downwards until we reach a point marked False in the Mask (let this be P2). The midpoint of P1 and P2 is chosen as the bottom-most point of the chair's backrest. At the point $(x3, y1)$ if the mask indicates a True value, we traverse diagonally upwards until we reach a point that is marked as False in the Mask (let this be P1). If such a value is found, we then traverse diagonally downwards until we reach the point marked False in the Mask (let this be P2). The midpoint of P1 and P2 is chosen as the bottommost point of the chair's backrest.

Graph Processor. The input to the Graph processor is the object skeleton obtained as output from the Object skeletonizer. The graph processor extracts the coordinates of the keypoints of an object from the previous module. From the coordinates obtained with respect to the canvas of the supplied image, the angles between various link segments are obtained. The output from the graph processor is further used to analyze the ergonomic features of the furniture under discussion, which, in turn is the determining factor for analyzing the efficiency of the object. We have used the chair backrest angle for analyzing the ergonomic efficiency of the chair.

Ergonomic Rule Engine (Object). The input to the ergonomic rule engine is the angle of inclination of the chair's backrest with respect to the seat. The output of the module is a thorough evaluation of the chair and the relation between the chair and the user and suggestions to improve the posture. This module consists of a set of rules with respect to the alignment and placement of office furniture viz. Desks, chairs and desktops. Each input will have to be checked against every rule contained in the rule engine.

If the value of chair's backrest angle is in the range of 95–115°, it is evaluated to be an efficient chair. If the user's back posture only happens to be moderate or inefficient, EPAS suggests leaning back on the chair. Else, it congratulates on having a good posture. If the value of chair's backrest angle is the range of 90–95°, it is evaluated to be a moderately efficient chair. EPAS suggests inclining the chair to about 5° away from the desk. If the value of chair's backrest angle is in the range of 115–120° it is evaluated to be a moderately efficient chair. EPAS suggests inclining the chair to about 5° towards the desk. For other angle ranges for the chair's backrest angle, it is evaluated to be an inefficient chair. EPAS suggests inclining it to about 10° towards or away from the desk depending on the angle.

4 Performance Analysis

This section presents the details of the test dataset, the evaluation metrics used and analyses the performance of the system.

4.1 Dataset

We have created a test dataset with 45 images, out of which 32 images are with efficient posture, 7 images are with moderately efficient posture and 6 images with inefficient posture, for this work.

4.2 Sample Outputs

A screen shot with a sample image detected correctly as inefficient posture is shown in Fig. 2. The image has a person sitting in incorrect posture. It can be seen from the screen shot that the system evaluates the human posture and tells that the knee is in efficient posture and the arm, back and neck are in inefficient posture. The calculated score can also be seen and the system says that the person is in an ergonomically inefficient posture. It also finds that the chair is in proper position and gives an overall analysis as 'Your back posture is inefficient, so remember to lean back on your chair'.

In Fig. 3, an ergonomically efficient human posture and chair position are correctly detected. The system gives an overall analysis as 'Good job with your posture'.

4.3 Evaluation Metrics

In this work, we have separated the images into three classes such as, efficient, moderately efficient and inefficient and have tested the system. We have classified the findings of the system as True Positive (TP) or True Negative (TN) or False Positive (FP) or False Negative (FN) based on the following criteria.True Positive (TP) correspond to

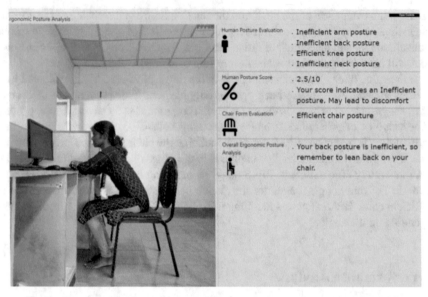

Fig. 2. Sample output for an image detected correctly as ergonomically inefficient

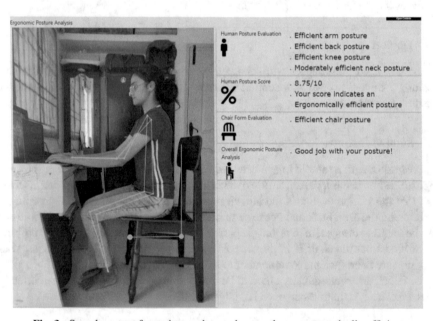

Fig. 3. Sample output for an image detected correctly as ergonomically efficient

images with ergonomically correct posture identified correctly as ergonomically correct. True Negative (TN) correspond to images with ergonomically incorrect posture identified correctly as ergonomically incorrect. False Positive (FP) correspond to images with ergonomically incorrect posture identified wrongly as ergonomically correct. False Negative (FN) correspond to images with ergonomically correct posture identified wrongly as ergonomically incorrect. The metrics used for the evaluation are sensitivity, specificity, precision, accuracy and F1 score.

Sensitivity (Recall). Sensitivity gives the percentage of the correctly identified ergonomically correct images out of the total ergonomically correct images.

$$Sensitivity(Recall) = TP/(TP + FN)$$

Specificity. Specificity gives the percentage of the correctly identified ergonomically incorrect images out of the total ergonomically incorrect images.

$$Specificity = TN/(TN + FP)$$

Precision (Positive Predictive Value). Precision gives the percentage of the correctly identified ergonomically correct images out of the images identified as ergonomically correct.

$$Precision(Positive\ Predictive\ Value) = TP/(TP + FP)$$

Accuracy. Accuracy gives the percentage of correctly identified images out of the total images.

$$Accuracy = (TP + TN)/(TP + FP + TN + FN)$$

F1 Score. F1 score is the harmonic mean of precision and recall.

$$F1\ score = 2\,{}^{*}(Precision\,{}^{*}\,Recall)/(Precision + Recall)$$

4.4 Performance Measures

The confusion matrix describing the performance of the system is shown in Table 1. From the confusion matrix, it can be seen that, for ergonomically inefficient images, the values of TP is 4, TN is 38, FP is 1 and FN is 2. For ergonomically moderately efficient images, TP is 7, TN is 25, FP is 13 and FN is 0. For ergonomically efficient images, TP is 20, TN is 13, FP is 0 and FN is 12.

The values of the calculated sensitivity, specificity, precision, accuracy and F1 score for the different classes are shown in Table 2.

For better understanding and explainability, each keypoint of the workspace setting that is considered in the problem is also evaluated for accuracy. Table 3 shows the accuracy got for different keypoints.

Table 1. Confusion matrix

	Ergonomically inefficient (detected)	Ergonomically moderate (detected)	Ergonomically efficient (detected)
Ergonomically inefficient (actual)	4	2	0
Ergonomically moderate (actual)	0	7	0
Ergonomically efficient (actual)	1	11	20

Table 2. Calculated performance measures

Class	Precision	Recall	F1-score	Accuracy
Ergonomically inefficient	0.8	0.66	0.72	0.93
Ergonomically moderate	0.35	1	0.52	0.71
Ergonomically efficient	0	0.63	0.77	0.73

Table 3. Accuracy for keypoints

Ergonomic posture point	Accuracy
Elbow	0.78
Spine	0.84
Popliteal angle	0.87
Neck	0.76
Backrest of chair	0.58

5 Conclusion

In this work, we have proposed an ergonomic posture analysis system that analyses images of human beings seated in an office kind of setup. The proposed system processes the images and tells the user if the posture is efficient or moderately efficient or inefficient. The contributions of the work are summarized as follows: Use of pose estimator to find key points and skeletonization of human figures, use of mask R-CNN for object segmentation, development of a novel algorithm for object key point selection and skeleton generation, graph processing of skeletons of human and objects and development of an ergonomic rule and scoring engine.

Many of the systems that have been developed earlier need the use of external devices and sensors connected or attached to the human body. Wearable devices cause discomfort and are expensive in most of the cases. Our work is advantageous that it does not require a wearable device. There is not much of work done related to ergonomics. Our system can be used in an office kind of setup where images of people working can be takes using fixed cameras and suggestions can be provided to the working employees. One of the limitations of our work is that it detects and analyzes only images with a side profile. In future, this can be extended to images with any orientation.

References

1. Tadayon, P., Felderhoff, T., Knopp, A., Staude, G.: Mobile system for the prevention, diagnosis, and personalized treatment of neck pain under a patient's everyday life circumstances. Curr. Dir. Biomed. Eng. **5**(1), 257–260 (2019)
2. Cunico, H.A., Dunne, J., O'Connor, J., Silva, A.: Personalized posture correction. Patent Pub. No. US 2019/0038215 A1, Pub. 7 February 2019
3. Li, Z., Chen, W., Li, Z., Bian, K.: Look into my eyes: fine-grained detection of face-screen distance on smartphones. In: Proceedings of the 12th International Conference on Mobile Ad-Hoc and Sensor Networks (2016)
4. Peng, J., Xie, J.: Method for warning a user about a distance between user's eyes and a screen. Patent Application No. US 9508005B2 (2015)
5. Hopkins, B.B., Vehrs, P.R., Fellingham, G.W., George, J.D., Hager, R., Ridge, S.T.: Validity and reliability of standing posture measurements using a mobile application. J. Manipulative Physiol. Ther. **42**(2), 132–140 (2019). https://doi.org/10.1016/j.jmpt.2019.02.003
6. Chung, H.-Y., Chung, Y.-L., Liang, C.-Y.: Design and implementation of a novel system for correcting posture through the use of a wearable necklace sensor. JMIR Mhealth Uhealth **7**(5), e12293 (2019). https://doi.org/10.2196/12293
7. Hirota, Y., Takahashi, N., Hayashi, T.: Posture measuring device, posture measuring method, image processing device, image processing method and image display system. Patent No. US 10,185,389 B2, 22 January 2019
8. Kim, M., Kim, H., Park, J., Jee, K.-K., Lim, J.A., Park, M.-C.: Real-time sitting posture correction system based on highly durable and washable electronic textile pressure sensors. Sens. Actuators A Phys. **269**, 394–400 (2018)
9. Zhang, J., Zhang, H., Dong, C., Huang, F., Liu, Q., Song, A.: Architecture and design of a wearable robotic system for body posture monitoring, correction, and rehabilitation assist. Int. J. Soc. Robot. **11**(3), 423–436 (2019). https://doi.org/10.1007/s12369-019-00512-3
10. Pamplin, J.C.: Device for assessing and recording posture. US Patent Application US15/726,432 (2006)
11. Van Wegen, E.E.H., de Goede, C.J.T., Kwakkel, G., Kordelaar, J.: Sensor assisted self-management in parkinson's disease: A feasibility study of ambulatory posture detection and feedback to treat stooped posture. Parkinsonism Relat. Disord. **46**(1), S57–S61 (2018)
12. Wenjing, C.: 3D human pose reconstruction for ergonomic posture analysis. Master's thesis, Concordia University (2018)
13. Heidari, H., Soltanzadeh, A., Asemabadi, E., Rahimifard, H., Mohammadbeigi, A.: Ergonomic posture analysis of different postures in laptop users at non-official places and related musculoskeletal disorders by rapid upper limb assessment method. Adv. Hum. Biol. **9**, 135–142 (2019)
14. Li, X., Han, S., Gul, M., Al-Hussein, M.: Automated ergonomic risk assessment based on 3D visualization. In: Proceedings of the 34th International Symposium on Automation and Robotics in Construction (2017)
15. Rasouli D, M.S., Payandeh, S.: A novel depth image analysis for sleep posture estimation. J. Ambient. Intell. Humaniz. Comput. **10**(5), 1999–2014 (2018). https://doi.org/10.1007/s12 652-018-0796-1

16. Yadav, S.K., Singh, A., Gupta, A., Raheja, J.L.: Real-time yoga recognition using deep learning. Neural Comput. Appl. **31**, 9349–9361 (2019). https://doi.org/10.1007/s00521-019-04232-7

17. Konar, A., Saha S.: Fuzzy image matching based posture recognition in ballet dance. In: Gesture Recognition. Studies in Computational Intelligence, vol. 724, Springer, Cham (2018). https://doi.org/10.1007/978-3-319-62212-5_3

18. Chin, L.C.K., Eu, K.S., Tay, T.T., Teoh, C.Y., Yap, K.M.: A posture recognition model dedicated for differentiating between proper and improper sitting posture with kinect sensor. In: Proceedings of the 2019 IEEE International Symposium on Haptic, Audio and Visual Environments and Games (2019)

19. Liaqat, S., Dashtipour, K., Arshad, K., Assaleh, K., Ramzan, N.: A hybrid posture detection framework: integrating machine learning and deep neural networks. IEEE Sens. J. **21**(7), 9515–9522 (2021). https://doi.org/10.1109/JSEN.2021.3055898

20. Ren, W., Ma, O., Ji, H., Liu, X.: Human posture recognition using a hybrid of fuzzy logic and machine learning approaches. IEEE Access **8**, 135628–135639 (2020). https://doi.org/10.1109/ACCESS.2020.3011697

Studies on Winding Number in Abstract Cellular Complex

R. Syama[1,2(✉)] 🆔 and G. Sai Sundara Krishnan[1] 🆔

[1] Department of Applied Mathematics and Computational Sciences,
PSG College of Technology, Coimbatore, India
syamar585@gmail.com, ssk.amcs@psgtech.ac.in
[2] Department of Mathematics, Bannari Amman Institute of Technology,
Sathyamangalam, India

Abstract. This paper the concept of the winding number and the computation of the winding number of the digital image in an abstract cellular complex is initiated. The notion of free homotopy on the abstract cellular complex between the loops is also introduced, and some of its properties are investigated by using the winding number of the loop with respect to a 0-dimensional cell.

Keywords: Bounding relation · Smallest open neighbourhood · Winding number · Abstract cellular complex

1 Introduction

In digital topology, Digital image being the main substance is defined [6] as a two-dimensional function $f(x,y)$, where the intensity of the image at the point (x,y) and the amplitude values of 'f' are all finite and discrete quantities. Let R represent a subset of these finite set of points in a Euclidean space with adjacency relation. This is the notion of a digital image which contains pixels. Rosenfeld [16–18] studied the basic topological features of digital images with adjacency relation. Kong and Rosenfeld [8] represented digital images with the concept of distinct adjacency relations to apply the foreground and background of digital images; however, the above representations comprehend the border and connectivity paradoxes.

For overcoming these boundary (border) and connectivity paradoxes, Kovalevsky [9,10] investigated locally finite space and established the concept of abstract cellular complex through lower dimensions cells. Syama et al. [20] studied the significance and efficiency of the lower dimensional cells of a combinatorial grid system through the basic topological concept is proved experimentally through the proposed MCC algorithm which is developed by defined mappings on the abstract cellular complex. Based on these mappings on abstract cellular complex without any flaw, the boundary of the digital image can be extracted by using the proposed MCC algorithm. The boundary of the digital image is too

I. Raman et al. (Eds.): ICC3 2021, CCIS 1631, pp. 179–188, 2022.
https://doi.org/10.1007/978-3-031-15556-7_13

substantial in the fields of computer graphics and animation. Many literature studies Bertrand and Malgouyres [1], Lee *et al.* [14], Mcandrew and Osborne [15], Boxer [3], Han [4], Edelsbrunner and Harer [5], Jaeger *et al.* [7] have shown that the concepts of algebraic topology in digital topology had given various applications in science and engineering field with a consistent result. For the classification of surfaces in the digital image is theoretically untroubled and gives the experimentally prevalent result while using the concepts of algebraic invariants.

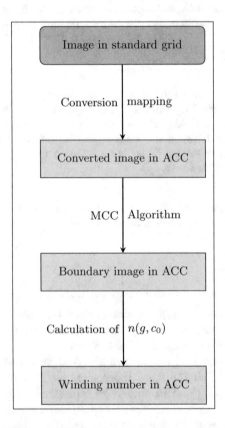

Fig. 1. Schematic diagram of the method

Boxer [2] discussed the properties of homotopy in digital spaces; however, this work was based on the concepts of adjacency and neighbourhood relation of pixels. Krishnan and Syama [19] discussed the implementation of homotopy in the abstract cellular complex gives a new way to the identification of different components of the digital images and initiated the following algebraic notions such as cellular homotopy, cellular path homotopy, cellular fundamental group, etc. in abstract cellular complex.

The winding number which is the topological number gives the detailed information of curves like the direction of the curve, the number of times the curve wind around the particular point, etc. Once the boundary or border of the digital image is identified in abstract cellular complex then the digital image features are extracted through the generalization of winding numbers in the abstract cellular complex which is best and effective in the following fields: computer vision, medical image analysis, robotic vision, etc.

Lee et al. [14] discussed the importance of winding number and euler numbers for 2D and 3D digital images. Winding number is topologically the exact influential information of the digital image and it prolongs the collection of closed curves. Hence, this information provides to the number of connected components in digital image and this study helps to initiate the biomedical applications like cavity detection and cavity structure identification, neuronal cells computing and counting through the abstract cellular complex. This inspires to study on winding number in the abstract cellular complex.

This paper the concept of free homotopy of abstract cellular complex between the loops is initiated and some of their properties studied through winding number of the loop with regard to a 0-dimensional cell. Correspondingly, the calculation of the winding number of the medical images is initiated. Fig. 1 is represented the phases of the calculation of the winding number in ACC by using MCC Algorithm.

2   Preliminaries in Abstract Cellular Complex

For the study of winding number the elementary definitions of Abstract Cellular Complex such as Locally finite space, Axiomatic Locally Finite space, Abstract Cellular Complex (ACC), subcomplex, open subcomplex, binary relation, boundary curves, smallest open neighbourhood, distance between the cells, loop, components, connected, continuous function on ACC, connectivity preserving map of ACC in [10–13], and so forth studied the following notions of cellular homotopy and cellular covering space [20].

Definition 1 [19]. *Let C_1, C_2 be the two abstract cellular complexes. Let f_1, f_2 be the two Continuous Connected Preserving Maps (CCPM) of C_1 into C_2. Suppose a map $G : C_1 \times [0, n]_{\mathcal{Z}*} \to C_2$ and there exist $n \in N$ such that*

1. $G(c, 0) = f_1(c)$ and $G(c, n) = f_2(c)$ for each $c \in C_1$.
2. For every $c \in C_1$, the induced map $G_c : [0, n]_{\mathcal{Z}*} \to C_2$ given by $G_c(t) = G(c, t)$ for all $t \in [0, n]_{\mathcal{Z}*}$ is CCPM.
3. For every $t \in [0, n]_{\mathcal{Z}*}$, the induced map $G_t : C_1 \to C_2$ given by $G_t(c) = G(c, t)$ for all $c \in C_1$ is CCPM.

Then, the map G is known as cellular homotopy between CCPM f_1, f_2, and is represented as $f_1 \simeq_C f_2$.

Definition 2 [19]. *Let g be the map from the ACC C_1 to the ACC C_2. Let g be a surjection and CCPM. Suppose there exists $\epsilon \in N$ and for any $e \in C_2$ such that*

1. *for some $\delta \in N$ and some index connected complex S, $g^{-1}(SON(e,\epsilon)) = \bigcup_{i \in S} SON(c_i, \delta)$ with $c_i \in g^{-1}(e)$;*
2. *if $i, j \in S$ and $i \neq j$, then $SON(c_i, \delta) \cap SON(c_j, \delta) = \phi$; and*
3. *the restriction map $g|SON(c_i, \delta) : SON(c_i, \delta) \rightarrow SON(e, \epsilon)$ is a combinatorial homeomorphism for all $i \in S$.*

The segregation of $g^{-1}(SON(e,\epsilon))$ into slices is a collection of $\{SON(c_i, \delta) : i \in S\}$. The $SON(e, \epsilon)$ is known as an elementary smallest open neighbourhood of e with some radius ϵ, which depends upon the bounding relation of C_2. Then the map g is called a cellular covering map (CCM) and (C_1, p, C_2) is called a cellular covering space (CCS).

Let $g : C_1 \rightarrow C_2$ be a CCPM and for some CCPM p from the ACC C_3 to the ACC C_2, as a cellular lifting of p from ACC C_3 to ACC C_1 is a CCPM $\tilde{p} : C_3 \rightarrow C_1$ such that $g \circ \tilde{p} = p$. The $SON(e, \epsilon)$ is the basic for the cellular lifting, $(SON(e, \epsilon)) \subset C_2$.

3   Free Homotopy and Winding Number of Abstract Cellular Complex

In order to study the free homotopy between the loops through the winding number of g with regard the 0-dimensional cell of the ACC the following example stated.

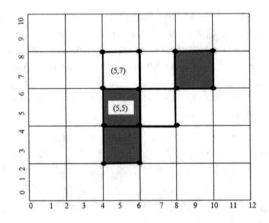

Fig. 2. The winding numbers of the incident path Γ_1 and Γ_2

The winding number, $n(\Gamma)$ of an incident path $\Gamma : [a, b] \rightarrow C$, is an integer number that counts the complete rounds of the path around the particular cell in counterclockwise sense. For example, In Fig. 2, consider the incident path $\Gamma_1 = \{(4,4), (4,5), (4,6), (5,6), (6,6), (6,5), (6,4), (5,4)\}$ and $\Gamma_2 = \{(4,4), (4,5), (4,6), (4,7), (4,8), (5,6), (5,7), (5,8), (6,8), (6,7), (7,6),$

$(8,6),(8,5),(8,4),(7,4),(6,6),(6,5),(6,4),(5,4)\}$ of the abstract cellular complex C_2. Then the winding numbers of Γ_1 and Γ_2 in the counterclockwise direction around at a 2-dimensional cell (5, 5) are $n(\Gamma_1) = 1$ and $n(\Gamma_2) = 3$.

The number of connected components of a digital image can be identified simply by using a defined winding number of abstract cellular complex with the modified chain code algorithm. Because the MCC algorithm provides the information of lower dimensional cells, the winding number of abstract cellular complex gives the details of the number of connected components, and the holes present in the boundary/border of the digital image. The graphical representation of the calculation of winding number of the boundary of a digital image is shown in Fig. 3 and Fig. 4.

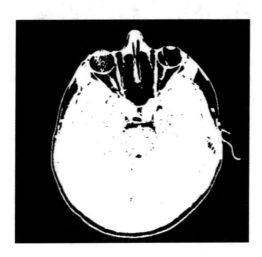

Fig. 3. Original image

The following is the process of calculating winding number:

1. Input the two dimensional image I.
2. Get boundary BI of an image I in the combinatorial grid system from the standard grid system by applying mappings on abstract cellular complex through the modified chain code algorithm.
3. Calculate winding number for the lower dimensional cells in the boundary of an image BI.

Initialize $n(\Gamma) = i$
If origin cell $c_{i,j} == (x, y)$ then $\Gamma \subset BI$
$n(\Gamma) = i + 1$
Else $n(\Gamma) = 0$
Endif

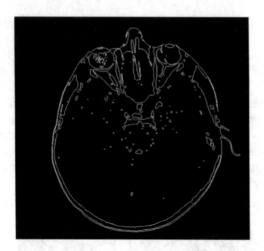

Fig. 4. Winding number of single component $n(\Gamma_1) = 1$ which is marked as red square in the Boundary of an original image traced through modified chain code algorithm

From the Definition 2 of cellular covering space and cellular covering map, the winding number of the abstract cellular complex is defined as follows:

Definition 3. *Let g be a loop in C^2, and c_0 be a 0-dimensional cell not in the loop g. Consider $f(s) = [g(s) - c_0]/(\|g(s) - c_0\|)$; then f is a loop in S^1. Let $g : C \to S^1$ be the CCM, and let $\tilde{f}$ be the lifting of f to S^1. The resulting value of the lifting of $f(1)$ and $f(0)$ is an integer and this integer is known as the winding number of g with respect to c_0, and is denoted as $n(g, c_0)$.*

Lemma 1. *Let S be a subcomplex of the two dimensional ACC C^2. Then the subcomplex S separates the ACC C^2 into four components and their boundaries are S_i where $i = 1, 2, 3, 4$.*

Proof:
   Let T be a subcomplex of C^2 which is the union of the components of S. Then the complex T can be written as the union of the following components: $T_1 = c_2 c_1 c_4 c_5, T_2 = c_2 c_5, T_3 = c_2 c_3 c_6 c_5$ in Fig. 5.
   That is union of the components T_1, T_2, T_3 gives the subcomplex T and they intersect in their end cells c_2 and c_5. The subcomplex T separates C^2 into three components whose boundaries are $T_1 \cup T_2, T_2 \cup T_3, T_1 \cup T_3$ respectively where $T_1 \cup T_2 = A, T_2 \cup T_3 = B, T_1 \cup T_3 = E$. Here $\overline{A}$ and $\overline{B}$ are connected and nonempty intersection of T_2, therefore $\overline{A} \cup \overline{B}$ is also connected. Moreover, the complex $\overline{A} \cup \overline{B}$ does not separate the abstract cellular complex C^2 also, $C^2 - T$ is the union of four disjoint components because these components are open in $C^2 - T$.
   Hence, the component A has $T_1 \cup T_2 = S_4$ as its boundary; similarly other components S_1, S_2, S_3 also have their boundaries respectively.

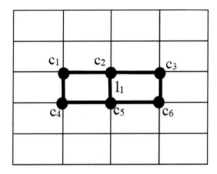

Fig. 5. Connected components of the subcomplex

Lemma 2. *Let S be the subcomplex of the two dimensional ACC C^2 and l_1 be the bounding cell of c_2c_5. Then (i) the cell l_1 lie in different component $C^2 - S$. (ii) An isomorphism of cellular fundamental groups is induced by the inclusion of $i : S \to C^2 - f_1 - f_2$.*

Proof: *From the Lemma 1, $S \cup c_2c_5$ separates the two dimensional ACC C^2 into three components $A, B,$ and E. Also, S be the subcomplex of the ACC C^2 and union of three components $A, B,$ and E gives the subcomplex S. The subcomplex S separates C^2 into three components whose boundaries are $T_1 \cup T_2, T_2 \cup T_3, T_1 \cup T_3$ respectively.*

Hence, the $T_1 \cup T_2$ is the boundary of the component and which is equals to the one of the components of $C^2 - T_1 \cup T_2$. Therefore, the cell l_1 lie in different component $C^2 - S$.

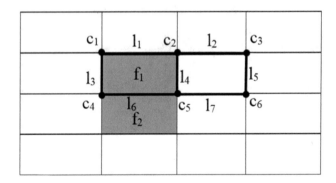

Fig. 6. Generator of the cellular fundamental group

Let $T = C^2 - f_1 - f_2$. Then the cells l_3, l_4 bounds the cells c_1c_4 and c_2c_5 respectively. Let $\Gamma_1 = l_3c_1l_1c_2l_4, \Gamma_2 = l_4c_5l_6c_4l_3$ be the bounding paths. Then the loop $\Gamma_1 * \Gamma_2$ lying in the complex S. In Fig. 6, the groups are infinite cyclic therefore, i_* is an isomorphism. Also, the homomorphism $i_* : \pi(C^2, l_3) \to \pi(T, l_3)$ is *surjective and gives the result that the loop $\Gamma_1 * \Gamma_2$ is a generator of the cellular fundamental group of T.*

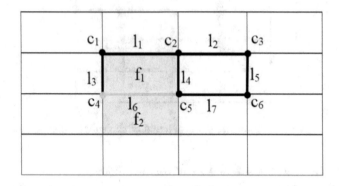

Fig. 7. Bounding path $L_1 = f_1 c_4 l_6 f_2$

Let $L_1 = f_1 c_4 l_6 f_2$, $L_2 = f_2 c_5 l_4 f_1$ are the bounding paths and let $A = C^2 - L_1$ and $B = C^2 - L_2$. From the Fig. 7 and Fig. 8, $T = A \cup B$ and $A \cap B = C^2 - L$, where $L = L_1 \cup L_2$ is a simple closed path. Therefore, $L = c_1 f_1 c_4 l_6 c_5 l_4 f_1 c_1$ and $A \cap B$ has two components also the cells l_3, l_4 which lie in the components of $C^2 - L$.

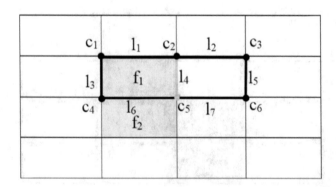

Fig. 8. Bounding path $L_2 = f_2 c_5 l_4 f_1$

The cellular fundamental group of T is infinite cyclic and the loop $\Gamma_1 * \Gamma_2$ is a generator of the cellular fundamental group. Therefore, the bounding paths Γ_1, Γ_2 are paths in A, B from l_3 to l_4 and l_4 to l_3 respectively.

Definition 4. *Let $G : I \times I \to C$ be a continuous connected preserving map such that $G(0,t) = G(1,t)$ for all t. The map G is known as free homotopy between the loops g_0 and g_1 if the map $g_t(s) = G(s,t)$ is a loop in C, for each t. The* *base point of the loop is allowed to move in the progress of the cellular homotopy since it is a cellular homotopy of loops.*

Lemma 3. *Let g be a loop in $C^2 - c_0$.*

1. *If $\bar{g}$ is the reverse of g, then $n(\bar{g}, c_0) = -n(g, c_0)$.*
2. *If g is freely homotopic to g', through the loops lying in $C^2 - c_0$, then $n(g, c_0) = n(g', c_0)$.*
3. *If c_0, c_1 belongs to the same component of $C^2 - g(I)$, then $n(g, c_0) = n(g, c_1)$.*

Proof: *(a) The sign of $\tilde{f}(1) - \tilde{f}(0)$ has changed in the process of computing, $n(\bar{g}, c_0)$ by replacing s by $1 - s$ in the free homotopy.*

(b) Let g and g' be a free homotopic which defines the map $F : I \times I \to S^1$ by the equation $F(s, t) = [G(s, t) - c_0]/(||G(s, t) - c_0||)$. By the continuous connected preserving, $\tilde{F}$ be a lifting of F to C. Then $\tilde{F}(1, t) - \tilde{F}(0, t)$ is an integer for each t which is a constant.

(c) Let Γ be the incident path between c_0 to c_1 in $C_2 - g(I)$. Then $g - c_0$ and $g - c_1$ are free homotopic of $g(s) - \Gamma(t)$ in $C^2 - 0$. Therefore, from the definition $n(g, c_0) = n(g - c_0, 0)$.

4 Conclusion

This paper introduced the concept of winding number of abstract cellular complex and investigated its fundamental features. The topological properties of a digital image, such as the computation of euler number, betti number in the abstract cellular complex, and so on, will be studied and implemented in the future. Furthermore, the properties and applications of these algebraic invariants can be extended to digital image analysis which is in various disciplines of science and engineering.

References

1. Bertrand, G., Malgouyres, R.: Some topological properties of surfaces in Z^3. J. Math. Imaging Vis. **11**(3), 207–221 (1999)
2. Boxer, L.: Properties of digital homotopy. J. Math. Imaging Vis. **22**(1), 19–26 (2005)
3. Boxer, L.: Homotopy properties of sphere-like digital images. J. Math. Imaging Vis. **24**(2), 167–175 (2006)
4. Han, S.E.: Digital coverings and their applications. J. Appl. Math. Comput. **18**(1–2), 487–495 (2005)
5. Edelsbrunner, H., Harer, J.: Computational Topology: an Introduction. American Mathematical Society. Mathematical Association of America Press, USA (2010)
6. Gonzalez, R.C., Woods, R.E.: Digital Image Processing. Pearson Prentice Hall, New York (2018)
7. Jaeger, G., Simon, D.S., Sergienko, A.V.: Topological qubits as carriers of quantum information in optics. Appl. Sci. **9**(3), 575 (2019). https://doi.org/10.3390/app9030575

8. Kong, T.Y., Rosenfeld, A.: Digital topology: introduction and survey. Comput. Vis. Graph. Image Process. **48**(3), 357–393 (1989)
9. Kovalevsky, V.A.: Finite topology as applied to image analysis. Comput. Vis. Graph. Image Process. **46**(2), 141–161 (1989)
10. Kovalevsky, V.A.: Axiomatic digital topology. J. Math. Imaging Vis. **26**(1), 41–58 (2006)
11. Kovalevsky, V.A.: Digital geometry based on the topology of abstract cell complexes. In: proceedings of the Third International colloquium on Discrete Geometry for Computer Imagery, pp. 259–284 (1993)
12. Kovalevsky, V.: Algorithms in digital geometry based on cellular topology. In: Klette, R., Žunić, J. (eds.) IWCIA 2004. LNCS, vol. 3322, pp. 366–393. Springer, Heidelberg (2004). https://doi.org/10.1007/978-3-540-30503-3_27
13. Kovalevsky, V.A.: Geometry of Locally Finite Spaces: Computer Agreeable Topology and Algorithms for Computer Imagery. Dr. Baerbel Kovalevski Publishing House, Berlin (2008)
14. Lee, C.N., Poston, T., Rosenfeld, A.: Winding and Euler numbers for 2D and 3D digital images. CVGIP: Graph. Models Image Process. **53**(6), 522–537 (1991)
15. McAndrew, A., Osborne, C.: A survey of algebraic methods in digital topology. J. Math. Imaging Vis. **6**(2), 139–159 (1996)
16. Rosenfeld, A.: Connectivity in digital pictures. J. Assoc. Comput. Mach. **17**(1), 146–160 (1990)
17. Rosenfeld, A.: Adjacency in digital pictures. Inf. Control **26**(1), 24–33 (1974)
18. Rosenfeld, A.: Digital topology. Am. Math. Monthly **86**(8), 621–630 (1979)
19. Sai Sundara Krishnan, G., Syama, R.: Algebraic invariants in abstract cellular complex. Results Math. **76**(3), 1–29 (2021)
20. Syama, R., SaiSundaraKrishnan, G., Yashwanth, R.: Mappings on abstract cellular complex and their applications in image analysis. Int. J. Comput. Math. **98**(8), 1521–1541 (2020)

COVID-19 Semantic Search Engine Using Sentence-Transformer Models

Anagha Jose[✉] and Sandhya Harikumar

Department of Computer Science and Engineering, Amrita Vishwa Vidyapeetham,
Amritapuri, India
anaghajose13@gmail.com, sandhyaharikumar@am.amrita.edu

Abstract. With the onset of COVID-19, enormous research papers are being published with unprecedented information. It is impractical for the stake holders in medical domain to keep in pace with the new knowledge being generated by reading the entire research papers and articles in order to keep pace with new information. In this work, a semantic search engine is proposed that utilises different sentence transformer models such as BERT, DistilBERT, RoBERTa, ALBERT and DistilRoBERTa for semantic retrieval of information based on the query provided by the user. These models begin by collecting COVID-19-related research papers and are used as an input to the pre-trained sentence transformer models. The collected research papers are then converted into embedded paragraphs, and the input query is sent to the same model, which in turn delivers the embedded query. The model uses cosine similarity to compare both embedded paragraphs and the embedded query. Consequently, it returns the top K most similar paragraphs, together with their paper ID, title, abstract, and abstract summary. The bidirectional nature of the sentence transformer models allows them to read text sequences from both directions, making the text sequence more meaningful. Using these models, COVID-19 semantic search engine has been developed and deployed for efficient query processing. The similarity score for each model was computed by averaging the top 100 query scores. As a result, the RoBERTa model is faster, generates a higher score of similarity, and consumes less runtime.

Keywords: COVID-19 · BERT · RoBERT · ALBERT · DISTILRoBERT · DistilBERT · Pandemic · NLP

1 Introduction

There has been accelerated growth of research papers released during the ongoing COVID-19 pandemic. In this paper, a semantic search engine is developed that optimises the contents of various research articles. To begin, the researchers collect these COVID19-related research publications and then feed them into the pre-trained BERT model along with the input query. This model transforms the research papers into embedded paragraphs and query into embedded query. The

I. Raman et al. (Eds.): ICC3 2021, CCIS 1631, pp. 189–200, 2022.
https://doi.org/10.1007/978-3-031-15556-7_14

conversion to the embedded is beneficial for semantic search and information retrieval because it allows for more precise extraction of answers that are appropriate to the question. Using cosine similarity, the model compares both the embedded paragraphs and the embedded query, then delivers the top K most similar paragraphs, together with their paper id, title, abstract, and abstract summary.

In this work, the machine-learning topic modelling methodology is used to analyse text data and create cluster terms for a collection of documents. The researchers also employed sentence transformers such as BERT, DistilBERT, Roberta, ALBERT, and DistilRoBERTa in this research to select the best model based on their score and the maximum time each model took to process. The model uses bidirectional and self-attention techniques which result in better accuracy. A sentence transformer-based semantic search engine is more efficient in text classification and for more accurate results. The sentence transformer models handle a large corpus of data. This semantic search engine is useful for health care providers and other COVID-19 workers who need to stay up to date with COVID-19 related information.

The BERT [2] is a transformer encoder stack which is pretrained. A self-attention and a feed-forward network are included in each encoder layer. The input from the encoder is passed through a self-attention layer, which then passes the output from the self-attention layer to a feed-forward neural network, which finally passes it on to the next encoder. The COVID-19 dataset [11] includes over 500,000 research papers, nearly 100,000 of which contain full text with regard to coronavirus. The BERT model takes data in a specific format as input. The model [2] employs a special token called [CLS], [SEP], [MASK] for the input formatting, Each sentence begins with a [CLS] token and ends with a [SEP] token. The framework consists of two steps: the Masked Language Model (MLM) and Next Sentence Prediction (NSP). MLM attempts to identify the actual value of a masked word, whereas the NSP determines whether sentence B is a continuation of sentence A.

In the proposed system, COVID-19 related research articles and query from users are collected and fed into sentence transformer models like BERT, DistilBERT, Roberta, ALBERT, and DistilRoBERTa. These models convert research papers and query into embedded paragraphs and embedded query. Cosine similarity has been used to compare embedded paragraphs and embedded query. Consequently, the model returns the top K similar paragraphs with their paper id, title, abstract, abstract summary. Further, various sentence transformer models are evaluated in order to determine the optimal semantic search engine. For experimentation, each model's similarity score is determined by averaging the top 100 query scores. It is observed that the RoBERTa model is faster, produces a higher similarity score, and requires less runtime as compared to other models.

1.1 Main Contributions

- Proposed a semantic search engine to retrieve most relevant articles from COVID-19 research papers based on sentence transformer models.
- Efficient query processing strategy chosen based on comparative analysis of five models namely BERT, DistilBERT, Roberta, ALBERT, and Distil-RoBERTa in the context of semantic information retrieval.

2 Related Works

The researchers collected the COVID-19 related dataset from the Kaggle website. This dataset [11] includes over 500,000 academic papers, across over 100,000 containing actual transcripts related to the corona virus. This dataset enables the world's artificial intelligence research community to utilise text and information extraction technologies to answer queries about the information contained inside and across it, with the goal of advancing ongoing COVID-19 response activities worldwide. This AI approach will help to create new insights to combat this infectious disease.

Manish Pate et al. [9] has built a semantic-search engine that can search for queries and rate content from most meaningful to least meaningful by utilising neural networks and BERT embeddings. In difficult queries for a given set of documents, the results demonstrate an enhancement over one existing search engine. The similarity score is calculated using a neural network while Kassim J. M. [3] proposed a semantic-based search engine that includes ontology creation, ontology crawler, application server, information retrieval, and query processor, but the authors do not use ontology to retain word structure and generate database information structures.

The Xiaoyu GuoJing et al. [6] created a model of semantic search, built on a recurrent neural network (RNN). In this model, each sentence is first broken down into individual words, and then these words are converted into word embeddings using GloVe vectors (global vectors for vector representation). It aids in the creation of vector representations of words. The GloVe extracts the semantic relationship between words from the co-occurrence matrix. After that, the embedded vectors are fed into the recurrent neural network (RNN). The RNN's output is then sent to the attention layer. Then it goes to the output layer, where it assists in determining the final output.

Priyanka C Nair et al. [13] addressed the survey of various jobs conducted on discharge summaries and the studied technologies. The discharge report contains detailed information about the patient, including his or her medical history, symptoms, investigations, therapy, and medicines. While the discharge summary is structured in general, it is not structured in a way that it can be processed by clinical systems. Several natural language processing (NLP) and machine learning algorithms were employed to extract various important bits of information from discharge summaries.

Remya R.K. Menon et al. [14] developed a predictive model-based strategy for constructing semantically oriented topic representations from a document collection. To begin, generate two matrices from the updated topic model: a matrix of document-topics and a matrix of term-topics. The collection of documents and the reconstructed documents are 85% identical. This may be shown by examining the reduced document-term matrix that was created from the two matrices. In topic models, the concept of themes is inferred from the regular appearance of concepts. It might be argued that the terms may not be semantically connected on the issue, even though they appear to be.

Akhil dev et al. [15] proposed a model for document data structure maintenance that makes use of a range of deep learning techniques. The same argument may be made for nearly all techniques. They can all be described by reference to their vector similarity. The research under consideration serves to improve the accuracy of documents by assessing alternate methods for maintaining document structure. Using the Doc2Vec model and applying TF-IDF produced better results than using the Tfidf model.

Paluru Asritha et al. [16] demonstrated the effectiveness of Intelligent Text Mining. Cyberbullying is described as the act of harassing, defaming, abusing, or threatening another person through the use of electronic communication. Censorship on social media has been increasingly important in recent years, and Twitter, Facebook, and Instagram are all at risk of cyberbullying. This can be somewhat minimised by isolating such frightening messages or remarks. The technique of sentiment analysis is used to determine whether a text is positive, negative, or neutral. It contributes to the establishment of a sentence's emotional tone. This paper describes a hybrid classifier technique for categorising these frightening messages, which distinguishes between good and negative assessments. According to the experimental results, the classifier is 89.36% accurate on the considered dataset.

The purpose of the feature extraction and processing system [17] is to extract information from english news stories and present it rationally to the user. Crawl and store the details of a preset set of websites. In between the lines of their publications, news organisations conceal a lot of information. Extracting data and arranging it in such a way that inferences may be drawn is crucial in analytics. The programme extracts identifiable elements such as the location, person, or organisation referenced in the news, as well as the headline and key terms for each article.

The document semantic representation based on matrix decomposition [18] addresses the critical issue of semantic text categorization for data acquisition in a data implementation. Often, search queries on documents look for pertinent information. Standard feature extraction techniques do not convey relevance and instead concentrate on phrase similarity for query processing. The difficulties inherent in semantic information in documents are in identifying critical aspects. The majority of strategies for detecting significant characteristics change the original data into another space. This results in a sparse matrix that is computationally inefficient. This approach identifies significant documents and terms in order to optimise data aggregation. Experiments on five sets of data demonstrate the effectiveness of this strategy.

3   Proposed Method

The architecture of the COVID-19 semantic search engine is shown in Fig. 1. The number of articles and research papers on the fight against the corona virus has increased in recent months. Health professionals find it difficult to follow the new information by reading all of these articles and research papers about the corona virus. This model aids in the discovery of answers to the query. By collecting the corona virus dataset from kaggle [11], they are converted into embedded paragraphs and the input query is sent to the same model, which in turn delivers the embedded query using the pretrained model's Robustly Optimized BERT Pretraining Approach (RoBERTa) [7]. This model uses cosine similarity to compare both embedded paragraphs and the embedded query. As a result, it returns the top K most similar paragraphs, together with their paper ID, title, abstract, and abstract summary.

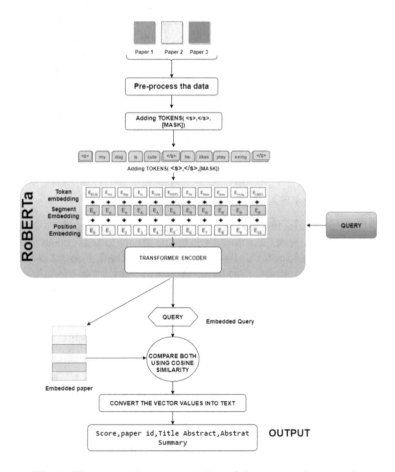

Fig. 1. Diagrammatic representation of the proposed approach

3.1 RoBERTa

RoBERTa [7] is an improved BERT Pretraining Approach. RoBERTa exceeds BERT by making the following changes:

- The training data used by RoBERTa is drawn from the large-scale text corpus (16G), news (76G), open-source recreation of the WebText corpus (38G), and articles (31G) databases.
- For the MLM aim, BERT masks training samples once, whereas RoBERTa replicates training sets 10 times and masks it differently.

Facebook has developed and published this model [7]. This pre-trained word representation language model can process long texts efficiently. It's bidirectional, so it can be read from both directions. Special tokens are used: $\langle s \rangle$, $\langle /s \rangle$, [MASK].

The Next Sentence Prediction (NSP) task, which is used in the BERT's pretrained model, is missing from the RoBERTa model. The NSP model is used to determine whether phrase B follows phrase A. The RoBERTa model employs a dynamic masking pattern, which duplicates the training data ten times and masks the word differently in each epoch, resulting in a change in the masked token during training. In the training procedure, larger numbers of training sizes have also been found more helpful.

The authors tested the removal/addition of NSP loss and found that removing NSP loss improves the model's task performance, possibly a bit. This RoBERTa model can process long texts, but it is very expensive, so we can only use a pretrained model. The comprehensive design and execution of each component is covered further below.

3.2 Explanation of the Block Diagram

Dataset: In this work, the researchers obtained the dataset from kaggle [11] related to the corona virus. The dataset is in the JSON format so the researchers convert this format into a CSV file and then divide the information into paragraphs. The RoBERTa model uses input data in a particular format. For input formatting, this model (Yinhan Liu, 2019) uses a special token called $\langle s \rangle$, $\langle /s \rangle$, [MASK]. The first sentence begins with a $\langle s \rangle$ token, and each subsequent sentence ends with a $\langle /s \rangle$token. The words are randomly selected from each sequence and mask those randomly selected words by using a [MASK] token.

Embeddings: The Highly dimensional vectors can be translated into a relatively low-dimensional space using embedding. The RoBERTa pretrained model (A Robustly Optimized BERT Pretraining Approach) [7] convert the paragraphs and user query into embeddings. In this research, the model uses token embeddings, embeddings, and position embeddings for the conversion of embeddings. The model adds the tokens in token embeddings and the number of the sentences that are encoded into a vector in the segment embeddings, and the position of a word within that sentence that is encoded into a vector in position embeddings. These values are concatenated by the model.

RoBERTa Transformer: The RoBERTa [7] transformer is a collection of encoders. Each encoder incorporates a self-attention neural network and a feed forward neural network(FNN). The concept of attention has aided in the performance of neural machine translation programmes. In order to help the encoder to look at the other words in the input sentence, a self-attention layer is used. A FNN is a network of neurons with multiple layers in which all information travels exclusively in the forward direction. It has three layers: input, hidden, and output. The information enters the input nodes first, then passes via the hidden layers, and ultimately exits through the output nodes. There are no links in the network to feed the information coming out of the output node back into the network.

Self Attention: The encoding of a single word in the self-attention layer enables the encoder to inspect other phrases within the input text. There are three vectors: the vector query, the key vector and the vector value.

The Following is the Processing Step Within Self-attention

- The vectors are produced by multiplying weight matrices.
- Calculate the score by multiplying the query vector by the key vector.
- Distribute the score according to the square root of the dimension of the key vector.
- For the best results, use softmax and then score is standardised by Softmax.
- Multiply the softmax score by each value vector.
- Add the weighted value vectors at this position to obtain self-attention output.
- The output of self-attention is subsequently transferred into the next neural feed network.

4   Experiments and Results

The model examines both the embeddings of the research paper and the query using cosine similarity, then returns the top K closest similar paragraphs, along with their paper ID, paper title, abstract, and abstract summary, as shown in Fig. 2. This work focused on experimenting with sentence transformer models such as BERT, DistilBERT, RoBERTa, ALBERT, and DistilRoBERTa, as well as SVD topic modelling using the Latent Semantic Indexing Model (LSI). When compared to other models, it is determined that the RoBERTa model produces the best results. The similarity score for each model was calculated by averaging the top 100 query scores. The RoBERTa model is faster, generates a higher similarity score, and requires less runtime, which represents the length of time required to finish the programme.

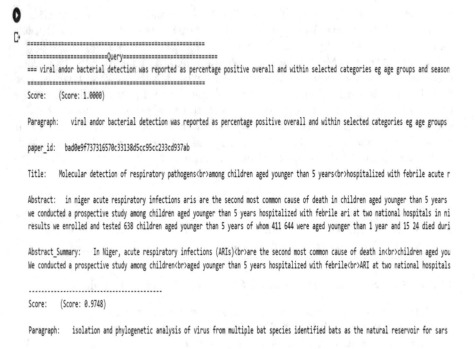

===
============================Query============================
=== viral andor bacterial detection was reported as percentage positive overall and within selected categories eg age groups and season
===
Score: (Score: 1.0000)

Paragraph: viral andor bacterial detection was reported as percentage positive overall and within selected categories eg age groups

paper_id: bad0e9f737316570c33138d5cc95cc233cd937ab

Title: Molecular detection of respiratory pathogens
among children aged younger than 5 years
hospitalized with febrile acute r

Abstract: in niger acute respiratory infections aris are the second most common cause of death in children aged younger than 5 years
we conducted a prospective study among children aged younger than 5 years hospitalized with febrile ari at two national hospitals in ni
results we enrolled and tested 638 children aged younger than 5 years of whom 411 644 were aged younger than 1 year and 15 24 died duri

Abstract_Summary: In Niger, acute respiratory infections (ARIs)
are the second most common cause of death in
children aged you
We conducted a prospective study among children
aged younger than 5 years hospitalized with febrile
ARI at two national hospitals

Score: (Score: 0.9748)

Paragraph: isolation and phylogenetic analysis of virus from multiple bat species identified bats as the natural reservoir for sars

Fig. 2. The result

4.1   Latent Semantic Indexing Model Using SVD

The Latent Semantic Indexing (LSI) [10] technique is utilised in document data to uncover hidden concepts.The elements connected to these concepts will subsequently be shown for each document and word as vectors. Each entry in a vector represents the extent to which the document or phrase participates in the idea.

The aim is to unify documents and terms so that hidden document, document-term and term-semantic relationships may be disclosed. To do matrix decomposition, the researchers utilise Sklearn's TruncatedSVD. The n components option can be used to specify the number of subjects/topics. This work employed Bokeh, a Python data visualisation package, to illustrate the LSI model. As shown in the Fig. 3, The LSI model identifies words and texts that are similar in meaning. Then identify the topics that are useful for a variety of applications, including document clustering, structuring online content available for data mining, and making decisions. Topic modelling is a text mining methodology that identifies co-occurring terms in order to summarise massive collections of textual information. It facilitates the discovery of hidden concepts in documents, annotating them with these topics, and organising massive amounts of raw data.

A topic model [10] is a form of statistical model used to uncover the conceptual "topics" that consist of a collection of texts. Topic modelling is a popular

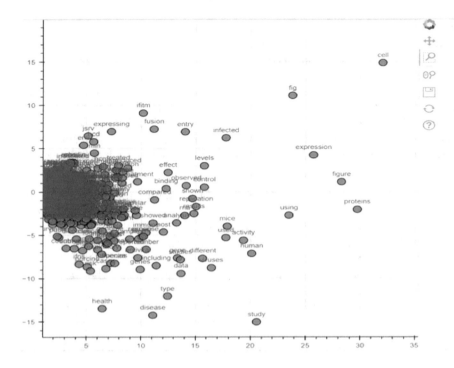

Fig. 3. The topics by using the LSI model

text-mining method for revealing hidden spatial features in a text. The Latent Semantic Analysis was used to identify 14 topics in this work. Topic modelling automatically detects hidden concepts in provided documents. It is used to find a collection of words from a given document. These word groups represent a topic. Figure 3 depicts the visualisation of different topics. The researchers used Python's popular NLTK library to import the stopwords into English. The stopwords are the frequently used words, so the researchers eliminate all stopwords to plot the most commonly used topics.

4.2   Sentence Transformer Models

BERT: The BERT [2] is a bidirectional transformer-based language model. The bidirectional nature of the sentence transformer model allows it to read text sequences from both directions, making the text sequence more meaningful. The BERT employs the NSP task, in which the model attempts to predict whether a sentence A is a continuation of a sentence B. To embed the research paper and input query, the model uses bert-base-nli-mean-tokens. Prior to input word sequences into BERT, the MLM replaces 15% of each sequence's words with a [MASK] token. The model then helps to identify the unmasked values of the masked words using the information contained in the sequence's non-masked words.

RoBERTa: The RoBERTa [7] is an improved BERT Pretraining Approach. It is bidirectional and self-attention techniques improve the efficiency and accuracy of the sentence transformer model in text classification. This language model can process long texts efficiently. The RoBERTa eliminates the NSP task, which in BERT's pre-trained model incorporates dynamic masking by duplicating the training data ten times such that each sequence is masked into ten distinct patterns. The authors tested the removal and addition of NSP loss and found that removing NSP loss improves the model's task performance a bit. To embed the research paper and input query, the model uses the nli-roberta-base-v2 package.

ALBERT: The ALBERT [8] model is a lite variant of BERT that beats assert models for a variety of benchmark datasets due to its minimal memory usage, although it takes longer to train. For evaluation, the researchers used the ALBERT base model, using a sentence transformer. When compared to equivalent BERT models, the ALBERT model has a decreased parameter size. In this work, to embed the research paper and input query, the model uses the twmkn9/albert-base-v2-squad2 package. When compared to other sentence transformer models, the ALBERT model takes a long time to compute.

DistilBERT: The DistilBERT [5], is a distilled version of BERT that uses the distillation method. The approach is then fine-tuned to execute similarly to its larger competitors on a variety of tasks. Pre-training a smaller, faster, and lighter model is less expensive. The whole output distribution of a big neural network can be approximated using a smaller network once it has been trained. To embed the research paper and input query, the model uses the nq-distilbert-base-v1 package.

DistilRoBERTa: The DistilRoBERTa [7] is installed using the Transformer package from the sentence transformer. To embed the research article and query, the model is implemented using the nli-distilroberta-base-v2 package. This model is a distillation of the RoBERTa-base model. It is trained in the same manner as DistilBERT. When compared to RoBERTa, this model uses four times less training data.

The Table 1 shows the similarity scores and programme runtime for each sentence transformer model. When compared to other models, the RoBERTa model is found to offer the best outcomes. The similarity score was obtained by averaging the top 100 query scores for each model. The RoBERTa model is faster and produces a higher similarity score. The runtime is displayed in seconds and explains how long it took to complete the programme.

When compared to the RoBERTa model, ALBERT has a slightly higher similarity score, but the processing time is much longer. So, based on the COVID 19 dataset, All these models conclude that RoBERTa is the best semantic search engine. Here, use the SBERT sentence-transformers package, which makes it extremely straightforward to use BERT, DistilBERT, RoBERTa, ALBERT and

Table 1. Sentence transformer models evaluation

Models	Score (approximate score based on 100 query)	Time (runtime of program in secs)
RoBERTa	0.99994	2081.515028476715
ALBERT	0.99997	7009.639680147171
DistilBERT	0.99873	3101.0192477703094
DistilRoBERTa	0.94985	1067.1314284801483
BERT	0.99901	5267.991491317749

DistilRoBERTa for sentence embedding. The researchers installed sentence - transformers using pip and bokeh, a Python data visualisation package, to illustrate the LSI model.

5 Conclusion

The COVID19 text classification is at the forefront of a number of NLP applications. In this work, a semantic search engine is proposed that utilises different sentence transformer models such as BERT, DistilBERT, RoBERTa, ALBERT and DistilRoBERTa. For the COVID19 semantic search engine, the researchers compared the performance of several techniques extensively. The results reveal that the RoBERTa outperforms the competition in this job. The researchers also use topic modelling to visualise the most important subjects in the acquired dataset. Instead of reading complete research papers and articles, this model provides answers to health-care employee's questions. Future studies could include assessing a semantic search engine employing OpenAI's Generative Pre-trained Transformer (GPT) models. These GPT models are some of the most powerful language models available.

References

1. Ait, C., Hubner, M., Hennig, L.: Fine-tuning Pre-Trained Transformer Language Models to Distantly Supervised Relation Extraction. arXiv preprint arXiv:1906.08646 (2019)
2. Devlin, J., Chang, M.-W., Lee, K., Toutanova, K.: Bert: pre-training of deep bidirectional transformers for language understanding. arXiv preprint arXiv:1810.04805 (2018)
3. Kassim, J.M., Rahmany, M.: Introduction to semantic search engine. In: International Conference on Electrical Engineering and Informatics, vol. 2, pp. 380–386. IEEE (2009)
4. Patel, M.: TinySearch- Semantics based Search Engine using Bert Embeddings. arXiv preprint arXiv:1908.02451 (2019)
5. Sanh, V., Debut, L., Chaumond, J., Wolf, T.: DistilBERT, a distilled version of BERT: smaller, faster, cheaper and lighter. arXiv preprint arXiv:1910.01108 (2019)

6. Guo, X., Ma, J., Li, X.: LSTM-based neural network model for semantic search. In: Yang, H., Qiu, R., Chen, W. (eds.) INFORMS-CSS 2019. SPBE, pp. 17–25. Springer, Cham (2020). https://doi.org/10.1007/978-3-030-30967-1_3

7. Liu, Y., et al.: Roberta: a robustly optimized bert pretraining approach. arXiv preprint arXiv:1907.11692 (2019)

8. Lan, Z., Chen, M., Goodman, S., Gimpel, K., Sharma, P., Soricut, R.: Albert: a lite bert for self-supervised learning of language representations. arXiv preprint arXiv:1909.11942 (2019)

9. Patel, M.: TinySearch-Semantics based Search Engine using Bert Embeddings. arXiv preprint arXiv:1908.02451. Twitter as a tool for the management and analysis of emergency situations: a systematic literature review. Int. J. Inf. Manag. **43**, 196–208 (2019)

10. Akashram. Topic-modeling (2019). www.kaggle.com/akashram/topic-modeling-intro-implementation

11. Allen Institute for AI. COVID-19 Dataset (2020). www.kaggle.com/allen-institute-for-ai/CORD-19-research-challenge/tasks?taskId=568

12. Alammar, J.: The Illustrated Transformer (2020). http://jalammar.github.io/illustrated-transformer/

13. Nair, P.C., Gupta, D., Devi, B.I.: A survey of text mining approaches, techniques, and tools on discharge summaries. In: Gao, X.-Z., Tiwari, S., Trivedi, M.C., Mishra, K.K. (eds.) Advances in Computational Intelligence and Communication Technology. AISC, vol. 1086, pp. 331–348. Springer, Singapore (2021). https://doi.org/10.1007/978-981-15-1275-9_27

14. Menon, R.R.K., Joseph, D., Kaimal, M.R.: Semantics-based topic inter-relationship extraction. J. Intell. Fuzzy Syst. **32**(4), 2941–2951 (2017)

15. Akhil dev, R., Menon, R.R.K., Bhattathiri, S.G.: An insight into the relevance of word ordering for text data analysis. In: 2020 Fourth International Conference on Computing Methodologies and Communication (ICCMC), pp. 207–213 (2020). https://doi.org/10.1109/ICCMC48092.2020.ICCMC-00040

16. Asritha, P., Prudhvi Raja Reddy, P., Pushpitha Sudha, C., Neelima, N.: Intelligent text mining to sentiment analysis of online reviews. In: ICASISET (2021). https://doi.org/10.4108/eai.16-5-2020.2303907

17. Karumudi, G.V.N.S.K., Sathyajit, R., Harikumar, S.: Information retrieval and processing system for news articles in English. In: 2019 9th International Conference on Advances in Computing and Communication (ICACC), pp. 79–85 (2019). https://doi.org/10.1109/ICACC48162.2019.8986223

18. Baladevi, C., Harikumar, S.: Semantic representation of documents based on matrix decomposition. In: International Conference on Data Science and Engineering (ICDSE) 2018, pp. 1–6 (2018). https://doi.org/10.1109/ICDSE.2018.8527824

Author Index

Printed in the United States
by Baker & Taylor Publisher Services